All Things
Wild and Wonderful

ALL THINGS
WILD AND WONDERFUL

Kobie Krüger

with illustrations by Rob Wishart

PENGUIN BOOKS

PENGUIN BOOKS

Published by the Penguin Group
Penguin Books (South Africa) (Pty) Ltd, 24 Sturdee Avenue, Rosebank, Johannesburg
2196, South Africa
Penguin Books Ltd, 80 Strand, London WC2R 0RL, England
Penguin Group (USA) Inc, 375 Hudson Street, New York, New York 10014, USA
Penguin Group (Canada), 90 Eglinton Avenue East, Suite 700, Toronto, Ontario, M4P
2Y3, Canada (a division of Pearson Penguin Canada Inc.)
Penguin Ireland, 25 St Stephen's Green, Dublin 2, Ireland (a division of Penguin
Books Ltd)
Penguin Group (Australia), 250 Camberwell Road, Camberwell, Victoria 3124,
Australia (a division of Pearson Australia Group Pty Ltd)
Penguin Books India Pvt Ltd, 11 Community Centre, Panchsheel Park, New Delhi
– 110 017, India
Penguin Group (NZ), 67 Apollo Drive, Mairangi Bay, Auckland 1310, New Zealand
(a division of Pearson New Zealand Ltd)

Penguin Books (South Africa) (Pty) Ltd, Registered Offices:
24 Sturdee Avenue, Rosebank, Johannesburg 2196, South Africa

www.penguinbooks.co.za

First published by Penguin Books (South Africa) (Pty) Ltd 1996
Reprinted 2000, 2002, 2003, 2004, 2006

ISBN-13: 978- 0-140-25929-2
ISBN-10: 0-140-25929-5

Typeset in 11/13pt Times by Iskova Image Setting
Cover photograph: Daryl Balfour
Printed and bound by Paarl Print, Cape Town
Cover: Mouse Design

For my mother, with love,

and

in memory of my father

CONTENTS

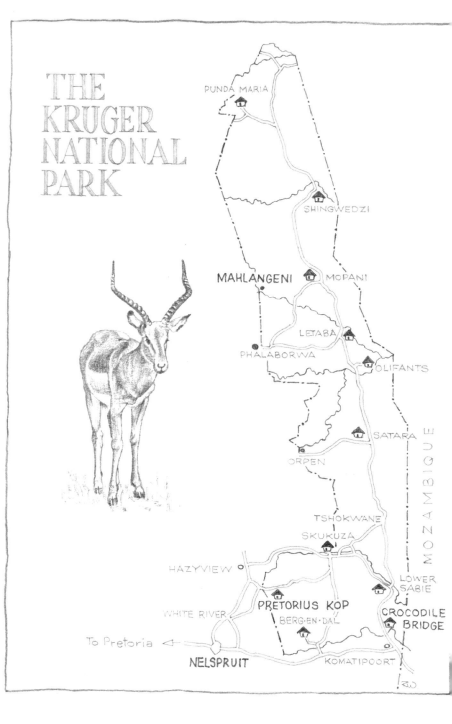

THE KRUGER NATIONAL PARK

PUNDA MARIA

SHINGWEDZI

MAHLANGENI   MOPANI

LETABA

PHALABORWA   OLIFANTS

SATARA

ORPEN

TSHOKWANE

SKUKUZA

HAZYVIEW

PRETORIUS KOP   LOWER SABIE

WHITE RIVER   BERG-EN-DAL   CROCODILE BRIDGE

To Pretoria ←

NELSPRUIT   KOMATIPOORT

MOZAMBIQUE

Goodbye, Sweet Solitude

I once read a French book — unfortunately I don't remember the title or even the author's name. Sadly, I don't remember much French either, but there was a sentence in the book that stuck in my mind. Someone was taking leave of a beautiful place to which he had lost his heart. And he decided that, in a deeply personal sense, the place would always belong to him even if he never saw it again. So he said: *Ici reste mon coeur*.

I thought it meant 'Here rests my heart' and that the Frenchman had buried his heart there — metaphorically speaking. Only later did I discover that *rester* was the French verb for 'remain' and not for 'rest'. 'Here remains my heart' was what he had actually said. But I could never shake off the idea that he had meant his heart was at peace there — in an eternal sort of sense. And so that French phrase lodged itself in my mind.

Years later, when we lived at Mahlangeni, it surfaced from the recesses of my memory and would play in my head like a recurring theme-song.

It came with the landscape.

Far from everywhere, Mahlangeni was a vast and beautiful place of wilderness and solitude.

I thought it was Elysium.

And I thought it belonged to me.

Perhaps it was the magic of its wild and lonely landscapes that affected my thinking — or maybe it was just that French phrase playing in my head.

Once, during our second or third year at Mahlangeni, when my husband Kobus suspected me of falling irrevocably in love with the place, he warned me not to forget that all game rangers get transferred sooner or later.

I promised I would not forget that.

But in the course of the years, that bit of unwelcome knowledge must have slipped to the hazier depths of my mind where it eventually sank into oblivion. Because when we heard, during our eleventh year at Mahlangeni, that we were to be transferred to Crocodile Bridge, I was dreadfully shocked.

For several days the idea didn't even bear thinking about. And the fact that I had become addicted to solitude didn't make matters any easier. I knew that only four other ranger stations in the Park were as remote and isolated as Mahlangeni, and Crocodile Bridge was not one of them. It even had a tourist camp.

I tried to be philosophical about it, but solitude is not something that one can give up overnight.

There is something about solitude, you see, that lets one discover the simple goodness of being. And, in time, this magic grows on you until you become so possessive of it that you cannot imagine ever having to forgo it.

Solitude, of course, also makes one people-shy.

After eleven years at Mahlangeni I was, in fact, more than people-shy: I was people-disorientated. I could no longer cope with the social expectations of strangers. They expected one to be entertaining, bright and amusing and lots of other things which I had forgotten all about. So I lay awake at night, worrying about the prospect of encountering strangers at Crocodile Bridge.

I didn't even know what the Crocodile Bridge section looked like. It was one of the few places in the Park I had never been to.

The map showed that it was in the south-eastern corner of the Park, bordered by the Crocodile river in the south and by the Lebombo mountains in the east.

A man who came to fix our water-pump told me that Crocodile Bridge was a lovely place. I wasn't consoled.

He pointed out that Crocodile Bridge was a lot closer to civilisation than Mahlangeni. I tried to hold back my tears.

He added that at Crocodile Bridge I would have neighbours less than one kilometre away. I was shocked beyond tears.

He mentioned that, in fact, I would have lots of friends since a whole farming community lived just outside the Park boundary on the south side of the river. I was stunned.

He added that the tourist camp was no more than a ten-minute walk from the house. I tried to be brave, but it wasn't easy. The place quite obviously hummed with humanity.

The well-meaning water-pump man also told me that I would even have a telephone in my new house. My misery was complete. I didn't want to talk on a telephone.

When our three daughters were told of the move, the first question each one of them asked, was: 'Will there be other people?' When told that there would be, they were dismayed. Although they enjoyed having lots of friends at their school hostel, they liked to think of home as a place that was far removed from the constraints and restrictions of a compact society.

Kobus also loved Mahlangeni but, being a game ranger, his loyalties reached beyond the boundaries of a single section. The Mahlangeni section had not been a particularly difficult one to manage — despite its considerable size. The Crocodile Bridge section, however, was a problem area because of its shared boundaries with Mozambique and with the Mpumalanga farming communities. Kobus knew that a whole new set of responsibilities awaited him, and he looked forward to the challenge.

He told the girls and me of the beautiful landscapes that lay at the foot of the Lebombo mountains and of the large herds of elephant, rhino and other game that grazed there.

I tried to picture the beautiful landscapes and the herds of wild animals but, instead of animals, I would see herds of humans.

Melancholia

We moved to Crocodile Bridge at the beginning of January 1991. I can't tell you how I felt when I said goodbye to Mahlangeni, because I don't remember. But even if I did, I wouldn't want to talk about it.

Crocodile Bridge is approximately 360 kilometres to the south east of Mahlangeni. We travelled east through the mopani woodlands to the Tsendze stream and then south through the vast mopani shrub savannah of the eastern region.

After crossing the Letaba river via the high-water bridge, we continued south through the tail-end of the mopani savannah to the Olifants river. As we drove across the high-water bridge over the Olifants, we left the mopani landscapes of the northern regions for ever behind us. Their domain ended at the river.

The wooded southern slope of the Olifants soon made way for the treeless savannah of the central region. Here, only clumps of stunted knob-thorn dotted the sweeping plain. I tried to appreciate its quiet austerity, but my nostalgia plunged deeper. I had left my soul behind in the mopani woodlands of the north.

Later, we reached the attractive tree savannahs of the south-eastern region. Herds of zebra and wildebeest grazed contentedly in the sweet grasslands, while giraffe and kudu browsed the foliage of marula and knob-thorn trees. It was a graceful landscape, and its complacent mood had a soothing quality. It sort of beckoned to my absent soul.

After stopping at the Satara camp for lunch, we headed further south towards Tshokwane and then east towards the Lebombo mountains. We travelled south along the mountain range and stopped a few times to admire the panoramic view of the bushlands below. Eventually we descended towards Lower Sabie and crossed the Sabie river. It was in this area — at the foot of the mountains and south of the Sabie — that we found the vast game herds that Kobus had told us about.

From Lower Sabie we continued south through the Delagoa thorn bushlands, and still the animals were everywhere — rhino, giraffe, elephant and many others. We came across two prides of fat lions, a pack of wild dogs with gorgeous puppies, and a newly married cheetah couple.

We reached our new home in the late afternoon.

We drove in through the gate and parked under a gigantic fuchsia tree. The parking area faced a subtropical garden where a troop of monkeys was reposing under a mkuhlu tree — much to the annoyance of our two dogs. They leapt from the truck and promptly evicted the squatters. Screams of monkey consternation filled the air.

A paved path led through the profusion of foliage and flowers to the front door of the house.

For a while I felt almost capable of liking the place. But within the next few moments a number of alarming facts came to my attention.

The first of these was that the sun was setting in the north. That bothered me a great deal. The second was that a Mozambique spitting cobra was lying at the front door. It reared its head, looked at us disapprovingly, and then slithered into a flowerbed at the side of the house. It was obvious that he was a permanent resident and that he disliked intruders.

The entrance to the house turned out to be the kitchen. The kitchen led to the lounge, where several bats were flying around amongst wooden beams that supported a ceilingless roof. There

were bats in every room. It appeared that they, too, were permanent residents.

It was an interesting house — old, but sturdy and solid. The criss-cross structure of heavy wooden beams under the high roof was particularly attractive, if one could ignore the bats. The layout of the rooms, however, was highly confusing. And the deeper one went into the house, the darker the rooms got. That was because most of the windows either opened on to screened verandas or looked straight into the foliage of shrubs and trees, keeping the daylight out. The interior gloom, along with the bats and the confusing layout, all contributed towards a feeling that reminded one vaguely of a cave.

I walked out into the front garden which looked on to the Crocodile river. The view was nice, but naturally it was no match for the view at Mahlangeni of the Greater Letaba river. The Crocodile river is mainly a gathering of streams that burble their way around islands of reeds. Reeds also cover most of the shores and the banks and, looking at them, they seemed to me to be too tall, too dense, and too everywhere. I don't trust reeds. Danger always lurks in dense reeds. Suddenly, I didn't like the name of the river either.

The garden was enchanting though, with its profusion of flowers, subtropical shrubs, green lawns and huge trees. As I walked the length of the front garden, I wondered whether wild animals still roamed free on the other side of the river — even though the land across the boundary belonged to farmers. I looked across the river, but the dense foliage on the far bank obscured most of the view beyond. Eventually I spotted a young bushbuck on the opposite shore — in a sandy spot between the reeds, and further along the bank I could see some monkeys playing tag in a mkuhlu tree.

But that was all — or so I thought, until I made a most alarming discovery. Further upstream, through a gap in the foliage on the far bank, I spotted part of what appeared to be a fenced-in garden. And right there, at that very moment, stood a PERSON.

It wasn't actually doing anything. It just stood there, contemplating a shrub or something. I couldn't tell whether it was a man or a woman — about 300 metres separated us. I stared at the disturbing sight with morbid fascination. After a while the stranger turned, spotted me and lifted its hand in greeting. I managed to wave back. But I was shaken. I had neighbours within waving distance! My only consolation was that the river separated us.

Then I noticed that the sun was still setting in the north.

I got a headache.

The headache lasted three months. After two months I went to see a doctor. He said it was tick fever.

I don't think it was.

I think it was melancholia.

Every morning for about three months when I woke up at Crocodile Bridge, I mourned not hearing Mahlangeni's Egyptian geese greet the day with their raucous trumpeting. I longed for the booming voices of the hippos, and for the lively early morning chattering of the neighbouring baboons. I missed the family of bushbuck who had often kept me company, and the three orphaned warthogs that we had raised. I missed the familiar birds, the squirrels and all the other sweet and strange creatures that had found solace and happiness in our garden.

The Crocodile river also had hippos of course, but the closest residential pool was several kilometres upstream from the house — and out of earshot. The neighbouring baboons seemed broody and quiet. And the birds, squirrels, bushbabies and other creatures in the garden were remarkably people-shy. When I greeted them, they'd give me a bewildered stare that said: 'And who are you?'

Another thing that deepened my early morning gloom at Crocodile Bridge every day was that the sun rose in the south.

I studied the Kruger Park map for a long time. The Crocodile river twists and turns a lot. In this south-eastern corner of the

Park it makes a ponderous U-turn in its search for a passage through the Lebombo mountains.

Our house, I discovered, stood on the western leg of the U-turn, facing east on to the river.

That, of course, was very confusing. The Crocodile river is the southern boundary of the Park, so naturally one would expect our house to be on the northern bank of the river, which, in fact, it was. But because of the U-turn, it faced east on to the river instead of south.

At Mahlangeni our house stood on the northern bank and looked south on to the river. For eleven years the sun had risen right out of the water in the east and sank right into the water in the west.

At Crocodile Bridge, the sun rose directly across the river. That scrambled my sense of direction completely, and no matter how hard I tried, I couldn't get it right. As a result, I often got lost when I went walking in the bush. I would look at the setting sun and tell myself 'that's west', but in my heart I knew it was north, and then utter confusion would set in until I could not for the life of me figure out where my house should be — or where I was, for that matter.

Apart from spending my first three months at Crocodile Bridge feeling sad, lost and confused and having a headache, I also suffered episodes of paranoia. They were caused by the behaviour of a neighbouring troop of baboons. Their abode was a sycamore fig tree on the river bank just outside our southern fence. (Actually it was the eastern fence, but you know what I mean.) For several weeks they sat around in their tree, watching my every move. The moment I left the house, I'd feel their eyes on me. It was unnerving. I knew they were merely inquisitive or something, but they certainly acted like a bunch of secret agents that had been commissioned to investigate me.

It was quite a while before I finally caught on to what their surveillance was all about. We had fruit trees all over the garden: papaws, litchis, mangoes, bananas, marulas and citrus. My two dogs followed me wherever I went, and the baboons were in fact doing an investigative study of the dogs to find out how seriously they intended to guard the fruit trees.

Wolfie, who is an Australian cattle dog (half dingo, half border collie), is a loyal and conscientious animal who takes all his responsibilities very seriously. Flenter, being a Staffordshire bull terrier, is a fighter as well as a fight-picker, and he distrusts all wild animals, especially baboons.

And so the baboons, being pretty intelligent observers, eventually concluded unanimously that the dogs were to be taken seriously, and the fruit trees to be avoided.

My headache finally went away one day, but the sun still rose and set in the wrong places. I still had neighbours across the river, and bats in the house, and the spitting cobra still dominated the entrance to the house, proclaiming sole ownership of the flowerbed at the side of the kitchen.

The Great Adjustment

One morning, shortly after we had moved in, I decided that the dogs' sleeping mats needed a spring clean. I picked up one of the mats to give it a good shake, and the resident cobra fell out of it. He landed on my foot, and my foot got such a shock that a ligament in the ankle got injured. The snake hurried away, disappearing into his flowerbed at the side of the kitchen.

His flowerbed was actually more than just a flowerbed — it also contained two trees, numerous shrubs and creepers and it was dense and overgrown to the point of being a perfect hangout for a snake. A whole community of frogs, lizards and geckos also inhabited it, so the snake had abundant food supplies right there in his own home which made foraging outside of it unnecessary. He liked to wander a bit though, and we often met him on the paved path in front of the kitchen.

He was a funny snake for a cobra. Ordinarily, the Mozambique spitting cobra is a nervous and highly strung snake. It can move and strike with remarkable speed, and its venom is extremely poisonous. It can also 'spit' its venom and reach its target (usually the eyes) over a distance of two or three metres with considerable accuracy.

Our cobra, for some or other reason, was neither very highly strung nor particularly aggressive. If you accidentally approached him too suddenly, he'd rear his head, ready to strike, but if you stopped in your tracks and remained frozen, he'd contemplate you for a while, and then slither away into his flowerbed. Apparently he had accepted the fact that he would always have human neighbours and that he had no choice but to tolerate them. His philosophy more or less coincided with ours, which was: We won't bother you if you don't bother us.

In accordance with our philosophy, my family and I always walked slowly and rather noisily along the paved path to give the snake ample warning that someone was approaching. He would keep his distance, and so neither party would be in danger of an unexpected dramatic encounter.

From time to time, when one of us accidentally surprised him, he spat his venom at us. This usually happened when someone rushed out of the kitchen to dash off somewhere, momentarily forgetting about the snake. If the snake was on his way out of the flowerbed, or resting somewhere near its border alongside the paved path, the sudden, unexpected movement close to him would frighten him and cause him to spit.

We usually got the venom on our legs, which was of course something to be grateful for. Other cobras would have spat in our eyes. But even if a snake spits only on your leg, you still need to wash the dribbles of venom thoroughly from your skin in case there's a scratch or other lesion through which the poison might enter your system.

During our first year at Crocodile Bridge I had trouble with a tooth which entailed three visits to the nearest dentist — 60 kilometres away. I was late for the first appointment because I got lost. I was late for the second and third appointments because I got spat on by the cobra and had to rush back inside to wash the spittle from my legs. I hate being late for an appointment, especially three times in a row. I apologised each time, explaining why I was late — even though the reasons themselves added to my embarrassment.

Wolfie, being a cautious dog, kept a discreet distance from the snake. Flenter, being a fight-picker, often tried to attack the snake but always got spat in the eyes. The first time this happened, our youngest daughter Karin dragged the dog to the nearest tap and held his face under the running water until all the venom was washed from his eyes. The second time, Flenter ran to the tap

himself and waited for one of us to get there and open the tap. On other occasions, when we didn't see the snake spit at him, he would howl at the kitchen door to let us know he needed help. As soon as one of us responded to his call, he'd run straight to the tap and hold his face upright, waiting for the relief of the cool water in his burning eyes.

Our policy of not bothering each other was understood by the snake, but not by the resident bats. They bothered us almost out of our minds.

Bats are mammals that can fly. That makes them pretty unique. But they are not very good fliers. Their navigating systems are hardly up to standard and, in fact, often pack up and go haywire. When a bat realises that he has miscalculated a chosen landing spot, he chooses a human as a site for the crash landing, preferably a human who is asleep (that is, horizontal and stationary). Sometimes even the crash landing goes awry, and the bat ends up in a waste-paper basket, a wash basin or some other container from which he cannot escape. Then he shrieks for help until you wake up. When you go to his aid (with murder in your heart), he looks so pathetic as he pleads with you please to help him out that you have no choice but to do so. As you lift him gently out, he bites your hand.

When bats get bored, which is often, they fly round and round and round in never-ending circles. The only way to stop them from driving everybody (including themselves) insane is to anaesthetise them temporarily.

This is done with a tennis racket. You plant yourself in a spot where, by holding the racket upright in the air, you are sure to invite a collision. You can also help the collision along a little if you wish. Once the bat is unconscious, you carry him gently outside and leave him on the lawn to recuperate.

Some evenings you'd find almost a dozen bats recuperating on our lawn.

In the beginning we tried very hard to persuade the bats to find themselves another home. But they made it clear to us that the house had belonged to their families for many generations, and that they would never dream of leaving it.

I think they mistook it for a cave. You couldn't blame them really. The house was dark and gloomy inside, and the roof leaked a little when it rained, adding moistness to the cave-like atmosphere. We tried spooking them out with an ultrasonic sound device. But it apparently didn't bother them. We tried gassing them out with chlorine, but they didn't notice. We tried worrying them out by keeping the electric lights in the house burning day and night for a couple of days, hoping it might open their eyes to the fact that the house wasn't a cave. It didn't. And remain they did.

In the end we gave up and conceded that the house was a cave and that it belonged to them.

Living as an intruder in a cave isn't easy. But one should always look at the bright side of things. Bats eat insects, including mosquitoes. So we had our own personal mosquito culling team.

Other culling teams also lurked in the neighbourhood.

One night a couple of prowling civets devoured my whole brood of bantam chickens. Only the cock escaped. I was so upset that I vowed never again to keep bantams. The cock decided that henceforth it would be safer for him to be a dog, so he shared the dogs' sleeping place in the garden shed at night, perching on anything that was directly above their heads. He gave up crowing and never ventured far from the dogs during the day. His survival instincts proved sound, for the civets left him in peace.

Another prospective culling team surprised me one night when I was alone at home. The girls had gone back to school and university, and Kobus was camping in the Lebombo mountains on an anti-poaching patrol.

I woke up in the middle of the night to a cacophony of sounds. I don't always wake up fully when I am awakened suddenly. My body reacts instinctively, but my mind sometimes takes a while to start functioning. So I found myself scrambling out of bed, grabbing my torch and pistol and running outside into the darkness — realising too late that I'd missed the pistol in my haste and had gripped an empty coffee mug instead.

I rushed towards the source of the uproar. Dogs were barking, horses whinnying, and a gate crashed open. Something was also growling, but that didn't register properly because about three-quarters of me was still asleep.

I was thinking only of our two horses. A few nights before a leopard had growled somewhere in the neighbourhood, frightening them so badly that they had crashed open the gate of their camp and fled headlong into the dark garden. One of them had collided with an iron structure that had made a deep gash in his flank. We had been doctoring the wound ever since.

Now, in my misty-mindedness, the only thought that surfaced clearly was that I had to prevent the horses from injuring themselves in the darkness again. They were out of their camp and were running along the eastern fence of the garden, straight towards the swimming pool in the south-east corner. Worried that they would stumble into the pool, I ran alongside them and tried to steer them away. The dogs were running along with me, barking their heads off.

My torch batteries were almost flat, and the faint beam of light didn't do much to relieve the inky blackness of the night. Something else was running along on the outside of the fence, but I was worried only about the swimming pool that was getting closer and closer, and the horses who were running faster and faster. Luckily the horses sensed the approaching pool and veered away in time, dashing through flowerbeds right up to the house, and then around to the back of the house.

Before following the horses I hurled the coffee mug at the creature that was trying to break through the wire of the fence. As the mug struck the mesh wire it made a nice clanging noise, and I hoped that it would frighten away the pestering prowler.

I found the panic-stricken horses at the back of the house and, after a lot of fuss, finally managed to calm them down and lead them back to the stable in their camp. I thanked the two dogs (who had barked themselves hoarse) for their loyal assistance and then went back inside to make myself a cup of good coffee.

The caffeine startled my mind awake and it was only then, as the fog of sleepy confusion lifted, that I registered the fact that I had actually heard the creature outside the fence snarling at one stage — just like a lion. But I dismissed the thought and went back to bed.

When Kobus came home the following morning, I told him how the horses had been disturbed again in the night, and how I'd had a really hard time calming them down and getting them back into their camp. Kobus promised he would do something about the gate right away so that the horses wouldn't be able to crash it open again. But first he went off to see if he could find out what it was that had worried them in the night. He came back a while later and told me to come with him. There was something he wanted to show me.

First he showed me several enormous lion pug marks along the outside of the eastern fence. Then he showed me a place in the fence where a lion had tried to get through the wire by hurling himself against it, leaving a large convex indentation in the mesh. He also showed me where a lion had hooked a piece of the wire with its claw and pulled it out towards him.

I was horrified.

Kobus thought that I had been pretty brave, running alongside the fence like that in order to protect the horses. So I didn't explain to him that I had actually been half asleep.

The animal population in the Crocodile Bridge area is enormous. One bumped into wild creatures virtually around every corner.

It is important, of course, that one should get to know the animals in one's neighbourhood and to become familiar with their habits and their haunts. That way one can take care not to bother them and avoid unfriendly confrontations.

Adjusting to the wild society at Crocodile Bridge took me a while, but it was nothing compared to my difficulties in adapting to the human society.

At Mahlangeni, my repertoire of social behaviour had consisted mainly of my relations with my husband and daughters and with the few Shangaan families who lived in the nearby staff village. I also kept in touch with some of the other game rangers' wives, but because of the distances that separated us we met only on rare occasions, such as the annual game rangers' function.

Kobus spent a lot of time working away from home and the girls spent their weeks at the school hostel during term time. So Kobus often had contact with his colleagues and my children saw their school friends during the week. It was only I who saw few other people outside of my own family. This led my subconscious to the conclusion that it no longer needed to store people's names and so it threw out that file along with the rest of the name-recalling program.

Whereas Mahlangeni was more or less in the middle of nowhere, our home at Crocodile Bridge was more or less in the middle of everywhere. It was only 90 kilometres from Skukuza and 37 kilometres from Lower Sabie, only two kilometres from the Crocodile Bridge gate, and less than one kilometre from the Crocodile Bridge tourist camp. It was separated only by the river from a whole farming community. And the village of Komatipoort was only 12 kilometres away.

So I had neighbours everywhere. And people dropped in all the time — mostly to see Kobus on official business but quite often also for a neighbourly visit.

Remembering names became a permanent nightmare for me. Actually, I couldn't even remember faces. A lot of people seemed to look alike.

People often turned up at our house to see Kobus when Kobus wasn't there. That was an ordeal for me, because most of the time I wouldn't know whether I had met the visitor (or visitors) previously or not.

After I had proved myself an idiot on several occasions by introducing myself to people who already knew me, I decided it would be best to greet everyone as if I knew them. If they turned out to be strangers, they would point out that we hadn't met, and I would then say: 'Oh sorry, I mistook you for someone I know!' At least that sounded as though I was a person who knew some people. This, at any rate, would be my strategy, and to a large extent it worked.

Except when the visitor, who didn't introduce himself (on the grounds that we'd met before), asked me to give Kobus a message from him. When Kobus came home, I was in trouble. All I could tell him was that someone had left a message that there were elephants on his farm, or whatever. Now Kobus would have to guess whose farm it was and then go out and herd the elephants back into the Park. Kobus would ask me for a description of the person, but since most people looked more or less alike, I could hardly help.

Naturally, Kobus insisted that I start to get interested in learning people's names. I explained to him that I was very interested, but that my mind had lost its name-recalling program.

Eventually I learned some names, but I would fit them to the wrong faces. I think my brain was storing names and faces in separate files.

At a school function I kissed the headmaster, mistaking him for one of our neighbours from across the river. And I introduced myself to my dentist — who then reminded me that not only did he know me, but he also knew my teeth pretty intimately.

One day Kobus warned me that someone from Skukuza — who happened to be a good friend of his — would be dropping in the following day, bringing his wife with him. Kobus told me their names and reminded me that I had met the couple on a previous occasion.

I was ready for them. I even baked a cake. When the car arrived the next morning, I rushed outside with a warm welcome on my face and hugged them both. 'I'm so happy to see you!' I babbled. 'Come right in, I've baked a cake!'

The lady looked alarmed. 'That's kind of you,' she stammered, 'but ... I don't know ...'

The man only said: 'Uh ...'

I realised they were the wrong people.

Kobus came out of his office, shook hands with them and introduced himself. The visitors explained that they had been commissioned by the Department of Water Affairs to research the status of the rivers in the area and that they needed some information from him.

Kobus invited them into his office.

The lady gave me a sympathetic smile. She probably thought I was so lonely for company that I spent all my days baking cakes and waiting for someone to visit.

I tried to comfort myself with the belief that things would get better as time went by. I reckoned that, once I got used to seeing lots of people, my social nervousness would decrease. But it didn't. It grew with each new gaffe that I made.

Remembering names and faces wasn't my only problem. It was the whole spectrum of social graces that eluded me.

Each time I opened my mouth, the wrong words came out.

But I don't want to give you any examples of these, if you don't mind. Some of them are too embarrassing to bear thinking about.

Despite my gaucherie, the farmers and their families from across the river always treated me with kindness and courtesy. Even when my blunders sometimes bordered on lunacy, they politely pretended not to notice. Unfortunately that didn't make me feel any better about myself, but I appreciated their forbearance. They were good, generous people. They brought us milk, eggs and vegetables from their farms, and the farmers' wives often sent me jams, preserves and other home-made delicacies.

It might perhaps interest you to know that, despite my people-shyness, I actually had one neighbour with whom I got on quite famously.

Her name was Ilse. She and her husband Willem lived right across the river from us. It was their garden that was visible from ours through the gap in the foliage on the far bank. I learned later that it was Ilse who had waved to me on that first day when I'd spotted her in her garden.

Although Ilse and I didn't meet in person for almost two years, we often waved at each other across the river.

I discovered eventually that it was actually quite nice to have a neighbour to wave to, even though she sometimes appeared to be an illusion. (At a distance of about 300 metres it's hard to tell what's real and what's not.) I might have suspected her of being a phantom neighbour if it weren't for the fact that we occasionally talked on the phone. She'd call to ask me to give my husband a message from her husband. Or I'd call her when I needed information such as where to find a library or a dentist or something.

And sometimes we'd discuss the weather or comment on the current happenings in the landscape between her house and mine — like the time a marabou stork stood on the shore for half a day watching a crocodile that had a huge dead fish dangling from its mouth. The marabou, being wise to the fact that the croc would have to open its jaws for the swallowing exercise, stood waiting for just that moment to snitch the fish from its mouth. And the croc, sensible of what was on the marabou's mind, refused to open its jaws. And so they spent the whole of the afternoon in each other's company, looking like two frustrated statues. Eventually it got too dark to see them and neither Ilse nor I ever knew the outcome of the standoff, because by the following morning they were gone.

Another time, an elephant mother chased an innocent buffalo bull right over the horizon after she'd got the absurd idea that he'd threatened her calf. Ilse thought that the calf had probably screamed in fright at the coldness of the water lapping at its feet and that the mother had misunderstood and thought the buffalo was the culprit. But I personally think the mother was simply being outrageous, the way elephant moms usually are.

Anyway, it was nice to have someone to discuss the scenery with.

We did eventually meet one day. After we'd been phantom neighbours for almost two years, Ilse heard the news that I had become foster mother to a lion cub, and she came over to meet the new arrival. About six months later, she paid me another visit to see how the cub was doing. And at the end of our third year at Crocodile Bridge, just before we moved to Pretorius Kop, she came over again to say goodbye and to tell me how sorry she was that we were moving. I was sorry too. She was such a compatible neighbour.

Although the Crocodile Bridge tourist camp is small compared to others in the Park, it is still a tourist camp, which means that there are tourist roads in the area and, of course, tourists.

A favourite pastime of mine has always been my late-afternoon walks with my dogs. It is a time to relax and to think of nice things.

At Mahlangeni I could walk the dogs wherever I wished. There were no tourist roads anywhere near the house. In fact, until shortly before we moved, there weren't even any tourist roads or tourist camps in the entire section. (The Mopani camp was completed in 1990 — the year before we moved. But it was 60 kilometres away.)

At Crocodile Bridge I could never relax completely when I went for a walk. I had to take care all the time to stay out of sight of tourist roads. If tourists spotted me walking in the bush with my dogs, they'd stop and study me through binoculars — and then go right ahead and report to the tourism official at the camp that they'd spotted a human in the bush.

There is a strict rule that tourists must stay in their cars and that they may drive only on approved tourist roads. Park personnel may under certain circumstances drive on unmarked roads or leave their cars, but only with permission from the local game ranger — and on condition that they do so with discretion. Once people get the idea that it's safe to walk in the bush, everyone might want to do it. And walking in the bush is, in fact, not safe. Unless you are armed and well-versed in the ways of the wilderness, you may get trampled, mauled or eaten. I'm not too clued-up myself, and I don't always carry a firearm, but my dogs are well trained and they are bush-wise. I rely on them to keep me out of harm's way.

The problem at Crocodile Bridge was that my dogs didn't know the rule about not being spotted by tourists. And since I had problems with directions, I sometimes got lost. You don't always see a tourist road from the bush. Trees and tall grass tend to obscure it. So sometimes, out of the blue, I'd hear a car approaching. If there was time, I'd call the dogs and we'd all flee out of sight. If there wasn't time, I'd fall flat behind the nearest shrub or tree and tell the dogs to do the same.

One day, when I was surprised by the distant sound of an approaching car, I looked at the setting sun and realised that I'd been heading towards the main tourist road linking Crocodile Bridge and Lower Sabie. I called the dogs but they were sniffing the ground vigorously a short distance away. I walked over and discovered lion pug marks leading — luckily — away from us towards the tourist road.

The dogs were having ambivalent feelings about the lion spoor: they were as eager to follow it as they were apprehensive of doing so. I commanded them to ignore the spoor and to follow me. The tourist car was approaching rapidly. I headed for a clump of trees that looked as though it might shield us from view, but before we got there, I heard the car stopping. It seemed a fair distance away, however. Hoping that I was out of sight by then, and not wanting to glance over my shoulder, I hurried along.

When I got home about half an hour later, Kobus was just arriving, and he told me that he'd been stopped by a tourist car at the T-junction where our private track met the tourist road. The tourists had excitedly informed him that they'd come across a pride of lions lying right next to the road some two kilometres to the north, and that they'd spotted a lady walking alone in the bush, not far from the lions. They urged Kobus to hurry off and save the lady from being devoured by the lions.

Kobus told them not to worry.

'The lady would be my wife,' he said. 'She gets lost sometimes.'

I still wonder what those tourists must be thinking.

Another of my adjustment problems at Crocodile Bridge concerned the telephone. In fact, the telephone alarmed and distressed me more than the bats, the snake, the out-of-orbit sun and everything else (except my social gaucherie).

But I'll tell you about that later.

Kobus and the girls adapted to our new home more readily than I did. Or perhaps they had less time to bother about adjusting than I had. Kobus was working too hard to take any notice of anything else, and the girls were too busy adjusting to life in the outside world. To them, the Park was still their haven, and as long as they could always come home to it, that was all that mattered.

The two older girls, Hettie and Sandra, were both at university (about 500 kilometres away) and weren't able to come home as often as Karin. Karin was in her first year at high school, and although her boarding school was 120 kilometres away in the town of Nelspruit, she was able to come home on the school bus every weekend.

Whenever they all came home, we loved to go camping with them at the foot of the Lebombo mountains — and to rediscover the therapeutic magic of wilderness and solitude.

A Trouble-sharing Friend

About six months after we had moved to Crocodile Bridge, another game ranger family from the north was transferred to the south. They were game ranger Flip Nel and his wife Annette and their two daughters.

Flip had been the district ranger at Shingwedzi for seven years. Annette, his wife, had been as happy at Shingwedzi as I had been at Mahlangeni. She loved the serenity and the solitude of the vast northern region of the Park, and she was as scared of the people-populated south as I was.

On the day that the Nel family arrived at their new home at Lower Sabie in the south, Annette burst into tears. Their house was practically next door to the Lower Sabie tourist camp and within viewing distance of the tourist road.

Lower Sabie, which was our closest neighbouring tourist camp, is only 37 kilometres from Crocodile Bridge. I looked forward to having Annette as a neighbour. We'd always been good friends, but up north the distance between her home and mine had been over a hundred kilometres. So we hadn't really seen much of each other.

A few weeks after the Nels had moved in at Lower Sabie, I drove over one morning to pay Annette a neighbourly visit.

When she saw my car driving in through the gate, she came out of the house to meet me.

'I've come to welcome you to the south,' I told her.

'Oh, how sweet of you,' she said. 'But it won't help. I could never feel at home here.'

'I understand,' I said sympathetically.

'I knew you would,' she said gratefully.

We went inside and made coffee while she told me of a terrible thing that had happened to her that very morning. She had walked out into her garden (still wearing her nightie) to look for her three-year-old daughter Narina. She spotted her playing in the sand under a tree in a far corner of the garden. As she walked towards her, she glanced up and noticed a tourist car parked at the side of the tourist road (less than a hundred metres from her house). And the tourists were leaning out of their car windows, studying her through binoculars!

I could hardly imagine such a dreadful experience and I sympathised sincerely with her. I told her that at least my house was not in sight of a tourist road but that I had other problems: I had neighbours everywhere, and people dropped in all the time. I told her that everybody thought me a blunderhead because I couldn't remember who they were. Annette agreed that this was most distressing.

She told me that, on a quiet evening, they could actually hear people talking and laughing in the tourist camp.

I thought that was really awful. I told her that tourists sometimes spotted me when I took the dogs walking. She sympathised and told me that her dog was suffering from a nervous disorder because it wasn't used to having so many people in the neighbourhood. I felt sorry for her dog.

I told her that I had a telephone in my house. She was shocked.

I also told her that, over at my place, the sun rose in the south and set in the north and that a snake lived in the flowerbed at the side of the kitchen.

She said that sounded bad, but not as bad as the telephone.

We were on to our second cups of coffee, and I was about to tell her that I also had bats in my house when, suddenly, we both sat bolt upright. Annette's dog Ngala was barking outside in a frenzied high-pitched tone. Game rangers' dogs only bark like that when something is terribly wrong. We put our cups down and rushed outside to see what it was.

And what we saw made us gasp.

Three young male lions were running along the outside of the fence, while Ngala, running along the fence on the inside, was barking her head off at them. The frisky young lions wanted only to get at the dog and teach it a lesson, and so they ran along the fence looking for a place to get in. They were running from south to north, directly towards the gate. The gate was wide open. About fifteen metres inside the open gate, three-year-old Narina was playing in the sand. When she saw the lions approaching, she jumped to her feet and stood frozen to the spot.

Annette shot forth like a launched rocket, sprinting towards Narina and the open gate. I ran after Annette but stopped at my car, which was parked near the gate, yanked the door open and grabbed my pistol. Annette had almost reached the gate by then, and so had the lions.

'I have a pistol!' I called to her. 'I'm coming!'

The lions stopped outside the open gate to stare curiously at the petite human female who was boldly charging them. Annette grabbed hold of the gate, swung it shut in their surprised faces and slammed the securing bolt into place.

The crisis was over.

The gardener, Abel, arrived on the scene brandishing a pitchfork and yelling abuse at the lions. Abel's colourful language coupled with the hysterical tone of the dog's voice got too much for the lions and they left.

Annette gathered Narina in her arms and we went back inside. Narina — a true child of the wild — thought it had been a rather interesting adventure. Nothing more.

Annette and I were both shaking. So we spooned more sugar into our coffee.

'You were very brave,' I told her. 'Those lions had a funny look in their eyes — it scared me to death.'

'Me too,' she said. 'When you shouted that you had a pistol I thought those were the nicest words I'd ever heard.'

We both laughed and felt much better.

I told her about my episode with the lions who'd tried to get at our horses one night.

Annette sighed and said: 'Northern lions aren't so cheeky.'

I knew what she meant. Northern lions don't often come into contact with humans and so they still have a natural fear of man.

We agreed that life in the south was no picnic.

But as I drove back home later that day, I found myself humming a happy tune. Life wasn't too bad really — not if you had an understanding friend to share your troubles with.

The Alarming Message Book

Crocodile Bridge was a place where things went wrong nearly all the time. There were too many humans and too many animals, and they constantly got into trouble or in each other's hair — the way maddening crowds tend to do.

I wanted only to get on quietly with my own life and to take no notice of the ongoing commotion. But my life didn't belong to me any more. It belonged to the telephone. Our number appeared to be some mysterious equivalent of 911.

People called all the time to report trouble or to complain about the state of things. And they called mostly when Kobus was away from home — which was most of the time. So I kept a large, thick message book next to the phone.

Apart from the animals, the tourists and the farmers — who all had their problems — another source of alarming events was the Nkongoma army base at the foot of the Lebombo mountains near the Mozambique border. The base was inside the Park and fell under Kobus's jurisdiction. I should mention though, that the army base also proved to be a blessing, for if I was unable to find Kobus or any of the local game guards to respond to an urgent call for help, I'd call the base and enlist the aid of the soldiers.

Kobus also found the base helpful: it provided him with an extra source of manpower to assist in apprehending armed poachers or to help fight devastating fires, especially those that often came rolling down the Lebombo mountains from Mozambique.

So naturally, and quite rightly, the soldiers also relied on me and Kobus for help when they encountered certain problems. A fair number of their troubles concerned the driving abilities of the young soldiers. Being young and being soldiers, they drove too fast. On no fewer than five occasions during our three-year stay at Crocodile Bridge, a soldier drove his truck too fast over the bridge and crashed into the Crocodile river.

We'd hear the resounding splash from our house and rush over to help get the soldiers out of the water (before crocodiles got them) and to tend to their injuries. Two soldiers got injured fairly seriously in one of these accidents, but fortunately none were hurt in the others. Trucks, however, got smashed up and the bridge itself was eventually so badly damaged that Kobus insisted the army pay up and fix it themselves.

On other occasions, soldiers crashed their trucks into trees or overturned them on winding tracks, and they would solemnly report to Kobus that their speed at the time of the accident had been exactly 40 kilometres per hour. I once overheard Kobus commenting to a soldier that 40 kilometres per hour was obviously the most dangerous speed on earth.

Apart from smashing up their trucks, soldiers also got lost in the mountains, or started accidental bush fires, or got stung by scorpions, or bitten by snakes, or something, and we'd help in whatever way we could.

And so everybody in the area had their troubles, and the telephone ensured that my stress levels remained permanently in the red.

I longed constantly and desperately for Mahlangeni — that faraway, magical place where no telephone ever interrupted the solitude.

When we first moved to Crocodile Bridge, the ringing of the telephone was such an alien sound to us all that it evoked no immediate response. Whenever it started ringing, we'd all look up, faintly surprised at the unfamiliar sound, and for a while nobody would move — until the signal finally registered. But even then we'd all be reluctant to respond to it. We were used to talking only on a radio.

The telephone confused us. Especially me. I would talk in abrupt sentences and say 'over' at the end of a paragraph. And I would forget that I could speak without having to wait for the other party to say 'over' first. It also disturbed my mind if the other person interrupted me. Interruption never happened on the radio. As long as you pressed your mike button in, no transmission was possible from the other party on the air.

Eventually, however, we all got used to the telephone. But then everybody went away and I was the one who was stuck at home, alone with the phone.

I was sorry when I'd lost that initial slackness of response to its ringing — it was nice when the sound still failed to unnerve me. Unfortunately, as soon as I was fully conditioned to the fact that about nine out of ten phone calls meant trouble, I found myself reacting to the signal at full speed and with an appropriate sense of dread.

If the problem was serious and required urgent attention, I'd try to contact Kobus on the radio or, if he was unreachable, to find game guards or soldiers from Nkongoma base to respond to the call for help. Sometimes I'd even respond myself (for example, if a tourist was injured, or if an animal in the area was reported to be ill, hurt, orphaned or lost).

If the problems were not serious enough to warrant immediate attention, I'd write them down in the message book. I often felt sorry for Kobus when he arrived home after a day (or sometimes several days) of hard work to find a list of frantic messages awaiting him.

My sister-in-law, while on a visit to us, was found one day reading the message book from cover to cover in one sitting. She said it was the most absorbing book of alarming messages that she had ever read.

During our three-year stay at Crocodile Bridge I filled four and a half 200-page books with messages.

In case you are interested, here are some of the entries for May 1992. (At that time, the water level of the Crocodile river was low, and wild animals frequently crossed over on to the bordering farms.)

16 May:

- Four elephants eating oranges and bananas on Ten Bosch farm. Please fetch.

- Herd of 200 buffalo grazing in sugar-cane lands on Whiskey Creek Farm. Please fetch with haste.

- Tourist frightened by bull elephant on Bume Road reversed into ditch. Hitched lift to camp with another tourist. Car still in ditch.

- Four-metre python eating chickens on Hensville Farm.

17 May:

- Willem's water-pump attendant dived into river to escape charging buffalo bull. Willem asks please fetch buffalo.

- Family of warthogs raiding mess tent at Nkongoma base.

- Komatipoort police report three elephant bulls walked through village — apparently on their way to Swaziland border post. (Without passports, I think.)

18 May:

- Customs official at Mozambique border post reports party of Mozambicans brought him present tied up in hessian sack. Official thought it was firewood. Wasn't. Was live crocodile. Presently in his tool-shed causing havoc. Please fetch.

- Tourist threatened by bull elephant on Bume Road near creek reversed into tree. Car damaged.

- Four-metre python still eating chickens on Hensville Farm.

- Two hippos taking up residence in irrigation dam Ten Bosch Farm. Please fetch.

- Large herd of buffalo turned up at municipal offices, Komatipoort.

19 May:

- Camp security guard Mabasa reports elephant in tourist camp eating sycamore fig tree. Also: Leopard tracks found in camp this morning.

- Warthogs still raiding mess tent at Nkongoma base.

- Herd of 20 elephant crossed river near confluence. Heading for Border Country Inn. Owner of inn asks what to do.

- Municipal clerk at Komatipoort says thank you for evicting buffalo. Unfortunately they have returned.

20 May:

- Camp security guard Mabasa reports following: (1) Leopard frightened him in camp last night. (2) Elephant broke southeast fence of camp again this morning. Ate remaining half of sycamore fig tree. (3) Some 'stupid tourists' threw oranges at elephant.

- Soldiers accidentally started fire in Lebombo mountains. Game guards on their way to check fire.

- Four elephants eating oranges and bananas on Ten Bosch Farm again.

21 May:

- Hensville farmer caught and brought over four-metre python in sack. It's in your office.

- Tourist startled by bull elephant on Bume Road reversed into car behind him. Both cars damaged.

- Soldiers report warthogs getting 'vicious'.

- Pack of wild dogs chased group of Shangaan women in sugarcane lands on Whiskey Creek Farm. (Huh?)

Note to reader: Wild dogs don't normally chase people. They probably followed the women out of curiosity.

22 May:

- Tourist bitten by monkey in camp. Security guard Mabasa says tourist was teasing monkey. Tourist says he wasn't.

- Aqua-culture researchers intimidated by crocodile while studying larvae. Ask your assistance — if possible tomorrow or Sunday.

- Tourist ambushed by bull elephant on Bume Road drove into ditch (again). Car still in ditch. (You'd better talk to that elephant!)

- Nkongoma soldiers and warthogs came to blows. Warthogs won.

23 May:

- Komatipoort police report three elephant bulls walking along road towards Mozambique customs office. (Probably the same trio who tried to emigrate to Swaziland last week.)

- Soldier overturned truck in Vurhami creek. (At 40 kilometres p.h.)

- Bume Road elephant slapped tourist car with its trunk. Big dent in fender. (Please talk to that elephant!)

- Two hippos in irrigation dam at Ten Bosch Farm again.

- Tourist car collided with impala ram chasing another ram across road in Gomondwane bush. Car door badly dented. Ram looks dead. [PS: Ram is fine. I checked. He's walking around in Gomondwane bush looking slightly dazed (and probably wondering where the other ram went).]

24 May:

- Bume Road elephant scared visiting Malawian diplomat and his wife. (!)
- Bulletin from security guard Mabasa: (1) Warthog sow charged tourist who was taking photograph of her in camp. (2) Camp gardener Elias Sibuyi slapped wife of gate guard Simeon Sibela. Sibuyi says Sibela's wife hit him on head with radio. (3) Snake found in linen room this morning.

25 May:

- Four elephants eating oranges and bananas on Ten Bosch Farm again.
- Sibela's wife wants to see you.
- More tourists report riotous elephant on Bume Road. (!)
- Sibuyi also wants to see you.
- Two hippos having love affair in irrigation dam at Ten Bosch farm. Farm manager asks please fetch them before they multiply.

26 May:

- Security guard Mabasa reports following: Baboon broke off aerial of tourist car parked at chalet no. 12 early this morning. Mabasa woke owner of car to tell him. Owner says he's not owner of car, it's a hired car and he asks letter from you to confirm baboon was culprit. Will need the letter to present to the car hire agency.
- Tourists report big tree felled across Bume Road near creek, blocking road. (Guess who did it!) [PS: I'm not taking any more messages concerning above-mentioned elephant. You'd better deport him.]
- Lone buffalo bull is back at Willem's place scaring pump attendant again.

There is only one entry in the message book dated 27 May 1992. As that entry concerned a message that had serious and dramatic consequences, I will leave it for the next chapter.

Lion Attack

The single entry for Wednesday, 27 May 1992 reads as follows:

- Wounded lion. Shot on Badenhorst Farm. Fled back into Park. Last seen in reeds northern bank 200 metres downstream Elsje's Point at 8.45 a.m.

In the early hours of the morning of 27 May, two lions left the Park and crossed the river on to the Badenhorst farm where they caught and killed a cow. Farm manager Hennie Minnaar came upon the feeding lions and fired a number of shots at them, killing one and wounding the other. The wounded lion escaped and fled back into the Park. Hennie Minnaar didn't know whether the lion had been fatally wounded or not.

I took the phone call from the farm owner, Phillipus Badenhorst, a few minutes after nine o'clock. I immediately called Kobus on the radio. He had left home early that morning to look up the Bume road elephant and read him the riot act. Luckily he was still on the road when I called and he answered my call on his vehicle radio. He promptly turned back and came home.

After collecting three of his most experienced game guards — Albert Maluleke, Wilson Ngobeni and Albert Malatyi — and our dog Wolfie, Kobus set out in search of the lion.

This was the second time during our stay at Crocodile Bridge that a farmer had shot at a lion and wounded it. It upset me enormously. It also distressed me that Kobus had to go out and find these animals. Tracking a wounded lion is a life-threatening situation — especially in dense reeds.

About mid-morning Kobus, the game guards and Wolfie met up with Hennie Minnaar at Elsje's Point. Hennie led them to the spot where the lion had re-entered the Park.

Kobus and his colleagues soon picked up the trail and, after checking their rifles, started tracking the wounded animal.

Wolfie sniffed his way through the long grass and the men followed silently.

For over two hours — as they followed the spoor through thick riverine bush, across sandbanks and rocky terrain, through tall grass and dense reeds — their senses remained on full alert and their adrenalin levels constantly at the ready.

Each time the spoor led them into dense thickets where visibility dropped dramatically, their adrenalin levels soared. Two hours is a long time. One eventually becomes adrenalin-drunk.

Eventually the trail led them to a dense stand of tall reeds.

All signs of the lion's spoor disappeared at the entrance to the thicket. Wolfie sniffed at the long stems while Kobus studied bloodstains on the reeds. The height of the stains indicated that the lion had been wounded either high up on his shoulder or his neck.

Still sniffing at the stems, Wolfie moved cautiously into the dense thicket. Kobus ventured into the reeds after the dog. Two of the game guards — Wilson Ngobeni and Albert Maluleke — followed him, while Hennie and game guard Malatyi waited at the edge of the thicket.

Kobus and his two colleagues moved cautiously through ankle-deep mud and sludge, their senses strained for danger signals as they moved ever deeper into the thicket. The visibility was less than two metres in any direction, and an eerie quiet had settled over the riverine landscape. They knew instinctively that the lion was close.

Wolfie, who was about two paces ahead of Kobus, suddenly stopped short and barked a furious warning, the sudden burst of sound almost exploding the heightened senses of the adrenalin-charged men. Three metallic clicks signalled the simultaneous release of safety catches. For a few eternal seconds the men stood waiting — rifles at the ready — expecting the lion a thousand times over. But nothing happened.

Kobus slowly parted the reeds ahead of him with his rifle barrel and spotted the lion about four metres away. It was in a crouching position, legs gathered beneath its body. It appeared to be resting. Kobus couldn't see the head, only the stomach heaving as it breathed heavily. He considered chancing a shot at the spot where he guessed the head would be, but decided against it. It was too risky — especially considering the nature of the terrain.

So Kobus signalled his colleagues to retreat. He would approach the lion from a different angle — one that might offer him a better view of the animal and of its injuries. If the injuries were not serious, he would choose to give the lion the chance to recover. Before turning back, Kobus studied the formation of the reeds around him, mapping the locality in his mind.

Moving carefully, the men doubled back out of the reed thicket. As soon as they were in safer, more open terrain, Kobus surveyed the stand of reeds from a vantage point, mentally plotting another route into it. In a bid to reassure himself of the lion's exact locality, he hurled some pebbles into the reeds. But no response came from the lion. Kobus told his colleagues to wait in the clearing and cover him with their rifles.

Accompanied by Wolfie, he ventured into the thicket once more, moving cautiously in a half circle around the lion's hiding place and searching for a spot where he might have a clearer view through the reeds. Heady with adrenalin, he perceived every tiny detail of sound, shape and movement in his surroundings with exaggerated clarity.

According to rangers' lore, a leopard is silent when it charges, but a lion will give a vocal warning before it attacks. Perhaps Kobus had misjudged his distance in the dense reeds, or maybe the lion had moved, but if it had, it had made no sound at all. Nor did it give a vocal warning as it charged. It was only Wolfie who growled a terrifying — but belated — warning.

The reeds exploded and Kobus saw a yellow blur hurtling at him.

The lion's jaws closed around his left calf just below the knee. As Kobus hit the earth, his rifle flew from his hands. The lion released his calf and bit into his leg above the knee. Kobus yelled and kicked at the lion with his free leg. The lion shifted its grip again and took hold higher up his thigh. Then it shook Kobus as a dog would shake a rat. There was no pain but Kobus knew that severe physical damage was being done.

Responding to the massive amounts of adrenalin coursing through his system, he lashed out with his fists. At the very moment when the lion was again adjusting its grip, Kobus struck the animal's open jaw with his left hand so hard that a canine ripped the flesh and tendons between his thumb and index finger. The lion suddenly let go and ran off through the shallows.

Perhaps it was that blow, added to his shouting and kicking, that saved Kobus's life. Or else, more likely, the lion had not been intent on killing.

Wolfie's coat was streaked with blood. He must have tried to get the lion away from Kobus, but Kobus couldn't recall in what way. All his attention had been focused on surviving and he had no recollection afterwards of what either Wolfie or the game guards had been doing at the time.

The game guards had, in fact, stormed into the reeds the moment they had heard Kobus's shouts. But when they saw the lion on top of him, they dared not shoot for fear of hitting Kobus. As soon as the lion let go of him they rushed to his aid but were so shocked at the severity of the wounds that they did not know what to do. Kobus told them he felt no pain. He took off his shirt and tore it into strips to use as bandages to control the bleeding.

Kobus's truck had been left behind on the dirt track a few kilometres away. Fortunately Hennie's truck was closer (about 300 metres away) so the game guards helped Kobus to Hennie's pick-up and Hennie drove Kobus to Komatipoort.

The game guards fetched Kobus's truck and followed.

Kobus told Hennie that he wanted someone to get a message to me.

So as Hennie drove past the Badenhorst farmhouse, he shouted a message to a young boy who was standing outside the house.

At about three o'clock that afternoon I drove to Komatipoort to collect Karin and Laudene (Annette's oldest daughter) at the bus-stop. It was the annual end-of-May long weekend, and both the girls had come home from school for the four-day break.

Shortly after the girls and I got home, Annette arrived from Lower Sabie to collect her daughter.

We were having coffee in the kitchen and were enjoying a nice trouble-sharing session when the telephone rang. An alarm bell echoed in my head as I rushed to answer it.

'Mrs Kruger?' the voice asked hesitantly. It was the voice of a young boy. 'I ... have to tell you,' he stammered, 'the lion ... it attacked your husband.'

Suddenly I could hardly breathe.

'How seriously?' I asked.

'I don't know,' the boy said apologetically.

'Where is he ... my husband?'

'Komatipoort. Someone has taken him to Komatipoort.'

'Yes,' I said. 'Thank you.'

I put the receiver down and rushed into the kitchen.

'What's wrong?' Annette asked.

'I'm going to Komatipoort,' I told her. 'That wounded lion, you know ...'

I didn't need to finish the sentence. There was instant comprehension in her eyes. She herself was a game ranger's wife.

'Let's go,' she said calmly. 'I'll drive you.'

As we rushed out of the house to Annette's car, I suddenly remembered Karin. She was in the garden, chatting to Annette's daughters. Karin saw me and called out, 'Hey! Where are you off to?'

I stopped, turned and walked over to her. 'I'm going to Komatipoort,' I answered carefully. 'Your father has been bitten by a lion. But it's not serious. I promise to call you on the phone as soon as I get there.'

Her eyes grew wide with shock. 'I want to come with you,' she said.

'No,' I said. 'I want you and Laudene to stay here and look after Narina.'

Karin didn't argue. But her eyes told me that she wanted desperately to come along. I felt sick with guilt. But if Kobus was badly injured, I wouldn't want her to see him. She was only fourteen years old. I had to know first, and cushion her from the trauma as best I could.

Annette drove very fast and talked to me all the way. I don't remember what she talked about but her voice had a calming effect.

For the first time since we'd moved to Crocodile Bridge, I felt grateful that we lived so close to civilisation. Komatipoort is a tiny village, but it has a clinic and a doctor and was only 12 kilometres away.

When we arrived at the clinic, the first thing I noticed was that Wolfie was standing at the door, as if guarding the place. There was blood on his coat. The three game guards were also standing silently near the door. They looked shocked. Game guard Malatyi — the youngest of them — was in tears. Hennie Minnaar, the farm manager, was there too. I greeted them all hurriedly and rushed inside, running through the clinic into the emergency room. The floor was covered with blood, mud and blood-soaked bandages.

Kobus lay on the examination table. My eyes flew first to his face and head. No injuries there. Relief swept over me. His shirt was off, his chest bare, scratched and streaked with splashes of mud and blood. I noted with relief that there were no injuries in the chest or abdomen. But the whole of his left leg, from thigh to ankle, was swathed in thick bandages.

His face was the colour of chalk but he greeted me with a smile and said, 'Don't worry. I'm fine.'

The doctor was busy bandaging his left hand.

I walked round the bed, taking care not to slip on the blood splashed floor, and reached for his undamaged hand. He was asking the doctor if he might use the telephone, explaining that he needed to inform the Park Warden that he would be absent from his section for a while. It amazed me that he could worry about his unmanned section at a time like this.

The doctor wouldn't let him get up, of course, so Annette went into the office and made the phone call.

An ambulance pulled up outside the clinic. Two men came inside, carrying a stretcher. After the doctor had secured the leg to a padded splint, they lifted Kobus on to the stretcher and carried him to the ambulance. I also climbed in, intending to accompany Kobus to the hospital at Nelspruit. And then I suddenly remembered Karin.

'Please wait for me,' I told the ambulance driver as I got out. 'I have to make a phone call.'

I heard the doctor saying, 'I don't think we should wait. Time is fairly important now.'

My heart missed a beat.

I stuck my head back inside the ambulance and told Kobus: 'I have to phone Karin. But I'll follow in my car.' As I said that I remembered that I didn't have my car there. 'I'll go back with Annette to get my car,' I added quickly. 'And I'll bring Karin along. We'll see you at the hospital.'

'No,' Kobus said firmly. 'Don't do that.'

'Why not?' I asked, alarmed.

'It's too far to Nelspruit. It'll be getting dark soon.'

'I'll drive carefully,' I promised.

'No you won't,' he said. 'You're too upset. Stay home tonight. You can call me on the phone.'

Before I could argue any further, the ambulance driver had closed the door, started the engine, engaged the siren, and sped off.

Annette was standing next to me. 'I think,' she said, 'that right now it's rather important that you do as he wishes.'

I hesitated. I badly wanted to go to the hospital to make sure that he was all right.

45

' is 120 kilometres away,' Annette reminded me. 'And
how hazardous that stretch through the mountains can
_ night.'

'Yes,' I said after a while. 'OK. I'll go tomorrow.' It didn't seem
a good idea for me to have an accident at that particular time.

Wolfie was licking my hand and the game guards were still
standing there, watching me anxiously.

I bent over Wolfie and tried to locate the source of the blood
on his coat, feeling carefully along the length of his back.

'It's not his blood,' one of the game guards explained quietly.

The doctor was about to leave. 'Are you OK?' he asked me.
'Would you like me to give you a tranquilliser?'

'No,' I said. 'But tell me about Kobus ... any chance that he
might lose his leg?'

He looked me in the eyes for a moment, summing me up, and
then said, 'A slight chance, yes. But there's a very good surgeon at
Nelspruit. He's not going to let it happen if he can help it.'

I turned to the game guards. 'It's all right,' I told them in
Tsonga. 'Kobus is going to be fine. Let's all go home now.'

The corporal, Albert Maluleke, had something on his mind,
but seemed hesitant to talk.

'What's troubling you, corporal?' I asked.

'We couldn't shoot,' he said miserably. 'The lion was on top of
him.'

I realised suddenly that the game guards were feeling guilty
because they had been unable to protect Kobus from the attack.

'Corporal,' I said, 'Kobus chose the three of you to accompany
him because he trusted you. He knew that you would have the
sense not to shoot a lion that was on top of him and risk killing
him as well.'

They looked relieved.

'Malatyi,' I asked hesitantly, 'why were you crying just now?'

Tears sprang to his eyes again and he couldn't talk.

Corporal Maluleke answered: 'He's young. He's never seen a
lion attack a human before.'

I felt sorry for Malatyi.

Annette drove me home while the game guards and Wolfie followed in Kobus's pick-up.

As soon as we got home, Annette made us some strong sweet tea and she stayed with me until — about an hour or so later — I got a call through to the hospital. They informed me that Kobus had arrived in a stable condition, that he was in theatre and would probably be there for a while.

I persuaded Annette not to worry about me and to go home before it got too dark. She left me reluctantly and on condition that I called her on the radio as soon as I had more news of Kobus.

She was such a good trouble-sharing friend.

Karin and I spent the rest of the evening discussing the events and making intermittent phone calls to the hospital.

Karin is a level-headed, sunny girl and her innate cheerfulness has often proved a blessing to me in times of stress. Throughout that long evening I found her company comforting and relaxing.

At about half past eight, Karin decided it was time we contacted her two older sisters to let them know what had happened to their father.

I agreed. So I picked up the phone to call Hettie's hostel at the Rand Afrikaans University, but my courage suddenly failed me and I dialled my parents' number instead.

My mother answered. I tried to break the news gently to her, but I discovered that there was no way, really, that one could soften either the word 'lion' or the word 'attack'.

My mother was shocked, but calmly asked all the right questions. Was the femoral artery involved? Were there bone fractures? What measures would be called for to prevent sepsis?

I couldn't answer all her questions yet, but promised that I would stay in touch and keep her updated on the prognosis.

Talking to my mother had, as usual, a calming effect on me. So afterwards I called Hettie. I told her the news as calmly as I could, but she gasped and dropped the receiver. When she'd retrieved it, she said: 'OK mom, don't worry. I'll see you tomorrow. I'll take the bus to Nelspruit.'

I was moved.

I still hadn't called Sandra, but decided not to.

She was in medical school and had called us a few days previously to tell us that the head of their department had told all his students to take a break over the long weekend and to get away. The class had been working extremely hard and had not had a break for many weeks. Sandra had asked us if she and four of her classmates might use our beach cottage in the Eastern Cape for their break, and we had agreed.

The cottage has no telephone, and the only way I could reach her would be to call an elderly couple who lived nearby and who normally kept our key and looked after our place for us. I'd have to ask them to drive over to the cottage and give Sandra the message. But I hated the idea of spoiling Sandra's short vacation with bad news and, knowing how dreadfully worried she'd be, I decided it could wait until after the weekend.

At about half past nine, when I made my fourth call to the hospital, Kobus was finally out of theatre and I was allowed to talk to the surgeon. He said the wounds were extensive but the good news was that there appeared to be no bone fractures. He had scrubbed the wounds and cut away the damaged tissue and he was treating Kobus with gram positive as well as gram negative antibiotics to inhibit sepsis. He added that he would scrub the wounds again on the following day and do further debridement if necessary. He felt confident that Kobus would not lose the leg.

I was also allowed to talk to Kobus, and although he was struggling to be coherent after the anaesthesia, he managed to assure me that he wasn't in pain and that he was looking forward to a good night's rest. He also spoke briefly to Karin.

Afterwards, Karin and I, both smiling with relief, decided it was time for bed. We intended to be up early the next morning to visit Kobus.

The Days After

Early the next morning, a spokesman from the broadcasting corporation in Nelspruit called to warn me that the story of the lion attack would be broadcast on the national news bulletins that day, and he wanted to make sure that the family had been informed. Surprised, I asked him how they had learned of the incident. He told me that the broadcasting office in Nelspruit regularly checked with the hospital for possible newsworthy events. He added that a lion attack was worth more than just local news and so the story had already been faxed to the Johannesburg office.

I had no choice but to get a message to Sandra.

If she were to hear the news on a national bulletin that day, it would spoil her vacation far more than a personal message from me would.

So I put in a call to Henk and Marie Jonker, the couple in the Eastern Cape who kept an eye on our cottage.

Marie Jonker answered the phone and I explained the reason for my call, asking her to tell Sandra that her father was feeling well, that the prognosis was excellent, and that she must enjoy her vacation.

Marie promised that she and her husband would reassure Sandra as best they could.

But as soon as Sandra heard the news, she rushed to the nearest phone booth and called the Nelspruit hospital. Kobus was most surprised to get a call from her all the way from the Eastern Cape, and he did a good job of convincing her that he was well on his way to a speedy recovery.

My mother had already informed Kobus's two sisters, so it was only his brother who still had to be told. (Kobus's parents are no longer alive.)

As I dialled my brother-in-law's number, I found myself shying away from the idea of telling him such awful news. He is sixteen years older than Kobus, and he cares very much for his younger brother. So I tried once again to think of a way to soften the words 'lion' and 'attack'.

I could say, for instance, that Kobus had been bitten by a cat. But naturally I would be asked what kind of cat. I could answer 'a big kind of cat', and if asked to name the cat, I could say *Panthera leo*, and so on. But in the end the explanation would still be 'lion', and the shock-value would hardly be diluted by the preliminary evasions.

I guess the reason why the idea of a lion attack is so shocking to most people, is probably because it raises terrifying primeval memories.

Karin and I had planned to drive to Nelspruit at first light that morning, but the telephone kept me busy and it was well past eight o'clock before we finally left the house.

On the way to the car, I spotted game guard Wilson Ngobeni approaching from the staff village. He was carrying Kobus's rifle and something else that looked like a bundle of dirty rags. Apparently Wilson had cleaned the rifle and was bringing it over to the house to be locked in the gun safe. The moment he spotted Karin and me, he dropped the rags behind a clump of grass and, without missing a step, continued on his way, pretending that the rags had never existed. I realised afterwards that the bunch of rags was in fact Kobus's shirt — or what was left of it after he had torn it into strips to use as makeshift bandages. Apparently Wilson wished to spare Karin and me the sight of those bloodied strips.

I was touched by his thoughtfulness.

As Karin and I got into the car, game ranger Flip Nel from Lower Sabie (Annette's husband) arrived and told me that he wanted to collect the game guards who had been with Kobus the previous day. He hoped they might help him find the wounded lion. I was grateful to Flip for caring about the wounded animal, but I worried about his and the game guards' safety, and I begged him to take care.

Karin and I arrived at the hospital about mid-morning and were relieved to see Kobus looking so well — until a nurse turned up to change the dressings on the wounds. Kobus warned us not to look, but I had seen some bad injuries in my time and I had never been squeamish about such things, so I looked on as the nurse removed the layers of bandages and padding.

The moment the first wound was uncovered I heard someone gasp in a strangled way. It turned out to be me. There was a quick rush of air inside my head and the world started spinning, making me feel airsick.

I cannot adequately describe my shock at the sight of the wounds. I cannot describe the wounds either. Not one of my numerous English dictionaries provides the words for it. Nor do my Afrikaans, German, French or Latin dictionaries. Obviously the compilers of dictionaries have never witnessed wounds inflicted by the jaws of a lion.

Kobus laughed at me when he saw how shocked I was. He assured me that he felt no pain. Apparently severe flesh wounds are painful only if they become septic. And then, of course, the pain is excruciating. But as long as lacerations are free from infection, there is no sensation in the damaged tissue.

Ironically, it was the lesser injury to Kobus's hand that eventually became painful. I think the surgeon was so concerned with preventing infection in the extensive leg wounds that he paid scant attention to the laceration between the thumb and index finger. And so it became septic. But prompt treatment soon stopped the infection and relieved the pain.

Kobus had been unable to stop worrying about the wounded lion, so he was pleased at the news that Flip and the game guards had set out in search of it again. He knew that the only reason it had attacked him was because it had felt threatened and wanted to protect itself. He felt sorry for the lion and wished that it could be receiving the same medical care and attention that he was.

Shortly after midday, Kobus was wheeled to the operating theatre again for further debridement of the wounds.

Hettie arrived at the hospital in the late afternoon. She had not come by bus as planned, but had persuaded a friend of hers who owned a car to drive her to Nelspruit. It was quicker than the bus.

She and her friend, a fellow student named Haddon, spent a couple of hours with us at the hospital, and in the evening we all went home.

We drove to the hospital again the following day. On that day, as indeed on the previous day, Kobus received numerous other visitors: reporters from the media, colleagues and friends from the Park and farmers and their families who lived across the river from us. It worried me that Kobus was getting so little rest.

He was scheduled for a third debridement operation in the evening, and after he had received his pre-med, we wished him luck, said goodbye, and drove home.

Soon after arriving home, Flip Nel called me on the radio and reported that, after two days of tracking, they had been unable to find the wounded lion. They had finally lost its tracks amongst other lion tracks in the area, and Flip assumed that the lion had rejoined its pride.

I rang Kobus at the hospital to tell him the news. We both hoped that the lion was doing well and would soon recover from its injuries.

On the Sunday Karin and I stayed home. Hettie and her friend would leave for Johannesburg shortly before midday and they planned to drop in at the hospital on their way.

Corporal Maluleke and game guards Ngobeni and Malatyi came over to the house in the early morning to enquire after Kobus. They also informed me that lions had caught and killed a buffalo on the river bank some 200 metres downstream from the house.

I thanked them for the information.

Whenever large predators were spotted in the immediate area, the game guards habitually informed me of their whereabouts. I think one of the reasons they did this was because they knew I liked to take the dogs walking, and they were probably concerned about my safety.

Later that same morning, I saw Karin and the dogs walking outside our garden fence down the bank towards the river. They were heading in the direction of the feeding lions. I immediately called Karin back to the house.

She came reluctantly, and I noticed that she was carrying a four-pound hammer.

'Why can't I go down to the river?' she wanted to know.

'Because there are lions feeding on the bank,' I told her. 'And why are you carrying that?' I pointed to the hammer.

'I know there are lions there,' she said. 'I saw the vultures early this morning. But I want to finish my tree-house.'

'What tree-house?' I asked in alarm.

She turned and pointed to a huge sycamore fig overhanging the river some hundred-odd metres downstream. 'I started building it two weeks ago,' she informed me. 'I would like to finish it this weekend.'

I was appalled. 'The lions are feeding less than a hundred metres from your tree!' I said. 'How can you even think of going there?'

'Goodness, why on earth would they want to catch me?' she asked. 'They have a whole buffalo to eat. And anyway the dogs are with me. And,' she added, lifting the hammer, 'I have this.'

By this time Hettie and her friend Haddon had joined us, and Haddon (who was a city person and therefore quite unfamiliar with the idiotic ways of Park children) gaped at Karin in sheer disbelief. 'It seems,' he said to Karin, 'that you have a morbid wish to follow in your father's footsteps.'

We all laughed. Karin dropped the hammer, sighed and said: 'OK. You win. I'll finish my house next weekend.'

I appreciated her consideration of my feelings. Actually, I don't think those lions would really have given her a thought if she had gone down to the river to complete her tree-house. They were, after all, too busy eating their buffalo. But after Kobus's dramatic episode, I really couldn't bear the idea of another member of my family going anywhere near a lion.

The Parks Board owns a flatlet in Nelspruit that may be used by Park personnel in times of crisis. I arranged with the office at Skukuza to use the flatlet while Kobus was in hospital.

So early on the Monday morning, I drove to Nelspruit again, dropped Karin off at her boarding school and moved into the flatlet.

It was nice to be so near the hospital. But living in a bustling, people-packed town with no quiet personal space of my own wasn't easy, and by the end of the week I was suffering from acute claustrophobia. My ears were also hurting, being unaccustomed to discordant and continuous sound. So when the surgeon agreed to let Kobus go home for a few days, I was very grateful. The condition, however, was that I would have to take over his nursing and clean and dress the wounds every four hours. The idea filled me with dread, but living in a town was even more dreadful, so I agreed.

Luckily Sandra and Paul, a classmate of hers from medical school, arrived at the hospital that afternoon to visit Kobus and to spend the weekend with us. I immediately commanded the two medical students to watch the nurse demonstrate the wound-cleaning and dressing procedure, so that they could take over the nursing for the weekend.

After picking Karin up at her boarding school, we all drove home.

It was awfully good to be home again. Kobus had not been able to rest properly in the hospital and he was looking forward to a really good rest in his own bed and his own house.

Sandra and Paul proved to be experts at cleaning wounds. They scrubbed their hands with disinfectant and put on sterile surgical gloves before touching the wounds or any of the instruments needed for the flushing and cleaning exercise.

I watched each time, hoping that by the end of the weekend I would be able to take over from them without wanting to faint all the time. The worst part of the procedure was inserting a tube filled with disinfectant right into the wounds and then squirting the solution into the surrounding tissue.

At about midday on Sunday, Sandra and Paul had to leave us and I was really sorry to see them go. They had been so very helpful.

For a number of days after this, I was full-time nurse to a lion attack victim and I am proud to say that I eventually became quite adept at flushing and dressing the wounds. The flushing was done with EUSOL, and I even manufactured my own when our supply ran out. I remembered reading once that EUSOL was made up of nine parts boiled water to one part ordinary household bleach. EUSOL was invented by medical students at Edinburgh University in Scotland — the name EUSOL is in fact an acronym for Edinburgh University Solution.

One day, as I was dressing his wounds, Kobus told me how difficult it was to tear a khaki shirt. He was referring to the day of the attack, when he'd had to tear his shirt into strips to bandage his wounds in an attempt to control the bleeding. No matter how hard he'd tugged at the fabric, he told me, it had simply refused to tear. Hennie Minnaar tried to help, but all that happened was that the sleeves came off. So Kobus had taken over again. If it hadn't been for the high level of adrenalin pumping through his system, Kobus reckoned, he would probably never have succeeded in tearing the shirt into strips.

(I think the manufacturers of khaki uniforms should take note here that a game ranger could bleed to death while trying to tear his shirt into strips.)

At the end of that week, on the 12th of June, I took Kobus back to the hospital. It was time for his skin graft operations.

Two days later I brought him home again, and a few days after that, on the 18th of June, I once again took him back to hospital for final skin grafting.

On the 22nd of June, almost one month after the lion attack, Kobus was finally discharged from the hospital.

Surprisingly, it was only then — when Kobus came home from the hospital for the last time — that he showed signs of delayed shock. For two days he couldn't eat, and then for two more days he wanted only to sleep. He slept almost non-stop for more than forty-eight hours, and when he finally woke up, he looked terrible but claimed that he was feeling better than he had felt during all the weeks since the attack. He wanted to know what was for supper and looked very happy when I told him I had made chicken soup. He even got up and walked to the kitchen to inspect the soup.

As we sat in the lounge sipping our soup, Kobus gave a contented sigh and said: 'You can't imagine how well I'm feeling.'

I looked at his pale, unshaven face, the dark rings under his eyes, his dishevelled hair and the equally dishevelled bandages hanging about his leg from thigh to ankle.

I smiled and said, 'I'm so glad to hear you're feeling so good because you can't imagine how awful you look.'

He looked down at his untidy bandages with a frown. After a while he unwound and removed the bandages and studied his leg. The scars were big and ugly, despite the very successful skin-grafting operations.

Still contemplating his leg, Kobus remarked, 'It probably won't win me first prize in a Mr Pretty Legs Competition. But no matter. It can walk.'

'Did you know,' I asked him, 'that there had actually been a possibility that you might lose the leg?'

He nodded. 'The surgeon told me, yes.'

We studied his scarred leg some more and agreed that it wouldn't get him far in a Mr Pretty Legs Competition, but that it most definitely was a prize-winning leg in every other respect.

The Foundling Prince

There was a hippo pool in the river some six or seven kilometres upstream from our house. A tourist road led to the area, and there was a spot where tourists were allowed to leave their cars and walk down to the water to view the hippos. A game guard was posted there every day to look after the tourists.

On the 1st of December 1992, security guard Daniel Mabasa had been on duty at the hippo pool. When he returned in the evening he reported to Kobus that, since the previous day, he had heard an animal crying somewhere along the rocky slope of the east bank of the pool. Kobus asked Daniel to mimic the cry, and after he had done so Kobus said that he believed it was the meowing call of either a lion or a leopard cub.

Worried that the cub might be in distress, Kobus drove to the hippo pool to investigate.

He left his truck on the nearby track, and as he started climbing up the rocky slope of the east bank, he heard the forlorn sounds of an abandoned cub calling its mother.

Guided by the meowing, he reached a wide ledge that led to a crevice underneath a boulder.

He listened carefully for any sounds that might indicate the presence of the cub's mother. Then, when he felt reasonably certain that the cub was alone, he moved across the ledge and reached into the crevice.

He found a tiny lion cub.

Its umbilical cord was still in place and not yet dry — the cub was no more than two or three days old. Its voice was hoarse from crying, and it was obvious that it had been calling for its mother for a very long time.

Kobus knew that if he left the cub there, it would die. It would probably be eaten by ants.

He gathered the little animal in his arms, wrapped it in his shirt and carefully carried it down the slope to his truck. Then he called me on the radio.

'I've found a lion cub abandoned by its mother,' he told me. 'What shall I do?'

I knew what that question meant. He was asking if I was willing to be its foster mother.

For one brief moment I thought: 'Me? Mother to a lion? Heavens, I'm just a harmless, vulnerable primate.'

But I said: 'Bring it home.'

I was terrified of lions. In fact, for many years most of my nightmares were about them. But that evening, when Kobus brought home the wretched little bundle that was crying its heart out for its mother, something strange happened to me: I turned into a lion-mother.

The cub was dehydrated and hypothermic, as abandoned carnivores usually are. We quickly bathed him in warm water and wrapped him in a thick towel. While Kobus dried and comforted the cub, I filled a sterilised baby-bottle with a solution of evaporated milk, boiled water and glucose.

We were worried that he might not be able to drink, but as soon as I'd managed to get the teat into his mouth, he started sucking and couldn't seem to get enough. Taking very few pauses for breath, he drank 60 millilitres in one sitting.

The cub didn't seem to know whether he should feel comforted or threatened by our presence. He hissed and even made brave little growling noises at us. When he 'growled', his whole face puckered into a fierce-looking crinkle.

We wrapped him in a blanket and put him in a pillow-lined cardboard box in our bedroom. Hoping that he was comfortable and would sleep for a while, we left him there and went to have our supper in the kitchen. But the moment the cub sensed that he was alone, he started meowing pathetically. So we fetched him and kept him in his box next to us. He was immediately comforted. Although his eyes were still closed, he appeared to be acutely aware of our presence. Perhaps our voices, or our smell, told him that we were there. If we touched him or picked him up, he would 'growl' at us, but the moment we left him alone in a room, he would start whimpering and calling to us.

That night he slept in his box next to our bed. He meowed a few times and I made comforting noises to let him know we were there.

Early the next morning Kobus and a number of his game guards set out in search of the cub's mother.

Combing a wide area around the cub's birthplace, they searched all day long. But they found no sign that the lioness had returned to look for her cub; in fact, they found no fresh pug marks anywhere in the area that could lead them to her.

And so Kobus was never able to determine the reason why she had abandoned her cub. Perhaps she had gone hunting on an adjacent farm and had been shot.

Meanwhile the cub was beginning to settle down, sleeping most of the time and drinking vast quantities of milk in between. After his first night with us, he no longer 'growled' or puckered his face at us.

He weighed only 1,2 kilograms — which is less than half the average weight of a new-born human baby. Considering that an adult lion weighs approximately three times as much as an adult human, I worried that the cub might be critically underweight.

Kobus phoned one of our vets, Dr Dewald Keet at Skukuza, and asked him for a recipe for lion's milk. He found us a recipe that had been formulated by an animal nutritionist, a Dr De Waal. The recipe consisted of Puppylac powder (a commercial substitute for dog's milk) dissolved in full-cream cow's milk, egg

yolk and cream. I was surprised at the high content of solids —
especially of protein and fat — in the formula.

The cub hiccupped after he'd had his first feed of this formula,
and I thought that it was probably too rich for him. So I diluted it
a little the second time round, leaving the cream out.

As it is against the Park's policy to keep wild animals in
captivity, Kobus went to Skukuza a few days later to see Dr
Willem Gertenbach — the director of Nature Conservation and
Research — to ask for permission for us to raise the cub.

Although we had been foster parents to an array of orphans
and strays over the years, we had never deemed it necessary to ask
permission to adopt them. The reason for this was that all our
foster children had belonged to species that adapted easily to their
natural lifestyles — despite having been hand-reared — and all of
them had eventually returned successfully to the wild.

Large carnivores are, of course, an entirely different matter.
Once they have been hand-reared, they are unable to fend for
themselves in the wild — unless a successful rehabilitation
programme can be provided. A male carnivore also needs a
hunting territory not yet occupied by other carnivores of the same
species. And, in the case of lions who are social animals, it also
needs hunting companions to help defend the territory. Reintro-
ducing a hand-reared lion into the wild, or at least finding a
suitable alternative home for it, can be a complicated business.

But we would worry about that later. First of all we needed
official permission to keep the cub.

Kobus told Dr Gertenbach that we were fully aware of the
problems of our proposed venture and assured him that we would
not take our responsibilities lightly.

After considering the matter and discussing it with the Park
Warden, Dr Joubert, Dr Gertenbach gave us permission to raise
the cub.

And so our foundling prince was granted the right to live.

Unfortunately, the first few weeks of his life proved to be a
struggle for survival. And I feel terrible to admit that it was my
fault.

I stupidly believed that the prescribed formula for his feed was too rich for him. Apart from the recurrent hiccupping, he was drinking less and less. That worried me, so I diluted the formula even further — leaving out not only the cream, but the egg yolk as well. He immediately started drinking more again, and so I believed that the problem had been solved.

What I didn't realise was that the reason he was drinking more was because he wasn't getting all the required nutrients and was hungry all the time.

He wasn't gaining weight properly, and after a week he started losing his fur. We thought that external parasites were the reason for this and so we took him to the vet, Dr Dewald Keet, at Skukuza. Dewald gave us a special shampoo to bathe him with and he also gave the cub an anti-parasite injection together with a vitamin A injection. The cub didn't mind the injections, but when the vet inspected his ears, he howled his little head off at the indignity of it all.

Unfortunately the cub didn't get better. He became weaker, lost more fur and his tummy started to become abnormally extended. I couldn't understand why. He was drinking well. In fact he was drinking between 50 and 70 millilitres every three or four hours. I actually wrote in my diary that he was a 'fierce drinker'. He would drink fast, clawing and slapping his bottle with his front paws in an impatient way.

Only later, with hindsight, would I realise that the reason he seemed so impatient with his bottle was because, no matter how much he drank, he was unable to satisfy his hunger.

On the morning of the 17th of December, when he was about two and a half weeks old, he woke up so weak and ill that he was unable even to crawl about. His little belly was enormous, but despite the acute discomfort that he must have felt, he never cried or complained. Kobus and I watched helplessly as the cub tried to get up — but failed — and it almost broke our hearts to see how stoically he accepted his fate.

Once again we drove him the 90 kilometres to Skukuza to visit the vet.

This time, Dewald diagnosed malnutrition and gave the ailing cub a steroid injection. He also gave me a copy of a scientific article on an analysis of lion's milk.

After reading the article I felt sick with guilt and quite appalled at my own stupidity.

In the wild, lion cubs feed only two to three times in a twenty-four hour period, allowing the mother time to hunt. That's why her milk is so rich in fat and proteins.

I immediately reverted to the prescribed formula and, as expected, the cub drank less of it than he had of the diluted version. He also drank more slowly and seemed less impatient with the bottle. Unfortunately the awful symptoms of malnutrition didn't disappear right away, and for several days the cub remained weak and ill.

He was such a good, uncomplaining baby that it hurt me to know that I had been responsible for his condition.

According to the article that Dewald had given me, the swollen belly indicated enlarged, blood-shot kidneys — a serious and often fatal condition in cubs suffering from malnutrition.

All through those critical days, our daughters, who had arrived home for the Christmas holidays, took turns with me to hold and comfort the cub. We believed that if he realised he was loved and cherished, he might fight harder to survive.

Happily, on the 20th of December — three days after the steroid injection — the cub started to show faint signs of recovery. He was getting used to the new milk formula and was drinking a little more of it than he had on the previous two days. He even became playful — lying on his back and offering his tummy to be tickled, he would swipe mischievously at us with his front paws.

We knew then that he was going to make it.

Unfortunately we ran out of Puppylac powder a few days later, and to our horror learned that no chemist in the area (not even in Nelspruit) had it in stock.

Kobus phoned the manufacturers in Johannesburg and told them he urgently needed a large supply of their product and that

he would fetch it himself later that day. He ordered eight kilograms of the powder.

Since I had only enough Puppylac powder left for two more feeds, I packed the cub in the car and we travelled the 550 kilometres to Johannesburg with Kobus.

The eight kilograms would cost us about a third of Kobus's monthly salary. Hopefully, it would last at least two months.

We were most surprised and grateful when the manufacturers gave us two kilograms on the house. (I think we were the first customers ever to turn up with a lion cub — and, moreover, a lion cub who allowed the staff to tickle his tummy!)

Afterwards we drove to my parents' house to spend the night, and another surprise awaited us: my parents had bought four kilograms of Puppylac from their local chemist and had it waiting for us when we got there.

When we drove home early the next morning, it was most comforting to know that we were armed with a three-month supply of Puppylac.

As the days went by the cub gradually started to gain weight and to grow new fur in the bald patches. By the age of six weeks he weighed five kilograms!

His eyes had opened on his fourth or fifth day of life (and how handsome he looked with those large, open eyes!) but until he was about four weeks old, they remained covered with a blue film. Unable to see properly, he would clumsily bump into things as he started exploring the house. When the blue film finally disappeared, his beautiful rust-coloured eyes became his most arresting feature.

We named him Leo. Or, to be truthful, we didn't really name him, we simply called him *Leeu* (which is Afrikaans for lion). To make it a real name, I decided that it should be spelled Leo — which is pronounced the same way as *Leeu*.

Nobly Born

Throughout the years, orphans and strays from the animal kingdom have often been temporary members of our family. I have been foster mother to a squirrel, a banded mongoose, a honey badger, three warthogs, a serval cat, two scrub hares, a marsh owl and several other wild birds. Of all my foster children, the hares had the lowest IQ and the least interesting personalities. But a mother's love is, of course, blind, and so she will care for even the most dim-witted of her children.

It's hard, however, to be a mother on a recurrent, full-time basis. Every time a charge reaches the age when it is ready to be launched into its own grown-up world, you suffer sleepless nights, worrying whether it is ready to cope with it all.

And I feel ashamed to say this, but one eventually becomes tired of being a mother. There comes a time when you think to yourself: 'All I am is a full-time mother. I need to be a person too.'

Time and again I resolved that, as soon as my current foster child or children became self-sufficient, I would resign as a foster parent. The next time Kobus brought home a stray or an orphan I would immediately find another home for it. There were lots of other game rangers' wives who would make perfect foster mothers. I wanted to become a full-time individual person and have the time to do some of the nice selfish things that a mother never has the time for.

The trouble is, the moment you set eyes on the wretched little creature that has lost its mommy, it is too late. Your maternal instinct takes right over — and before you know it, you have turned into a dedicated mother all over again.

I must admit, though, that each one of my foster children has enriched my life in some way or another (even the stupid hares). I have, over the years, spent countless delightful hours watching my orphans play and marvelling at their individual personalities. Some of my foster children were surprisingly intelligent, all of them were affectionate and amusing. They have left me and my family with wonderful memories.

Despite my many years of experience as a foster mother, nothing could have prepared me for the intensity of emotions and the level of involvement that come with being a foster parent to a lion.

A lion cub is the strangest, most undemanding creature I have ever known. It doesn't scream for its bottle (like some of my other foster children did — especially the warthogs), nor does it demand attention or ask for affection. In fact, it doesn't ask anything of you. It is totally contented just to know that you are around somewhere. Occasionally it may come looking for you, and when it finds you, it will look at you with an expression of perfect contentment that says: 'Ah, there you are! How nice.'

Often, when I found the cub staring at me with those enormous, expressive eyes, I'd ask: 'What is it you want, Leo? What can I do for you?' And his gaze would become soft and sweet with an expression that said: 'I only wanted to know where you were.'

How can one not love a creature who talks with his eyes and who asks nothing of life, except to know that he has a mother?

Although Leo was a totally contented baby, he was by no means a sedate one. He possessed a great talent for living joyously and abundantly, and all of his waking hours were spent playing himself into a state of exhaustion.

He had an assortment of toys: a tattered teddy bear, a ball of wool, an old rag doll, a tennis ball, an empty coffee tin and a stuffed toy duck. He loved his toys passionately, and the moment he woke up he would rush straight to them. I kept them in a basket for him, and he would dive right into the basket — often with such speed and clumsiness that the basket would topple over and roll some distance with him inside it.

Most of my other foster children had instinctively respected or feared any animals bigger than themselves. Not Leo. Coded with the knowledge that he was the king of them all, he perceived other animals either as lesser creatures or as admiring fans and treated them accordingly.

We introduced him to our dogs when he was six days old and he took it for granted that dogs would naturally love lions. The dogs instinctively took fright at the smell of the cub and backed off. But as soon as they realised how tiny and harmless he was, they approached him cautiously and, as a gesture of welcome, licked him all over — proving what the cub had known all along: dogs love lions.

The horses were quite shocked at the sight and smell of the creature that we brought over to show them. But after a while they approached carefully, studied it in the aloof way horses have and decided that if a lion was to become part of the household, then that was that — as long as it wasn't expected that they should love it.

At the age of five weeks, Leo had his first contact with animals outside the household.

We had been invited by Kobus's brother and his wife to spend New Year's day with them on their farm near Lydenburg. Not wanting to leave the cub alone at home, we packed him, his bottles, his formula, his sleeping box, pillow and blanket, and his beloved toy duck into the car and set off.

Leo spent most of the three-hour journey on a lap (either mine or one of the girls') contentedly sucking a finger. (He was an incurable finger-sucker.)

When we arrived at the farm, I carried Leo out of the car to the barbecue area where the family was assembled. After everyone had had a chance to admire and cuddle the cub, I found myself a chair near the edge of the patio and sat Leo down on the grass close to my chair.

An arrogant little dachshund came trotting out of the house, spotted the cub sitting on the grass — and charged right over, barking his head off. I was about to rescue Leo but saw to my surprise that he was totally unruffled by the approach of the hysterical dachshund. He sat calmly, happily, waiting for it. As soon as the dog was within slapping distance, up came Leo's front paw — one swift, well-aimed swipe — and the dog was making a hasty U-turn in mid-air and clearing the distance back to the house a lot faster than is normal for a dachshund.

The silly dachshund had no doubt mistaken the cub for an alien dog and got the shock of his life when he realised it was a lion. Perhaps in future he will be more discreet about picking a fight with anything that catches his fancy at a distance.

Leo was still sitting where I had placed him on the grass, looking dignified and, as usual, totally contented with life. (He knew, of course, that lions — like all good royalty — never get hysterical.) I was awfully proud of our cub.

A short while later, two turkeys and a bunch of farmyard chickens came over to inspect the cub. Although they seemed unable to grasp that he was a lion, there appeared to be something in their primeval memories that was sending them urgent messages. Unable to decipher the messages properly, they spent a long time circling the cub (at a safe distance), necks stretched forward, eyes blinking rapidly, and all the while discussing the strange visitor excitedly amongst themselves. Leo sat like a prince, contemplating his admiring audience with an air of dignity.

When he got sleepy, I gave him his bottle and put him to bed in his box with his pillow, duck and blanket. This seemed to persuade the fowls that Leo was a human baby, and so they lost interest in him and resumed their everyday business.

When we got back the following day, Leo recognised his home and was so happy to be back that he spent a whole hour gambolling and cavorting all over the place and checking every room to see if all was still the same. He was a clever boy. He knew that a lion belonged in its own territory.

At the age of about six weeks he became interested in hunting, and so his toys became 'practice-prey'. Taking advantage of any cover available (such as a couch, curtains or a potted plant), he would carefully stalk a toy that was lying unprotected by itself and, waiting patiently for just the right moment, would pounce on the unsuspecting toy and maul it to death. The coffee tin, however, gave him a few scares. Instead of perishing after receiving a vicious slap, it would roll aggressively towards him. The tin's behaviour startled and confused him, so he concentrated on his other toys instead. Once they had all been successfully demolished, he tried once more to attack the coffee tin but it wouldn't co-operate, so he looked about for more obliging prey. He soon discovered a host of them: pillows, books, baskets, shoes, towels and so on.

Until he was two months old Leo was a house-lion. He would venture outside only if accompanied by one of the family. Luckily he was easily house-trained. With the fastidiousness of all cats, he preferred to make his little puddles and messes outdoors. As he got older and no longer needed encouragement from us to do his bathroom routine, he would — at the call of nature — march out through the veranda door and use the daisy border at the side of the patio. Considering that he never left the house on his own except when he needed the bathroom, I think he was a very good little lion. The daisies died eventually, but at least the house remained free of lion puddles.

At the age of about three months he started venturing outside on his own more often to explore the garden, but still only within close range of the house.

Belonging, as he did, to a species of competitive, territorial predators, he was coded with the knowledge that a lion should stay within the boundaries of his family's established range. Stumbling into the territory of an alien pride could mean trouble — especially if the dominant males weren't kind to interlopers.

And so Leo deemed it wise to stay close to the house until he learned where the boundaries of his home range were.

One day, during one of his outdoor explorations, he discovered a young papaw tree growing near the kitchen door. The tree fascinated him — probably because of the way its large, flat leaves moved in the breeze. He lowered himself into a crouch, and after creeping carefully up to the tree, pounced on a large leaf and mauled it into pitiful shreds. For several days the tree remained his favourite practice-prey until, eventually, it looked more like a weeping willow than a papaw tree.

Leo lost interest in it and decided that dogs and humans were more fun to practise on than a weeping willow. He chose the snake's flowerbed at the side of the kitchen as his favourite spot to lie in ambush. It was a good choice, of course. It was right alongside the paved path — the main approach route to the kitchen door. And so any unsuspecting human or dog who happened to be approaching or leaving the house got pounced on by a lion — or spat on by a cobra, as the case might be.

Even at a tender age, Leo proved to have a good memory. He never forgot his favourite people. When Hettie and Sandra went back to university at the start of the new term, they wondered if the cub would forget them. He never did — regardless of the length of their absence. He was always overjoyed to see them again and would greet them with a prolonged display of affection. Karin came home every weekend, and the moment she stepped out of the car, he would rush into her arms for a fond greeting and a cuddle.

Annette (my trouble-sharing friend) fell desperately in love with Leo and tried her best to persuade me to trade him for any or all of her personal possessions, including her husband. I wasn't willing to trade of course (not even for her husband — he's a great guy, but I already had one), so I said thanks a lot, but no. She accepted her fate stoically, but often came over with her younger daughter Narina to play with Leo. Leo grew very fond of Annette and Narina, and even when he started treating other people as outsiders, he always treated them as family.

Often, while Annette and I were enjoying a nice trouble-sharing session over coffee, Leo and Narina would stalk and chase each other all over the place until both of them collapsed with exhaustion. Then Narina would climb on to her mother's lap to rest, while Leo climbed on to mine to suck my finger.

Whenever Leo got tired or sleepy he needed a finger to suck. He would not ask for one, he would simply climb on to an available lap and seize the owner's hand. Gripping it between his front paws, he would select a finger for himself. Once your finger was in his mouth, you were stuck. Caught between his tongue and palate, the finger would remain firmly in place — glued by suction, so to speak. And any indication from you that you wished to extract your finger would prompt the razor-sharp dew-claws to tighten their grip on your hand. The only way to get your finger back was to wait patiently until he nodded off, and then take care not to awaken him while extracting the finger.

It was cute, of course, but exasperating — especially if he took a long time to fall asleep and you had other things to do.

Annette suggested I buy him a dummy, and I often considered doing so, but I remembered reading in Joy Adamson's book, *Born Free*, that Elsa had sucked Joy's finger until she was a mature lioness.

I didn't want Leo to become an incurable dummy-sucker. Moreover, what would visitors think if they saw our lion walking about with a dummy in his mouth?

I also wanted to bring Leo up in a way as close as possible to what his real mother would have done. Not being a lion myself, I wasn't quite sure exactly how she would have gone about it. I could only guess.

But I knew at least that she wouldn't have bought him a dummy.

A Royal Cubhood

At the age of four months Leo was a boisterous, affectionate little lion with an immense personality.

He possessed the spontaneous gaiety of one who never doubts his own adorability. He loved being hugged and cuddled and would often leap from the ground into our arms to embrace us fondly and to lick our faces.

But in addition to being totally adorable, he was also inexhaustibly playful and, being a lion, he could never resist stalking us and pouncing on us. We developed the habit of glancing nervously over our shoulders. If we noticed him frozen in a crouched position with intent, mischievous eyes, we would hastily brace ourselves for the impact of the pounce. Running away did not help — he was faster than us.

Initially he was a bit rough and careless with his claws, and our arms and legs often got scratched rather severely.

In repose, a lion's claws are sheathed and they are exposed only in deliberate attack. The razor-sharp dew-claw, the equivalent of our thumb, is a most vicious weapon.

Fortunately, Leo soon developed more control over his claws and learned to keep them sheathed when playing with us. In fact, by the time he was six months old — and quite capable of inflicting serious injury — there was far less chance of lacerations than when he was younger.

Leo had a beautiful nature and he never showed any signs of aggression towards us. If he did something that we didn't think was a good idea for a lion, we disciplined him verbally or with a smack.

He accepted this and did not bear any resentment. In fact, if he knew he had done something wrong, he would try to make amends by rubbing his body against our legs and uttering soft, sorrowful moans. He was extremely sensitive to a harsh tone of voice, and on the few occasions that I scolded him rather severely for stealing my washing off the line, I felt so guilty when I saw the hurt look in his eyes that I resolved never to get angry with him again.

Leo wouldn't give up his bottle until he was almost four months old, and the only reason he gave it up then was because he had chewed up all his bottle teats and I refused to buy him new ones.

After that, he continued to lap milk from a bowl for several months more.

When he was three months old, we judged his teeth big enough to chew meat, so we decided to introduce him to his traditional fare and offered him an impala chop. He was delighted, even though he wasn't sure what it was. He stared at it and sniffed it, and eventually gave it an experimental lick. It tasted good. So he settled down and, gripping the chop between his front paws, continued to lick it for a while. Then, as another experiment, he chewed it a bit. That was even better than licking. In fact it made so much sense that he closed his eyes in concentration and enjoyment.

We decided to leave him to it and went back inside. He gathered up the chop in his mouth and ran after me.

'No,' I told him. 'You have to eat that outside.'

He looked at me nervously, and I realised that he was scared to be left alone with his meat. He needed me to protect him from other predators or scavengers. I knew that our dogs would not steal his meat, and of course there were no predators or scavengers lurking in the garden. But how was he to know that? So I sat down next to him and waited until he had finished eating his chop.

For many weeks after this, I had no choice but to 'guard' him and his meat while he ate.

At the age of five months Leo was satisfied that the boundaries of his pride's established territory were the fences around the garden, and he was delighted with his wooded playground of almost one acre. The many trees, shrubs and flowerbeds offered a nice variety of cover for a lion whose favourite game was stalking unsuspecting prey (us, the dogs, visitors and any washing left unguarded on the line).

Although we had started taking him for walks in the bush when he was three months old, he never ventured outside the garden on his own, even though the gates always stood open during the day.

Visitors were often surprised that we left the gates open and would ask us if we weren't worried that the lion would escape.

I am sure the question would have mystified Leo. Why would he want to leave his family and his safe haven? Where would he want to go?

Although Leo saw a lot less of Kobus than he did of me, he was extremely fond of him. Whenever Kobus spent a day or two at home to catch up on office work, Leo was delighted. Every half hour or so, throughout the day, he would bound into the office for a fond greeting and a cuddle.

It sometimes happened that Kobus would be talking to a colleague on his office radio at the very moment that Leo came charging into the office. It is impossible, of course, to avoid a boisterous cub who wants to cuddle. And so Kobus would find his head clasped firmly between large paws and his face smothered with lion-kisses, making it impossible for him to talk into his microphone.

Kobus's colleagues got quite used to his sudden silences on the radio. They knew that he was simply being strangled by an affectionate lion.

Initially, Leo shared our bedroom at night, but at the age of three months his sleeping box got too cramped for him, so he went in search of a better arrangement. He tested the guest bed on the screened veranda and found it to his liking. In fact, he enjoyed his new-found comfort so much that he abandoned his habit of getting up at dawn to greet the family. Instead, he would stretch out on his back, paws dangling in the air while the rays of the early sun played on his chest and tummy. Often, when we found him there — stretched out on his bed like a lazy prince — he would look at us with an expression that said: 'Why are you up so early? It's so nice to be in bed still!'

We didn't mind him sleeping on the bed. In fact we thought it a nice idea that he had a bed all to himself rather than have him trying to climb into bed with us. But two months later, when he was about five months old, he discovered that his mattress was great fun to chew, and so he demolished it. When he started hauling mattresses off other beds to play with, we realised it was time to teach him to sleep outdoors. (By this time he had already demolished several pillows, shoes, books and other valuables and had even left tooth marks on some of the furniture. Our house was beginning to look very lion-inhabited.)

We fetched a large wooden crate from our store room and set it on its side on the patio outside the veranda. I put Leo's bedding inside the crate, together with his toy duck (that, for some or other reason had escaped demolition — it must have had sentimental value for him). We also spread a tarpaulin over the crate to make it rain-proof.

The first night that Leo was banished from sleeping in the house, I spent half the night in the crate with him (while he sucked my finger). On the second night I spent only an hour or so in his crate with him and on the third night less than half an hour. After that he was left on his own. Luckily, he soon accepted his fate of having to sleep there. As he grew bigger and more bold of the great outdoors, he would more often sleep outside in the open, even when it rained. He didn't mind rainy weather at all. In fact he loved it.

One night, when we were having a rather frightening thunderstorm, I went outside with my torch to see if Leo was all right. I couldn't find him in the garden, and so I went to check his crate. Not wanting to shine the torch right into his eyes, in case he was in there, I got down on all fours and, while calling his name, stuck my head inside the crate. Receiving no answer, I decided he wasn't there after all, but a huge paw suddenly seized my shoulder and pulled me right into the crate. The next moment a very rough lion tongue was licking my face in greeting.

A lion's tongue is like sandpaper. Our necks, faces and arms often bore the scars of Leo's friendly attentions.

Leo still enjoyed having toys, so I stuffed a few hessian bags with rags, tied each to a length of rope and hung them from trees. These proved to be excellent as practice-prey and also as swings.

When Leo was six months old, we introduced him to an old tyre. He would rush after it as it was rolled along the ground and try to trip it up with a circular swipe of the front paw. As soon as the tyre was downed, he would pounce on it triumphantly. Once, when I rolled the tyre along the downhill slope of our front lawn, the tyre gained speed too rapidly and Leo was unable to catch up with it. It crashed into the garden fence and, as it bounced off the mesh, it came rolling back straight towards Leo. Believing that the tyre had suddenly turned aggressive and was chasing him, Leo uttered a startled grunt and fled.

After that he didn't trust the tyre for quite a while and refused to run after it when it was rolled for him.

The older Leo got, the more demonstrative he became. By the time he was six months old, he insisted on greeting each member of the family several times a day with a ceremonial touching of heads and cheek-rubbing.

We had to kneel for the greeting ritual, of course.

But we didn't mind.

He was, after all, a prince.

Leo and Wolfie

One day Leo and Flenter were both chasing a tennis ball. When Leo got to the ball first, Flenter tried to take it away from him, but Leo slapped him on the head with his front paw. This sent Flenter into a rage and he attacked the cub. Surprised and hurt by his friend's aggressive reaction, Leo slunk off. When he returned a little while later to make amends, Flenter would have nothing to do with him.

Flenter was actually becoming a bit of a problem dog. He had never really cared much for wild animals, and the bigger the cub got, the less Flenter liked him. Being a Staffordshire bull terrier, he wanted to be the leader of the pack. But since his pack consisted of one Australian cattle dog and one fast growing lion, he had a bit of a problem.

Wolfie he could handle, for although Wolfie was bigger and heavier than he was, Wolfie was not a fighter and chose to be submissive rather than to invite attack. But Leo wasn't getting any smaller, and so Flenter was worried. How was he to control his pack if its youngest member was already twice as big and strong as he was? (And there was obviously no end in sight to his ever-expanding size.) Moreover, he had a nagging suspicion that the outsized youngster was related to the king.

The poor dog didn't know how to cope with his troubles, and so he vented his frustrations on Wolfie, attacking him at every opportunity and demanding total submission from him. But no matter how often Wolfie pledged submission, Flenter was never satisfied.

Eventually Wolfie wasn't even allowed to play with Leo any more. Flenter would attack him.

Wolfie started slinking about the place, trying his best to keep out of sight of Flenter. It wasn't that Wolfie was a coward. He had proved on more than one occasion that he would protect his family with his life if necessary. It was simply that he hated fighting and preferred to avoid any unpleasantness.

The whole situation was becoming intolerable, and we knew that something would have to be done about it.

There was a farmer across the river, Johan Boshoff, who had a strong affinity for Staffordshire bull terriers. He admired them for their courage, tenacity and strength, and he found them incomparable as guard dogs and companions. He owned a Staffordshire bitch and was looking for a mate for her.

Whenever Johan came over to see Kobus, he would spend some time playing with Flenter. One day he asked us if we would consider selling Flenter to him, and Kobus and I both said no, sorry.

But as time went by and Flenter's repeated attacks on Wolfie became unbearable, we reconsidered.

Although Flenter did not tolerate other animals, he loved humans and took easily to strangers. Wolfie, on the other hand, was tolerant of all wild animals, but he did not take to strange humans. He loved only his own family. If strangers tried to befriend him, he would look the other way with a distrustful, suspicious glint in his eyes. He especially hated having a stranger pat him on the head. He would lift his upper lip at one corner, exposing a canine. It was only a fair warning, to be translated as: 'If you try to become any more familiar with me, I'll bite you.' Wolfie was the kind of dog one could never dream of giving away. It would be too cruel.

But would Flenter mind all that much? He seemed genuinely fond of Johan Boshoff.

So, one morning, after Flenter had again attacked Wolfie and bitten him rather severely, we asked Johan if he still wanted the dog. He did. And he offered to pay any price that we wanted. We wouldn't have dreamed of selling our dog; we only wanted a good home for him.

And so, for the first time in our lives, we gave a dog away. It was a very hard thing for us to do. I remember the day that Johan came to fetch Flenter: as he was driving out the gate with Flenter on the back of his pick-up, I called out to my dog and waved goodbye, tears streaming down my cheeks.

But Flenter was too busy sniffing the deck of the pick-up to pay much attention to me. Johan's Staffordshire bitch must have left her scent there, and Flenter was very intrigued by it, because he didn't so much as look up when I called his name in farewell.

Johan kept in touch with us and we learned that Flenter had adapted well to his new home and was, in fact, charmed with his girlfriend.

When Wolfie finally realised that Flenter was not coming back, he stopped slinking about the place and became a very happy and relaxed dog, smiling most of the time. And he enjoyed being able to play with Leo again without being attacked by Flenter.

In due course, Wolfie became Leo's most trusted friend and companion.

People often asked us how a lion's intelligence compared with that of a dog. I think a dog is more intelligent in terms of its relationships with humans. It can learn to understand a fair amount of human vocabulary and to respond to vocal commands.

Leo appeared to have a very limited capacity for understanding the vocal index of human language, but his ability to interpret body language was remarkable. It was a sensitivity that enabled him to recognise a variety of human moods and emotions and to appreciate differences in human personalities.

Leo had a unique relationship with each member of the family.

Kobus was his father — and the dominant male of the pride. Leo loved, respected and admired him. I was his mother, much loved but not respected as much as his father. He trusted me and depended on me for motherly love and care but, in a mischievous mood, he would tease and bully me. He never bullied his father.

Karin was his favourite sister. She came home more often than the others to play with him, and her sunny, boisterous nature always provided for a lot of fun.

Sandra was the sister for whom he had the most respect. He sensed her quiet determination of spirit, and although he played with her and challenged her as he did everyone else, one harsh look or stern warning from her would instantly turn him into a well-behaved lion.

He sensed Hettie's passionate nature and he showed remarkable perception in his responses to her moods. If her mood was joyous, he would be an exuberant clown, and the two of them would play with such happy abandon that I sometimes feared Leo would unintentionally hurt her. (There were in fact a few accidents, but fortunately nothing serious.) If her mood was wistful, he would sit quietly beside her, groaning softly or licking her arms and face to comfort her. He would never tease her or try to play with her when she was in a melancholy mood.

Sandra's classmate at medical school, Paul Meyer, had since become a regular visitor, accompanying Sandra whenever she came home. Despite the fact that he had grown up in a town, Paul took to our way of life right away. I was rather surprised that he did, considering that my family is slightly bush-mad (not counting me — I'm the only sane one). In fact, after only a few visits, it was quite obvious that Paul had become as bush-struck as the rest of the family.

To Leo, Paul was the best brother any lion could wish for: Paul not only knew how to play wonderfully wild and rough lion-games, he also had a talent for inventing them. Whenever I was awoken in the early hours by the sound of human feet racing around the house followed by the thud-thud of lion paws, I would know that Paul and Leo were playing Cops and Lions again, or Lions and Crooks, or whatever. (Paul usually carried a water pistol for self-defence.)

Leo also had a unique relationship with Wolfie. Wolfie was his trusted companion and friend, his tutor and his mentor. He respected Wolfie and never broke the rules that Wolfie set down

for him. Even when Leo eventually weighed a solid one hundred kilograms more than the dog, he still regarded Wolfie as his superior.

Wolfie could be strict with Leo at times, but for the most part he was extremely tolerant of him. He often allowed the lion to pester him to a point that no other dog would dream of enduring. Whenever we went walking in the bush, for instance, Leo would often run directly behind Wolfie and try to trip him up with circular swipes of his front paw. Wolfie, ignoring the discomfort of a hind leg getting swiped from underneath him every now and again, would earnestly continue his own business of sniffing the ground and running along whichever spoor he was following. Only occasionally, when the tripping-game truly hampered his exploratory endeavours, would he pause momentarily to turn his head slightly towards Leo, lifting his upper lip at one corner to expose a canine. In the international language of animals that gesture means: 'Do that one more time and I'm going to bite you!' Leo understood every nuance of the gesture and would back off immediately and behave himself.

Leo loved excursions into the bush. Whenever we told him that we were going for a walk or a drive, his eyes would light up with excitement. But being unable to distinguish between the words 'drive' and 'walk', he would pay close attention to Wolfie's reaction to see which it was to be. If it was 'walk' Wolfie would head for the gate, and if it was 'drive' Wolfie would leap on to the truck. And Leo would do whatever Wolfie did.

Leo seemed to realise that Wolfie understood a lot of human language, and so he relied on the dog as his interpreter.

It was very useful to have Wolfie as an interpreter. Whenever we wanted to give Leo a specific command, we would give it to Wolfie instead, knowing that Wolfie would respond and that Leo would follow his example. Wolfie eventually realised that we were using him as an interpreter, but he didn't mind. Being a conscientious dog who took all his responsibilities very seriously, he co-operated as best he could − even though the job sometimes required a lot of patience. If Leo wasn't paying attention, for instance, Wolfie would have to repeat the required action several times until Leo got the message.

One of our favourite Sunday afternoon outings was to drive to Panamana, a beautiful pan at the foot of the Lebombo mountains. The pan was home to a family of hippos who always performed dramatically at the sight of us. They plunged and splashed about, raising gaping jaws in our direction and bellowing threats at us. Leo loved to sit and watch the hippos perform.

The trouble was that when we wanted to go home, Leo always wanted to stay longer. Wolfie, loyal, obedient dog that he was, would respond promptly to the command to get on to the pick-up, but Leo would pretend not to hear. Until he was about six months old, we were still able to carry him to the truck if he refused to listen. But as he grew heavier and stronger, he eventually got wise to the fact that if he struggled while we carried him, we had to release him immediately.

And so we had no choice but to rely on Wolfie to get Leo on to the truck. We would ask Wolfie to please disembark, fetch Leo and jump back on to the truck again. Wolfie would jump off, go over to Leo, look him straight in the eyes to get his attention, then turn and run back to the truck and jump on it again. Leo seemed to reckon that if Wolfie wanted him to get on to the truck so badly, then there probably was a good reason for it. And so he would follow. But when Leo was in a difficult mood, Wolfie sometimes had to repeat the performance several times before Leo would obey.

Eventually Wolfie became so conditioned to this procedure, that whenever he jumped on to the truck and realised that Leo wasn't following, he'd jump right off again — without waiting for a command from us — and repeat the performance until Leo eventually followed him.

It was during these outings into the bush that we realised that Leo considered Wolfie to be his tutor and mentor.

Lions are born with the hunting instinct, but they are not born with the skills of hunting. This they learn from their mothers. It is a fine and complicated art, and a lion mother spends up to two years teaching her offspring to hunt successfully.

Something in Leo's instinctive memory must have told him that there were important things in the bush for him to learn. For some or other reason, he didn't look to Kobus or to me for an education, but to Wolfie. He strongly suspected Wolfie to be the guy who knew all the things that it was crucial for a lion to learn.

But he was mistaken. There is nothing, really, that a herding dog like Wolfie can teach a lion about hunting and survival. And Wolfie had no idea that Leo was looking to him for an education. So he would run about the bush in crazy zigs and zags as dogs do, sniffing the ground and reading all the messages left behind by hordes of wild life. Leo would follow Wolfie like a shadow, but instead of sniffing the ground like a dog, he would watch Wolfie's face and body language intently, hoping to pick up some useful clues of whatever secret knowledge Wolfie possessed. If Wolfie started digging furiously into abandoned termite hills or aardvark burrows, Leo would stand right in front of Wolfie and study the dog's busy face with a look of intense puzzlement that seemed to say: 'Huh? What are we doing now?'

In the bush Leo often had that huh? expression on his face. Poor chap. We felt sorry for him. He was badly in need of a proper tutor.

Wolfie never chased or harassed wild animals, but on the few occasions that he was surprised by a sudden close encounter with mongooses, warthogs or other small game, he would herd them for some distance — and then leave them in peace.

One day Wolfie poked his head into a burrow to check who was inside and out charged a warthog mother, followed by three warthog babies. Wolfie, making a hasty retreat, reversed into Leo who was standing right behind him but nevertheless managed to get out of the way in time. Not Leo. He was still saying 'Huh?' when the sow collided heavily with him. She made a hasty U-turn and headed in the opposite direction, followed by her screaming children. As soon as Leo recovered from the surprise of the sudden blow inflicted by the sow, he realised that Wolfie was in hot pursuit of the warthogs. He bounded after them and, being a lion, soon caught up with them.

By this time Wolfie was running alongside the warthog family, doing his herding act. Good student that he was, Leo followed suit and ran alongside the startled warthogs, watching them with an expression of happy achievement on his face. He obviously thought he was learning fast.

The dog and the lion herded the family of bewildered warthogs for some distance, and then Wolfie decided generously that enough was enough and gave up the chase (or the herding act). He came trotting back to us, followed by Leo. We always praise Wolfie for being kind to animals and for not hurting them. On this occasion we had no choice but to pat Leo on the head as well. We knew, however, that this was not helping his education along.

Leo was growing up to be a herding dog.

This worried us. He was already way behind in his educational curriculum. It was time we started teaching him the things his mother would have taught him. He would never be a successful lion if he continued to believe that his food came from the refrigerator and that the bush was a place where a herding act was required.

The problem was how and when to teach him. A game ranger is on call twenty-four hours a day, every day of the week. Kobus was lucky if he had more than an hour a day free to spend with Leo. Obviously a lion's mother spends a lot more than an hour a day teaching her offspring the skills of hunting.

The only solution, it seemed to me, was that I would have to take over our lion's education. Kobus could give a helping hand whenever he had some time to spare.

A Confused Scholar

There were numerous game trails to the north and west of our house, and I liked to follow them when walking with Leo and Wolfie, knowing that we would come across the local waterbuck, wildebeest, kudu and impala populations who would be on their way either to or from the river.

I loved the way the animals stopped and stared at us with a big question mark on their faces: 'What is this primate doing in the company of a fat wolf and a lion?'

In the beginning the sight of Leo gave them a fright and they would flee. But Leo never gave chase — for the simple reason that Wolfie didn't. And so he would stand and stare at the animals with that huh? expression on his face. The animals soon caught on to the fact that this was a duff lion and so they lost their fear of him.

Even though the local game populations grew quite used to the sight of the three of us together, they never stopped wondering about us. And while they were standing and staring, we would walk carefully up to them until we were almost close enough for a friendly chat. Then we would all stand and stare at one another.

I, for one, enjoyed these encounters immensely.

There was one waterbuck bull whose curiosity eventually got the better of him. Throwing all caution to the wind, he approached us nonchalantly, stopping very close to us and studying us with a perplexed expression, sometimes stamping a hoof impatiently on the ground — demanding an explanation. I loved to deepen his bafflement by crouching between Wolfie and Leo and putting my arms around them. Wolfie didn't altogether trust the arrogant bull and on a few occasions when the bull came too close for his peace of mind, he growled a soft warning at him. The bull retreated, rejoining his family of two cows and two calves who preferred to remain at a safer distance.

The impalas, being the least intelligent of the antelope species, often forgot that they had seen us together on previous occasions and bounded away upon sighting or smelling us. But as soon as they realised that we weren't giving chase, they would stop and stare — and that same question mark would be on their faces.

Now when I decided that it was time to start Leo's hunting lessons, I was troubled by a moral question. How could I, after having won the trust of the local antelope populations, now do an about-face and start teaching my lion to hunt them? It didn't seem very fair. Yet, how else could I teach Leo to hunt? Not being a lion myself, I wasn't really sure how to stalk animals. Stalking these semi-tame antelopes would at least be a lot easier than stalking wild ones who didn't trust me.

I felt like a traitor. But I had my responsibilities as a lion-mother. So I tried to harden my heart and decided to go for the impala. At least they were less intelligent and more forgetful than the others.

This is how I tackled the first hunting lesson.

It was late afternoon and the three of us were following a game trail, looking for the herd of impala who would be on their way back from the river at about that time. As soon as we spotted them, I crouched in the long grass and commanded Wolfie to do the same. He sat down obediently and Leo — Wolfie's faithful shadow — copied the dog. The herd was moving towards us at a leisurely pace, grazing as they did so.

'Stay here,' I whispered to Wolfie, and I moved off towards the river, keeping well out of sight of the impalas — and leaving behind one obedient dog and one puzzled lion. Testing the wind, I moved carefully in a semicircle around the herd until I reached a spot where I was directly opposite Wolfie and Leo with the herd between us. I knew that the wind would soon carry my scent to the impala. Fortunately Wolfie and Leo were still hidden from sight in the long grass.

When I felt confident that the impala were getting my scent (some of them had turned and were looking in my direction with alert expressions), I jumped to my feet and waved my arms. Snorting with fright, the impalas fled from me — straight towards Leo and Wolfie. I shouted to Wolfie to go for them, and he shot forth from his hiding place, followed by Leo. The startled impalas almost collided with the dog and the lion, and I hoped with all my heart that Leo would respond to some inborn instinct and grab an impala.

He didn't. He stopped in his tracks, an expression of uncertainty and excitement on his face. His instincts were obviously signalling that something very important was happening and that there was something urgent that he should do. But he couldn't fathom what it was. Then he spotted me, and with a look of sheer delight, he charged right through the herd and caught me! As I tumbled to the ground I experienced a brief moment of instinctive panic — which was, of course, totally unnecessary. Leo was only playing, and enjoying the new game immensely.

Meanwhile Wolfie, who had herded the impala back towards the river, returned to look for Leo and me. He found us in the long grass where I was struggling to get away from Leo's playful and somewhat excited attentions. Wolfie must have wondered what this whole exercise had been about.

I realised then that teaching a lion to hunt wasn't going to be easy. And it would probably cost me some bruises.

In the late afternoon of the following day, Leo, Wolfie and I were once again waiting in the same spot along the game trail for the herd of impala to return from the river.

As soon as they came into sight I crouched in the grass, commanding Wolfie to do the same. As the three of us waited quietly in ambush, I realised that I didn't know what to do next. Repeating the previous day's performance didn't seem like a good idea, but I could think of no other plan. And then, as the unsuspecting impalas came closer, I noticed that Leo was up to something. Crouching, he gathered his hind legs beneath him and made himself very flat. Then he slowly glided along close to the ground, stopping after five or six metres, frozen in a flat crouch.

My heart started beating a lively crescendo.

Soon a ram was grazing almost within pouncing distance of the lion.

Leo didn't move as his eyes focused on the ram.

Wolfie and I sat very quietly, hardly breathing as we watched and waited. The impala ram remained totally unaware of our presence. He grazed and munched the grass, occasionally stamping a hoof on the ground or flicking his short fluffy tail.

Leo remained in a low crouch, his eyes never leaving the ram.

We waited ... and waited ... and waited.

The tension became unbearable.

What was Leo waiting for?

'Go Leo!' my mind said. 'Catch him!'

My attempt at telepathy didn't work. Nothing happened.

The unsuspecting ram started moving away. Leo stood up, turned and gave me a perplexed look that seemed to say: 'Please tell me what it is that I am supposed to do!'

The ram saw him and fled.

I was almost in tears. It had been so close. And my poor cub had not known what to do. Was I supposed to have given him a demonstration?

I just couldn't see myself leaping on to an antelope and biting it to death.

For the first time since adopting Leo, I realised that, as a lion-mother, I was a failure. I felt so sad.

A few days later, I walked Leo and Wolfie down to the river. Looking forward to an hour of relaxation while being entertained by my two amusing companions, I made myself comfortable on the sand.

The sandy beach along the water's edge was one of Leo's favourite spots. He loved the feel of the moist sand and the smells and sounds of the riverine landscape. He also enjoyed tripping

Wolfie up as Wolfie rushed about the shore, studying the myriad animal signs in the sand.

I was admiring a handsome grey heron descending on to the opposite bank when a rustling sound in the tall reeds some distance upshore caught my attention. I quickly got to my feet, commanding Wolfie to stay close to me. Leo raised his nose to the wind, and there must have been something in the air that told him something, for he suddenly bounded off and disappeared into the reed thickets.

Wolfie uttered a soft yelping noise.

'No,' I told him. 'Stay with me.'

I stood quietly, straining my senses for some clue as to what might be going on inside those ominous thickets — and worrying about Leo. Where was he? What was he up to?

Another rustling noise made me jump, but nothing happened. The landscape appeared to have frozen in time. And then some sixth sense told me to get out of the way. As I turned and fled towards the high river bank behind me, the reeds exploded and a herd of buffalo came stampeding across the shore. I sprinted up the bank. As soon as I reached the top, I turned and saw the herd running downstream along the shore — followed by a playful lion doing a perfect herding act.

After a while I sent Wolfie to fetch Leo.

Wolfie scampered down the bank and across the shore after his friend. When Leo heard Wolfie's barks, he turned and came bounding back towards him. I had never seen Leo look so proud of himself. As he met up with Wolfie, he touched heads with him in greeting and told him all about it. Then he came running up the bank towards me and the happy expression on his face said: 'Did you see what I did, hey? Wasn't I good?'

'Come along,' I heard Karin saying to Leo late one afternoon. 'You're not a cattle dog. You're a lion. And I'm going to teach you to hunt.'

I saw the three of them leaving through the gate. Karin, Wolfie and Leo.

I wondered how she was going to accomplish her mission. And I was sorry I couldn't go along to observe her teaching methods but I had other urgent chores to attend to.

Later, when dusk started to settle, I began to worry about them and set out to look for them. Luckily I spotted them as soon as I walked through the gate. They were on their way home. Wolfie came trotting towards me, followed closely by Leo who was trying to trip him up.

Karin approached with stiff-legged strides, swinging her arms in the way she does when she's irritated. Her face, clothes and arms looked dusty.

I went to meet her.

'So,' I said. 'How did it go?'

'He's so stupid,' she replied. 'I organised a perfect hunting situation for him. I crept up to a couple of resting wildebeest and chased them right towards him. They never even saw him. They almost collided with him. But do you know what he did? He charged right past them and caught me!'

'I know just how you feel,' I said sympathetically.

Some days later Kobus had a few hours to spare and he decided it was a good time to help with the hunting lessons.

We set out in the pick-up with Wolfie and Leo on the back.

We encountered lots of animals along the way: waterbuck, wildebeest, giraffe, kudu, zebra, impala and warthogs. But Kobus was looking for guinea fowl. They are the most muddle-headed birds on earth, so Kobus reasoned that they would be a sensible choice as practice-prey for a slow-witted lion.

Some ten kilometres from home we finally came across a big flock of guinea fowl. They were marching down the track right in front of us. Kobus drove off the track, kept alongside the parade for a few metres and then turned back on to the track again, stopping more or less in the middle of the procession. Leo and Wolfie bounded off the truck and started chasing the front half of the flock. The startled fowls fled down the road, sprinting

comically on their short legs, necks stretched forward and intermittently taking off in short bursts of flight.

Leo enjoyed the chase, thinking it was a new game. Unfortunately the idea of catching a fowl never entered his head. After a while Wolfie decided to turn back. Guinea fowls weren't all that much fun to herd — they were too idiotic.

As Wolfie came running back towards us, so did his faithful shadow, Leo.

Kobus and I turned to see where the other half of the flock had gone, and discovered that they were standing right behind us! Apparently they had been watching the proceedings down-road with as much interest as we had. But as soon as they realised that the dog and the lion were advancing rapidly, they turned and fled up-road. Wolfie and Leo again gave chase — and again, after a short while, abandoned the effort. The front line of the flock had meanwhile returned to the site of the commotion, and as we turned we found them right behind us, gawking at the proceedings up-road. So, of course, Leo and Wolfie went right ahead and herded the current audience down-road again. Meanwhile the up-road half of the flock returned to watch the proceedings down-road. A while later Leo and Wolfie returned and chased the new audience up-road again. And the down-road half of the flock returned to watch the proceedings up-road ... and so on. It was most amusing. But it had the makings of a never-ending story. So, after a while, we called Leo and Wolfie back on to the truck and drove home.

Although it had been another unsuccessful attempt at lion education, it had at least been a lot of fun.

The next day Kobus took us for another drive and shot a guinea fowl for Leo. The fowl had been sitting in a tree, and as it fell to the ground, Wolfie rushed towards it, followed by Leo. Kobus told Wolfie not to take the fowl, and the good dog obeyed, leaving it for Leo. It took Leo a while to catch on to the fact that the fowl was dead and that it was his. When the idea finally hit home he was elated. He snatched up the dead fowl in his mouth and ran off with it — where to, no one knew. Not even Leo himself. After a while he returned, the dead fowl still dangling from his mouth, and looked at us with a quizzical expression: 'What should I do with it?'

I suggested to Kobus that he cut the fowl open so that Leo might realise it was edible. But Leo was very possessive of the fowl and wouldn't let Kobus touch it.

When we decided to go back home Wolfie had to do his get-on-to-the-truck routine several times before Leo obeyed. But as Leo jumped up the fowl slammed into the side of the pick-up and fell out of his mouth to the ground. With a yelp of anguish Leo leapt off the truck to retrieve his fowl, and poor Wolfie had to do several re-runs of the getting-off/getting-on act again before Leo finally followed, the fowl gripped firmly between his teeth.

When we got home, Leo spent the rest of the day running all over the garden with the dead fowl in his mouth, tossing it into the air from time to time, catching it, rolling on it, wrestling with it and even sitting on it (to keep it dead, I suppose). It was quite obvious that Leo had gone a little mad. Eventually the fowl started to disintegrate, and it was distressing to see its entrails, feathers and limbs being scattered all over the place. Leo himself was a disgusting sight: feathers and bits of entrails sticking to his coat and whiskers. Ugh.

He never ate the guinea fowl.

Karin remained quite adamant that her friend should learn to hunt, and so she spent most of her winter school vacation trying to teach him some basic rules. On one occasion Leo almost caught a hare — but that was only because Wolfie practically chased it right into Leo's open jaws. (Leo had merely watched the chase with his huh? expression, mouth hanging open.) But unfortunately he slammed his mouth shut at the wrong moment.

After numerous other failed attempts at hunting lessons, we realised that we were unsuccessful teachers and that Leo was a confused scholar.

We knew, of course, that there were other more effective methods of teaching a lion to hunt, but they seemed cruel to us and so we were not willing to use them.

A Riotous Adolescent

On the first day of Karin's spring school vacation, she looked forward to spending the afternoon relaxing in the garden. She carried a book, a cassette player and a blanket outside and made herself comfortable under a shady tree.

Leo spotted his favourite sister on the lawn and bounded over to her. Pouncing on her blanket, he yanked it out from underneath her and made off with it. Karin gave chase, screaming at the lion to bring back her blanket.

I was inside the house doing some sewing, and I watched the comedy show through a window at my side.

Karin returned a while later, carrying her blanket and looking angry, followed by Leo. After threatening the lion with murder if he didn't behave, she made herself comfortable on her blanket again and proceeded to read her book. Leo lay quietly on the grass next to her, pretending to be a very good lion.

After a while one of his paws sidled ever so slowly on to the blanket, and then the other paw followed. Soon the rest of his body started to move in gradual instalments. Karin reached out to pat his head, and as she did so, he snatched her book and ran off with it.

'Hey!' Karin yelled as she jumped up and ran after him. 'That's a library book! I'll get into trouble!'

A few minutes later she finally returned, carrying her library book, looking very angry and, of course, with Leo in tow. He had an apologetic, almost sorrowful look on his face, as if he himself couldn't believe his own naughtiness.

'OK,' Karin muttered crossly as she sat down on the blanket. 'I'll give you one last chance. But if you dare to even think of bothering me, I'm going to punch you on the nose.'

Leo looked even more regretful.

'And look at this!' she added, shoving the library book under his nose. There were lion tooth marks through the cover. 'How will I explain that to the librarian?' Leo looked at the book and his face was a study in self-recrimination.

Karin settled down to her book and her music. Leo lay quietly at her side, trying his best to be a good lion. And for a while he actually succeeded.

But after about five minutes the effort proved too much for him, and he started irritating Karin in small ways. One paw edged forward, just an inch or so at a time, until it ended up either on her book or her cassette player. Karin slapped the offending paw away, muttering threats. And for a while Leo would try to behave again. But it was hard for him. He couldn't stand the fact that she would rather read than play with him.

Suddenly the urge to play was overwhelming. He leapt up, pounced on her and, as she rolled over to get away from him, he sat down on top of her. But Karin wasn't having any of it. She punched him on the nose. A short, fierce wrestling match followed — human and lion limbs flailing in all directions. Karin ended up the winner — sitting on the lion's chest and pinning his paws to the ground above his head. She bent over, bringing her face very close to his, and then she hissed at him — like an angry cat. That was more than Leo could bear. He moaned in a tone that seemed to mean: 'Please don't hiss at me like that! It frightens me.' Karin let go of him, rolled over on to the blanket and continued reading her book. Leo decided that it would be better for him, after all, to behave. So he lay peacefully next to her on the blanket, and she stroked his fur.

At the age of ten months Leo was a handsome youngster with a strong and determined character. And he was even more boisterous than ever before. But for a lion he was actually very obedient. He seemed to realise that he had to co-operate with us.

We, in turn, tried to limit any restrictions on his behaviour and to raise him as a lion — not as a domestic pet. For his own sake, as well as for ours, we wanted him to remain the unfrustrated, even-tempered animal that he was.

He was still as affectionate and demonstrative as ever, and he enjoyed being close, often either leaning against us or actually sitting on us. Any parting, regardless of its duration, involved on our return a lengthy ritual of head-touching, cheek-rubbing, embracing and cuddling — accompanied by a series of soulful grunts and groans. After a shopping trip I would take care to leave the shopping bags in the car until the greeting formalities were over — or else the groceries would get squashed. (The greeting ritual often ended with Leo sitting on me to prevent me from going indoors.)

He still loved bounding into Kobus's office for a hug and a cuddle, but he was now so huge that he would just about knock the desk over jumping on to Kobus's lap. If Kobus was talking on either his radio or his telephone, it would end up on the floor along with anything else that was in the way. At the end of the fond greeting the whole office would be in chaos.

Leo also still loved chasing and jumping on us, but he was so heavy now that he often brought us crashing to the ground. So we had to teach him to respect the fact that we were a lot more fragile than he was. Eventually he learned that we didn't want him to chase and catch us any more, but the idea baffled and perplexed him. It was such fun — why give it up?

He couldn't altogether bring himself to give up his favourite game, but he was willing to modify it: he would stalk us and launch himself at us, but slam his brakes on in time to break the impact of the pounce. And so he would catch us more 'gently', clasping us around our waists with his enormous paws. We didn't mind that too much, as long as he didn't try to drag us down for a playful wrestling match — which he often did. Unfortunately he also possessed a rather exasperating sense of humour: whenever he spotted someone bending over, he would sneak up from behind and give the unsuspecting bottom either a playful chomp or a toppling shove.

The flowerbed at the side of the kitchen was still his favourite ambush spot, and since he loved to test the reactions of strangers, I was forced to go out and meet all visitors at the parking area and escort them safely indoors. Fortunately, Wolfie always barked to announce the arrival of visitors, acting as our official doorbell.

I love gardening, but when Leo also became interested in this activity, things got complicated. He only wanted to help, of course, but our ideas tended to clash, and so a newly planted flowerbed would end up looking like an excavation site.

Moreover, the telephone often interrupted my gardening, and whenever I dashed off to answer it, Leo would think I was inviting him to a game of catch. I would spend so much time and energy wrestling the lion off me that, by the time I answered the phone, I'd be too breathless to talk.

One beautiful morning in October, as I was trying to do some gardening, the telephone started ringing. And, as usual, Leo caught me long before I reached the house. After a short but vigorous battle I managed to disentangle myself from the lion and, with a stern warning to him to leave me alone, I tried once more to reach the house. Breathless, I arrived at the paved path — and a lightning movement at the edge of my vision froze me.

It was the cobra.

Rearing himself up high, he fixed me with a cold reptilian stare. I stopped breathing. He was much too close. While the steely eyes studied me carefully, judging my case, I remained as frozen as I could, praying that the noisy pounding of my heart wouldn't annoy him to the point of pronouncing me guilty. Meanwhile, Leo evidently thought that the reason I had stopped running so suddenly was because I wanted to play some more. The snake had just reached his generous verdict of 'not guilty' and was about to retreat, when the lion caught me from behind and brought me tumbling to the grass.

The snake didn't like that at all, and spat at us. The venom spray caught me on the leg. I kicked the lion off me and hastily got to my feet to inspect the damage. The poisonous venom was dribbling down my leg straight towards a bleeding scratch on my ankle. Keeping the ankle raised, I hobbled over to the nearest tap and managed to rinse the poison off before it reached the scratch. My head was spinning and my heart was doing flip-flops from the crazy variety of shocks that I had just experienced and — I could hardly believe it — the stupid telephone was still ringing its head off! I rushed inside, snatched up the receiver and tried to make my voice sound normal.

I was rather surprised to hear the voice of a dear friend, Riaan Cruywagen, at the other end.

Riaan and I had been to school together, and many years later, when he had become a well-known television broadcaster, I had contacted him to ask him to do the voice-over for a documentary film that I had made about baboons. Ever since that time we had kept in touch, writing to each other about once a year.

On this day, while I struggled to regain my breath, Riaan told me the reason he was calling was that he had just made a most alarming discovery. He'd been to the dentist that morning, he said, and as he paged through an old magazine in the waiting room he came upon an article telling the story of a game ranger who had survived a lion attack. When he read that the game ranger was Kobus, he almost fell out of his chair. He checked the date on the magazine and saw that it was June 1992. He then remembered that he had been on vacation at that particular time — which was the reason why he had not heard about the attack. Even so, he said, he felt awful about it and hoped that I hadn't thought him terribly insensitive for not having called at the time to offer condolences and to enquire about Kobus.

I was about to tell him not to worry, that had all happened a long time ago, but if he still wished to offer condolences, he might offer them to me: I had just been attacked by a lion *and* a cobra.

But naturally I couldn't expect him to believe that, so instead I told him that he needn't feel bad, I had been meaning to write to him about the lion attack but time had simply been getting away from me.

So we chatted some more and eventually I told him about the cub we were raising.

While Riaan and I were talking, I heard Wolfie barking outside, but I forgot to pay attention. It was only after I had put the receiver down that I suddenly got the feeling that I had ignored an important signal. And then it struck me — the doorbell! I rushed out of the house to warn the visitors about our lion.

Too late. Leo had already caught himself a soldier and they were wrestling on the lawn.

The soldiers from Nkongoma base all knew about our lion, but this was a new recruit, and judging from the look of alarm on his face, he had not known about our lion. I rushed to his aid and got Leo off him.

'I am so terribly sorry...' I stammered. 'Are you OK?'

Scrambling to his feet, he assured me that he was.

He was a young boy, barely out of his teens. I admired his gracious attitude, and told him so.

He confessed that the sight of the lion rushing at him had been quite a shock. But fortunately, he said, the lion had caught the dog first. And since it hadn't eaten the dog, things looked a little brighter than they would otherwise have done.

I invited him in for a cup of sweet, strong tea — which I was sure he needed. But he declined, saying that he was in a hurry to get back to the base. He had come to deliver a letter to Kobus from his commanding officer. As he said that, he realised that he'd misplaced the letter. He turned to look for it and spotted the envelope caught between the leaves of a bush-fern in the flowerbed. As he bent over to retrieve it, I tried to warn him not to — but, again, it was too late. Leo chomped him in the rump and the cobra peeked out from behind the bush-fern. Fortunately the snake decided to retreat, disappearing under the leaves of a neighbouring delicious monster. I snatched up the envelope and, after further apologies, sent the soldier on his way before things got any worse.

I realised that we would have to take better care of our visitors in future. So I decided I would put up a sign next to the paved path: BEWARE OF THE LION AND THE SNAKE.

But this struck me as sounding a little dramatic, so I thought that perhaps BEWARE OF THE FLOWERBED would sound better.

But I wasn't sure.

In a World of His Own

We often tried to introduce Leo to other lions — at a respectful distance, of course. But until he was almost eleven months old, Leo had never seen another lion in his life.

That, however, was not our fault. We had come across lions in the bush several times, and as soon as we'd spotted them, we had tried excitedly to show them to Leo. But instead of looking in the direction that we were pointing, he would stupidly stare at the finger that was doing the pointing. On a few occasions we actually grabbed hold of his head and swung it in the direction we wanted him to look, but he would roll his eyes upwards and look at us instead.

Often, when lions roared close to the house at night, I would rush outside into the garden with my torch to see how Leo was reacting. I usually found him sitting up and listening — not too intently really, but at least with some interest. I'd put my arms around him and say: 'Do you hear that, Leo? Those are your people! Do you understand what they're saying?'

But Leo would yawn, or lick my face. Apparently he found the calls quite interesting, but not *that* interesting. I realised later that he showed about the same amount of interest (or lack of it) when he listened to hyena or jackal howling in the night.

This worried me. Did Leo realise he was a lion? If not, what did he think he was? A dog? Or a human? I desperately wanted him to know that he was a lion. It seemed very important to me. But how could I teach him that?

I thought back to the days when he was still a young cub, and I couldn't help believing that, in those days, he had been closer to realising he was a lion than he was now. Could it be that the long period of his association with us was responsible for the fading of his instinctive memories? Did his total acceptance of us as his family blot out all earlier knowledge? If so, it was most important that we started making serious efforts to introduce him to other lions.

Kobus came home late one afternoon and told me that he had spotted a pride of lions resting in the Vurhami creek — only two kilometres from the house.

We called Wolfie and Leo and set out immediately in the truck, hoping that we might at last be able to introduce Leo to his own kind.

When we got there, the lions were still resting on an open stretch of sand in the creek, some 150 metres upstream from the causeway. Kobus parked the truck on the causeway and we got out quietly. As Wolfie and Leo jumped off the back, we commanded them to stay close to us.

Kobus took his rifle from the cab, checked its magazine and slung it over his shoulder. I noticed that there was an R4 rifle in the cab as well, and on the spur of the moment I decided to take it along — just in case Leo might need some protection.

We climbed down the side of the causeway on to the sandy creek bed. Two of the lions spotted us but remained lying down, just lifting their heads to study us. They had probably had a recent good meal, and were feeling full and lazy.

We approached them slowly. Taking care to look casual and relaxed, we hoped to communicate to them with our body language that we meant them no harm.

Leo and Wolfie kept close to us. Leo appeared apprehensive, his gaze fixed warily on the lions. Wolfie was his usual composed self.

The landscape was very quiet, the only sound being the sand crunching underneath our feet. The Vurhami is a beautiful creek with its scattering of perennial pools, its wide sand bed and its high, densely vegetated banks.

All the lions were wide awake now and studying us with alert, curious expressions. The pride consisted of five lions (or so we thought at the time): one adult male, two adult females and two sub-adults who appeared to be only a few months older than Leo. The closer we got to them the more restless they became. For a while, however, their bafflement at the sight of a young lion in the company of two humans and a fat wolf overrode their fear of us, and so we were able to get quite close to them before they decided to turn tail.

I was about to ask Leo what he had thought of the lions when a shocking, reverberating growl immediately to our left shattered the afternoon silence. As we spun around to face its source, a lioness burst forth from the dense undergrowth of the bank and charged us.

Our reflexes taking over, Kobus and I raised and aimed our rifles, releasing the safety catches. I was standing directly behind Kobus. Wolfie launched himself at the lioness. Three cubs appeared from nowhere and fled up the bank. The lioness turned to see where her cubs were going, and Wolfie ran up the bank after them. With an angry growl, the lioness turned and charged again, coming at us in a yellow blur of speed — abruptly pulling up very close to us. Then she suddenly turned and ran after Wolfie and her cubs.

Kobus shouted to Wolfie to come back. He needed no persuasion and came tearing down the bank towards us. (Had he gone after the cubs in an attempt to lure the lioness away from us?)

The lioness and her cubs disappeared over the top of the bank.

Kobus and I relaxed our aims, feeling extremely grateful that it had not been necessary to fire a shot.

We looked about for Leo. He was missing. As we turned to look towards the causeway, we spotted him jumping on to the back of the truck. He had cleared the distance between us and the truck in record time — even for a lion.

Poor fellow. His first meeting with wild lions had not gone well.

Walking back to the truck, I realised with surprise that I wasn't shaking too badly, and I wondered why that was. I used to be so terrified of lions that I would be in deep shock each time we came across them in the bush — even if they had been the first to back off. But that was before we had Leo. Was I starting to lose some of my fear of lions?

When we reached the truck, we patted and hugged Leo and tried to tell him that lions weren't usually so aggressive, and that the only reason the lioness had charged us was to prevent us from getting any nearer to her cubs.

Leo rubbed cheeks with us and, in his own language of grunts and groans, shared with us his personal views of the adventure. And although I don't speak Lionese, I knew he was telling us that he had never been so scared in his life.

A few days after our encounter with the lioness, I overheard Kobus discussing the incident with two of his colleagues, Tom and Brian. They obviously didn't know I was near, or else they might have used nicer language. Anyway, as I listened to the conversation, it struck me — not for the first time — how strange are the minds of men.

This is how the conversation went:

Kobus: Then all hell broke loose: a lioness burst from the thickets and charged us, and — directly behind my back — I heard a metallic click. That was Kobie, releasing her rifle's safety catch . . .
Brian: NO!
Tom: AAUGH!
Kobus: I felt too threatened to breathe . . .
Brian: @*%#!
Tom: Aaugh! Crisis! What a nightmare . . .
Kobus: Yes. Caught between two excited females, and each with so much destructive power . . .

At this point I decided that I didn't need to listen to such chauvinistic nonsense, and so I walked out of earshot.

Leo was almost twelve months old (and weighing close on a hundred kilograms) when it finally dawned on him that he was stronger than his parents. It had taken him a surprisingly long time to realise this, but when he did, the idea gave him so much self-confidence that he started challenging rhino and elephant.

Late one afternoon, as we were driving home after a visit to Panamana, we came across a rhino bull grazing right next to the road. As was our habit, we stopped to let Leo and Wolfie admire the animal, but to our surprise, Leo jumped off the truck and playfully charged the rhino. With a startled snort, the bull spun round, lowered his head and charged — a most formidable horn aimed at Leo. We held our breath. Leo was really asking for trouble. But fortunately he realised right away that the rhino's sharp end was to be avoided. Dashing around the rhino in figures of eight, he succeeded in scrambling its sense of direction. Soon the spinning, horn-swinging bull began to feel a little dizzy, and so he had to stop and stand still for a while to reorientate himself to his surroundings.

At that moment Leo darted away and, with swinging tail and comical body language, invited the rhino to chase him — which the rhino promptly did. But Leo disappeared into a thicket and the rhino charged right past him. As he slammed on his brakes, wondering where the lion had gone, Leo reappeared. And so the game — with its prelude of dizzy-dancing — started all over again. Eventually the rhino got tired of it and, totally ignoring the pestering lion, began grazing again. Leo tried his best to persuade the rhino to play some more, but the beast had had enough and, after a while, started moving off into the bush.

Leo decided to follow him and we called to him to come back. But he ignored us, moving ever deeper into the bush with his new-found 'friend'. Dusk was setting in and we wanted to go home. Kobus even started the truck's engine to let Leo know we were about to leave without him. It didn't help. He probably didn't believe us. We called again, but we knew that when Leo was in an arrogant mood, he wouldn't even understand his own name.

We were not keen to send Wolfie after Leo — the rhino might decide to take his frustrations out on the dog. After a while we began to get worried, and so the three of us set out together to look for our errant lion. We walked some distance into the knob-thorn thickets, but found no sign of either Leo or the rhino. It was getting too dark to see properly, and so in the end we had no choice but to rely on our faithful dog to find our lion for us.

'Wolfie, please fetch Leo,' we told him, and off he went.

About fifteen minutes later the splendid dog returned with the naughty lion in tow.

We decided (as we had on numerous previous occasions) that Wolfie deserved a gold medal.

From that day on, Leo could never resist challenging rhino and elephant, and so we no longer stopped the truck when we came across these animals but instead tried to get past them as fast as possible. On a number of occasions when we got held up by elephants in the road, Leo jumped off the truck and challenged them. I almost died of fright each time a screaming, trumpeting giant charged my cub. But Leo would nimbly hop out of its way and caper about in zigs and zags, teasing and confusing the elephants until they got thoroughly fed-up with the silly game and decided to move on.

Leo evidently enjoyed himself enormously, and it always took a lot of persuasion from Wolfie to get him back on to the truck again. I am sure Wolfie often prayed as hard as we did that we wouldn't encounter elephant or rhino along the way.

On a hot morning in November, Sandra and Paul — who were home for their summer vacation — decided to go fishing.

'Come along, Leo and Wolfie!' they said. 'Let's go fishing.'

Leo loved fishing, but being a little dim in the verbal department, he thought they'd said 'Let's go jogging'. So he said no thank you. It was much too hot a day for a lazy lion to go jogging. And he knew Paul and Sandra: they would jog all the way to the Vurhami creek and back without stopping for a rest. Now why would a lion want to give up his snooze for that?

'Come on,' Sandra persisted. 'You'll be sorry you stayed behind.'

Leo lifted his lazy head from the ground, gave her a fond gaze as a gesture of thanks for her concern, but again declined the invitation. He definitely wasn't in the mood for jogging.

Eventually they left without him.

There was no gate leading from our front garden down to the river, so one had to leave through the back gate and walk all the way around the western and southern fences to reach the trail that led to the river bank.

Enjoying his snooze, Leo registered distant sounds coming from the direction of the river. He opened one eye and spotted three figures disappearing over the river bank. Good heavens — they were going fishing! With a surprised grunt he leapt up and ran towards the eastern fence, calling out to them to wait for him. But by this time they were over the bank and unable to hear him above the sound of the river.

'Auh-wu! Auh-wu! Auh-wu!' Leo called.

But they didn't come back. He ran all the way to the back gate, and called again. No good. The gate didn't even face the river. So he summoned all his courage, walked out through the gate (something he never did on his own), ran along the fence, turned the southern corner to face the river, and then stopped. Surely it would be too dangerous for a lion to venture any further on his own? So he stood there, calling his heart out. He so much wanted to go fishing with them!

When he realised that no one was coming back for him, he decided to go and tell his parents.

'Auh-auh! Auh-auh!' he called while running back to the house.

Kobus came out of his office and I came out of the house to see why our poor lion was crying so pathetically.

'Leo!' we called. 'What's the matter?'

He came running straight to us, grunting and groaning a stream of complaints.

Game guard Albert Maluleke, who had been cleaning his rifle in the garden, told us the whole story, explaining that the children and Wolfie had gone fishing and that Leo had misunderstood the invitation to go along with them.

'Don't be such a baby, Leo!' I told him. 'You can go down to the river by yourself!'

'Au-wuh, au-wuh,' he moaned.

'But you play with rhinos and elephants,' I reminded him. 'So what are you afraid of?'

He looked at me with huge, innocent eyes that said: 'I don't know exactly. But I think I'm still too young to go so far from home on my own.'

In the end, Kobus and I walked him down to the river. As we went down the bank, Leo spotted the children and Wolfie on the shore and ran to them, complaining loudly at their lack of consideration for his feelings. Paul offered him a fish, and so Leo forgave them.

Leo was an avid fisherman — not that he fished himself, but he would sit quietly next to Paul and Sandra, his gaze fixed on the line. As soon as a fish was pulled out, he would leap up, ready to lend a helping hand if necessary. If not necessary, he would study the fish with an expert eye and nose. He knew he was allowed only to look and smell, and not to taste. He was, however, allowed to guard the catch, and if a fish tried to get away he would slap it right back where it belonged. It was worth the trouble, of course, for in the end he would be rewarded with a fair share of the catch. Occasionally, when he thought no one was looking, he would quickly open his mouth in case a fish wanted to jump inside. But he would never blatantly steal a fish.

Leo adhered to a strict code of ethics concerning his and his family's food. It was not something we had taught him. It was an inborn code. He would never try to pilfer our food, nor would he even expect us to share with him while we ate. (We often enjoyed our meals outside in the garden.) At the same time, Leo was very possessive of his own food and would not allow anyone too near him while he fed — that is, anyone except me. He trusted me completely. I guess he knew that I — his mother — would never steal his food from him.

Kobus occasionally shot an impala for Leo, but most of Leo's food was donated by the Park's Research Department. Whenever the veterinarians required a carcass, they would ask Kobus to shoot the animal for them, and since they needed only the stomach and occasionally the lungs for their research purposes (which was to check for signs of tuberculosis or other diseases), they would donate the rest of the carcass to Leo.

There was a small kitchen attached to our guest cottage in the garden, and we converted it into a 'butchery' for Leo's meat. A carcass could hang there overnight to be cut up and stored in Leo's freezer the next day. We couldn't afford the luxury of letting Leo have a whole carcass to feast on. He wouldn't be able to finish it by himself in one sitting, and so a lot of meat would go to waste.

Our policy of not wasting any meat helped to ensure that Leo never had to go hungry. There were times, however, when the meat supply ran low, and if Kobus wasn't home to shoot an impala for Leo, I had to buy him chickens from the market in Komatipoort. To Leo, a whole raw chicken was always a special treat. Whenever offered a chicken for his meal, he would snatch it up and bound straight on to a flat-growing wild iris bush in the middle of the snake's flowerbed — his favourite spot for eating chicken. (The wild iris is not normally a flat bush — it only becomes flat if it is often sat upon by a lion.)

One morning in early November, an army truck from Nkongoma base turned up at our gate. Two soldiers came up to the house and told me that their truck had collided with an impala ram and that it had been killed on impact. They offered their apologies and wondered if it would be OK if they donated the carcass to our lion.

Leo's meat supply was running alarmingly low at the time, and I had been thinking of driving to Komatipoort to buy him some chickens, so naturally I was rather grateful for the unexpected meat delivery.

I asked the soldiers if they would be so kind as to off-load the carcass at the door of Leo's kitchen and help me hang the carcass inside.

Looking embarrassed, they confessed that they had made the mistake of off-loading the carcass at the edge of the lawn near the parking area and that Leo was already feeding on it.

I thought to myself that at least Leo was getting a proper chance to appreciate what it felt like to have a whole carcass to himself, but I also knew that a lot of meat would go to waste if I didn't try to salvage at least part of the carcass. It was a very hot day and, if left outside, the meat would soon become smelly and attract hordes of blowflies.

I went off to assess the situation. The moment Leo saw us approaching, he clutched the carcass to him, flattened his ears and growled a distinct warning at the soldiers. I warned them to stay well away. I walked carefully up to Leo but he showed no signs of aggression towards me. He remained wary of the soldiers, however, so I suggested to them that they retreat and wait out of sight for a while.

At that moment, Karin, who was home for the weekend, came out of the house and I called to her to bring me a large kitchen knife.

As she approached with the knife, Leo became nervous of her presence and so I told her not to come closer. I walked over to her to get the knife.

There was a shrub border at the edge of the lawn, about two metres from the spot where Leo was feeding. I asked Karin to creep quietly up to it from the other side and then hide amongst the shrubs. I would cut off a chunk of the carcass for Leo and, when he wasn't looking, I wanted her to reach out, get a grip on the rest of the carcass and carefully pull it away into the shrub border.

I felt rather flattered that Leo didn't mind my presence at his 'kill' and that he even allowed me to sit on it as I started cutting it up. He probably thought I wanted to share in the feast, and since I was his devoted mother who would never allow her cub to go hungry, I was welcome to share. I noticed that he had been chewing on various parts of the carcass, apparently unable to make up his mind where to start. So I cut open the stomach for him, and as the entrails spilled out, he took an immediate interest in the mess. That kept him busy for a while, so I started cutting off a whole hind leg for him.

After a while he became interested in the hind leg I was cutting off and decided to sample it. By the time I finally had the leg free from the rest of the carcass, Leo was happily chewing on it and Karin reached out from her shrub cover behind us and started pulling the rest of the carcass slowly towards her. It was too heavy, however, and I had to lend a helping hand. Very slowly we pulled the carcass towards the shrubs. At one stage Leo turned his head, contemplated the altered position of the carcass, and then looked at me with an expression that seemed to say: 'It's OK. Have some if you want it.'

So we pulled the carcass away and, concealed from Leo's view by the shrubs, we lifted it on to a wheelbarrow and wheeled it to Leo's kitchen.

The soldiers came over and helped us hang it inside.

If Leo realised that a big part of the carcass had gone missing, he didn't seem to mind. He probably reckoned that I had eaten it all. No matter. His tummy was already feeling so full that breathing was becoming difficult.

Until he was a year old, Leo's fare had consisted mostly of impala, chicken and the odd antelope that had to be destroyed. On the 28th of November — which we presumed to be his birthday — the Park veterinarians asked Kobus to shoot a buffalo for them. They needed to do a spot-check for tuberculosis on a certain herd in the area. So, Leo got his first taste of buffalo meat as a birthday present.

A buffalo is an incredibly big animal, and since only about a third of the meat would fit into the freezer, we donated the rest of it to the local game guards and field staff.

Being so large, the carcass couldn't be accommodated in Leo's kitchen, so it was hung on a thick iron hook from a high branch of the mkuhlu tree at the barbecue area.

Leo looked on with wonder as Kobus and the game guards hoisted the enormous carcass into the tree. We didn't usually skin carcasses but cut them into lion-size chunks, leaving the skin on so that Leo would have a fully balanced lion diet. But since two-thirds of the buffalo would go to the staff village, part of the carcass had to be skinned.

Leo watched the skinning and cutting-up procedure with immense interest. He wasn't sure whether the buffalo belonged to Kobus or to the game guards but, whichever, he accepted that it wasn't his, and so he was a very well-behaved spectator. Eventually Kobus offered him the entrails, and Leo gratefully accepted the generous gift.

Dashing off with his savoury fare, he found himself a 'safe' hiding place around the corner of the house where he could enjoy his feast in peace.

They were the best entrails he had ever tasted, so after devouring them he went back to watch the proceedings — just in case another hand-out might be considered.

Kobus offered him a chunk of liver, and Leo accepted with much gratitude. A while later he returned again — just in case.

By the end of the day, his stomach was practically dragging on the ground. He was a very full and a very happy lion on his first birthday.

Early the next morning, Leo noticed that a large piece of the buffalo skin was hanging from a low branch of the mkuhlu tree. It was within easy reach — but to whom did it belong? Dashing over to Kobus's office, Leo called to him: 'Auh-wuh! Auh-wuh!'

Kobus came out of the office to see what Leo wanted.

Leo led him to the tree and showed him the skin.

'You want the skin?' Kobus asked.

Leo rubbed his body against Kobus's legs, uttering soft, pleading grunts.

'OK,' said Kobus. 'You're such a good boy. You may have it.' He reached up, pulled the skin down and handed it to Leo.

Leo's heart almost burst with happiness. He spent the rest of that day and most of the following week dragging the buffalo skin all over the garden, wrestling with it, rolling on it, sitting on it and parading it to anyone who happened to come along.

We wondered why the buffalo skin made him so happy. Was he playing a game of make-believe, pretending to himself and everyone else that he had killed the buffalo single-handedly? He certainly acted like someone parading a trophy. We all played along, pretending to believe him. Only Wolfie refused to be taken in by Leo's preposterous story and paid him and his 'trophy' scant attention.

At the age of one year, Leo's large, rust-coloured eyes were still his most captivating feature. They were expressive and intelligent; they could be warm and soft with love and trust, and they could light up with joy or glint with mischief. Leo 'talked' with his eyes, and it was a magical language that expressed his thoughts and feelings so effectively that I never doubted what he was telling me when he looked at me.

It was only when Leo looked at the sky that I didn't know what he was thinking.

He often looked at the sky. Curious to know what he was seeing, I would look up myself. And I would spot a bird — usually far, far above, circling lazily in the great blue yonder.

It was obvious that Leo had exceptional vision. But why did he study the heavens like that? I have never seen a dog or any other animal contemplate the sky. In fact, I have never seen wild lions look up at the sky like that either. But then I have never really been in the company of relaxed wild lions.

Sometimes I would ask him: 'Leo, what do you think of when you look at the sky like that?'

He would turn to me and, concentrating his gaze on me with love and trust, would seem to say: 'I am only dreaming — the same as you do sometimes.'

And I would find myself reacting with a mixed-up feeling of wonder, joy and sadness at the knowledge that such an exquisite bond was possible between a human and a lion.

bove left: The foundling prince.
bove right: By the age of two months, Leo's eyes were his most arresting feature.
elow: Portrait of an upbeat trio – Wolfie, Karin and Leo.

Above: Leo and Hettie entertaining each other.
Below left: Travelling in regal style.
Below right: Leo clowning with Sandra and Paul.

bove left: Wolfie teaching Leo herding techniques.
bove right: A big hug from Karin.
elow: Leo and Wolfie watching baboons on the other side of the fence.

Kobus and Leo (Photograph: Daryl Balfour).

Above: A special bond…(Photograph: Daryl Balfour).
Below left: Karin was Leo's favourite sister.
Below right: Leo striding over the top of Shabeni.

Onward, Leo. Pamuzinda, 1994.

bove: Resting with Hettie. Pamuzinda, 1994.
elow: Leo's joyful reunion with Kobus. Pamuzinda, 1995.

Above: The Royal Family: Fat Cat, Leo and Happie. Pamuzinda, 1995.
Below: A portrait of The King. Pamuzinda, 1995.

Sandra's Wedding

A few months after Paul and Sandra had first started dating, they made the astonishing discovery that Paul's mother and I had been best friends at university. She and I had lost contact shortly after we had both married and moved away to far places. I didn't even know that she had a son named Paul, nor did she know that I had a daughter named Sandra. So naturally we were both bowled over by our children's discovery. And shortly afterwards, Paul's mother drove all the way from Lichtenburg to look me up.

And — although I know this sounds like a fairy-tale — Paul's mother's name is Sandra. I had named my second daughter after my erstwhile best friend.

The renewal of our friendship was such a success that we decided to have a proper family get-together as soon as possible.

Paul and Sandra had started their university careers as medical students, but after completing two years of medical studies, they had both decided to change their courses. Paul changed to veterinary science and Sandra to nutritional science. Although their two years of medical training gave them some discount on their altered courses, several years of study still lay ahead for both of them. Neither wanted to wait that long before getting married, and so they consulted us, asking if we would give them permission to marry at the end of their third year. Naturally we gave our permission — and our blessing.

So when Paul's family arrived for the promised visit in July, we celebrated the engagement.

To Sandra senior and to me, our children's engagement seemed indeed like a fairy-tale come true.

The wedding date was set for the 11th of December.

The children decided they would like a simple, small, rural-style wedding. Paul suggested that it be held in our garden. Kobus agreed that a garden wedding was a wonderful idea. But Sandra (junior) pointed out that she didn't fancy being pounced on by a lion in the middle of the ceremony. Paul promised that he would protect her with his water pistol. But Sandra said no, that would look too silly for words and, anyway, she wouldn't like Leo to pounce on any of the guests during the ceremony either. Hettie reminded us that Paul's father was a medical doctor and so casualties could be treated on the spot but, even so, she said, a garden wedding probably wouldn't be practical. There was the cobra to think of as well.

I also sided with Sandra. I wouldn't want our guests to be looking over their shoulders and worrying about the whereabouts of the lion instead of paying attention to the sermon.

And so it was settled that the two of them would get married in the quaint little stone church in Komatipoort.

The sugar-cane farmers across the river owned a community hall on the southern bank of the Crocodile river, and we asked them if we might hire it for the reception. The farmers generously offered to let us have it free of charge for the occasion. The hall was set in a beautiful garden surrounded by bush and had a magnificent view of the river and the Park beyond it.

Sandra and Paul made their own invitation cards, sending them to relatives and close friends. All in all, we expected between fifty and sixty guests. My trouble-sharing friend Annette offered to bake the wedding cake, supply the flowers and to turn the reception hall into fairyland with the assistance of her sister Lien who has a magic touch with flowers.

The church ceremony was scheduled for five in the afternoon and the reception for about an hour later.

We held a family meeting to discuss the menu. Paul suggested barbecued meat with *pap* (traditional maize porridge). Kobus seconded Paul's proposal. But Sandra said *aikona*, no *pap*. I sided with her. *Pap* was daily fare in our household, but I knew that a lot of city people didn't eat it and I felt we had to consider our guests.

Paul mentioned timidly that he would enjoy his own wedding so much more if he could have *pap*, and he wondered if he might not cook it himself. Sandra threatened instant divorce if he did, and so that settled that. No *pap* at the reception.

We decided on a menu of barbecued meat, a delicious mixed salad, home-baked bread (which Paul's mother graciously offered to supply) and chocolate trifle for dessert. Paul's father kindly offered to provide the drinks.

It was agreed that Sandra would make the pudding, while Hettie and Karin would prepare the salads on the morning of the wedding.

My task was to make the wedding dress.

Fortunately, Sandra's taste is pure and simple to the point of austerity. So the pattern was actually quite easy and straightforward. Even so, it took me ages — and a good deal of agony — to get the dress made. I so much wanted it to be perfect. But contrary to what everybody thinks, I don't like sewing and I'm not good at it. I only do it because I have three daughters — and because a game ranger's salary is not big enough to allow for a clothes budget.

The preparations for the wedding started in all earnest at the beginning of December. Everything went smoothly until two days before the wedding.

Then everything went less smoothly.

The mercury rose to 44°C in the shade. I couldn't get on with my sewing as my hands were slippery with perspiration and I was terrified it would leave stains on the satin. The wedding dress was almost finished — but not quite. I decided to wait until dark and continue in the cool of the night.

I still had nothing to wear to the wedding myself. But fortunately my mother had once given me a trunk of pretty dresses that she had owned when she was young. So I unpacked the trunk and discovered a beautiful dark blue dress in a sheer, silky fabric. It had long sleeves and a high collar — which wouldn't do in the suffocating heat. But that was no problem. I would cut off the sleeves and the collar and make a few other alterations, and — *voilà*!

Hettie found a lilac-coloured dress of soft sateen in the trunk and decided right away that it would be her outfit for the wedding. She looked lovely in it, the pale lilac setting off her silky blonde hair and blue eyes. Karin tried on some of the stuff in the trunk, but eventually decided that at her age she looked a little incongruous in such old-fashioned outfits. So she drew all her birthday money from her savings account and bought herself a short, white chiffon skirt with a dark blue silky linen top. It was the first outfit she had ever bought herself (all her clothes were either inherited or home-made). She looked striking in it and I was very proud of her taste.

All my daughters were going to look so beautiful at the wedding — the very thought of it brought tears to my eyes. We had never before, as a family, all dressed up like this for an occasion.

I waited for nightfall to get back to my sewing. Apart from the final touches to Sandra's dress, there were still the alterations to be made to my own outfit.

Then a sudden thunderstorm just before dark brought a terrific gale that upended a large coral tree in the garden. It crashed into the power lines, cutting off our electricity! I couldn't go on with my sewing.

Kobus and the game guards spent most of the next day sawing the fallen tree into transportable chunks and carting them off.

Just before noon the power supply was finally turned on again and by that time the mercury had once again risen to above 40°C. Paul's parents, brothers, sister and sister-in-law arrived at midday and Leo tried to pounce on all of them, so we had our hands full.

At two in the afternoon a film crew from the BBC arrived. They were filming a documentary for a programme called 'The Really Wild Show'.

The director, Joanna Sarsby, had phoned us all the way from London a few days earlier, asking permission to film our cub for their documentary. Kobus had told her that we were anxious not to expose our lion to publicity for various reasons, one of them being that hand-rearing a lion in the Park is a sensitive issue. Joanna explained that the theme of the programme was in fact a debate on the issue of hand-rearing wild lions and the question of whether they should be reintroduced to the wild or whether suitable alternative homes should be found for them. She added that the programme would be screened only in England.

Kobus nevertheless asked her to contact the Park Warden first and seek his permission. She did this, and permission was granted. So she called again and asked if she and her crew could come on the 10th of December (the day before Sandra's wedding!). Unfortunately no other date suited them, but they promised not to keep us more than two hours at the most.

Naturally we were curious to know how these people had learned about our lion. It turned out that Joanna had heard from a friend, who had heard from an acquaintance, who had heard from a colleague, who had heard from — none other than Gareth Patterson!

Goodness.

How did Gareth Patterson know about our lion?

The answer came that same afternoon.

I answered a telephone call, and was immediately entranced by the caller's British accent and the melodious inflection of his speech. When he told me that he was Gareth Patterson, I was naturally most surprised. I said that we had been wondering how and where to contact him but that, quite frankly, I hadn't thought it possible to actually make contact with a mythical person — especially not one who lived in the middle of nowhere, somewhere in the wilds of Botswana.

Gareth told me he was calling from Pretoria and that he had just been interviewed by the same BBC crew who were on their way to us. He explained that he had heard about our lion from an acquaintance, who had heard from a friend, who, on a recent visit to the Park, had met a game ranger who had mentioned our lion.

Thus doth news travel in Africa.

Anyway the reason for his call, Gareth said, was to enquire about our future plans for Leo. I told him that that was the very reason why we had been hoping to contact him — to discuss Leo's future. We needed help.

Gareth said he was on his way back to Botswana right then, but promised that he would contact us again early in the new year.

Now to get back to the day before the wedding.

As soon as the BBC crew arrived, Leo turned into a mischievous monster.

He stalked and caught each one of the four crew members while Kobus and I were trying to introduce ourselves to them. They had just come from Letaba Ranch, a ranger's outpost in the north of Gazankulu where they had filmed three other hand-reared lions. These were lazy, well-behaved adult lions who were kept in a large fenced-in camp near the ranger's house. The crew were surprised (or perhaps horrified) to find that our lion not only roamed free, but also behaved abominably.

While we were trying to explain the 'rules' to them — don't bend over, don't crouch, never run away, stay together in a group and avoid eye contact — they more or less broke all the rules.

Naturally Leo had a field day. Joanna saw him coming at her and tried to run, but he caught her around the waist and dragged her down. The sound-man was bending over his equipment, so Leo chomped his behind. The cameraman, setting up his camera, was also bending over, and he not only got chomped in the rear, but as he spun around, Leo grabbed him round the waist, pulled him down and sat on him.

Paul's family wisely stayed indoors, watching the goings-on through the windows. When Paul realised that Kobus and I were having a really hard time trying to control Leo, he came out to lend a helping hand. The moment Leo spotted his favourite brother, he charged at him. Paul, being an accomplished athlete, dashed round the house, Leo hot on his heels. When they turned the last corner and came into sight again, Leo caught up with Paul and pulled his shorts off, exposing his green underwear. The cameraman was happily impressed. But Paul had had enough. He was camera-shy anyway and not at all anxious to appear on British TV in green under-garments, so he disappeared back into the house.

Meanwhile Leo disappeared into the flowerbed, emerging a few seconds later as a yellow blur and landing on top of me. I was getting really cross with Leo, but I didn't want the British visitors to realise that I had no control over him. And they probably wouldn't believe me if I told them that Leo had never been as naughty as this in his whole life.

As Leo proceeded to make it as difficult as possible for Kobus and me to protect the crew from him, I considered asking Paul to bring his water pistol. Not that the water pistol was the final answer to controlling Leo, but it was helpful in that as soon as Paul squeezed the trigger, Leo would open his mouth to catch and swallow the sprays of water, giving his victims a chance to get away. But camera-shy as he was, I knew Paul would be reluctant to appear on British television shooting a lion with a water pistol.

Now Joanna wanted the narrator, Chris, to interview Kobus and me. For over an hour, this proved quite impossible as Leo simply wouldn't let up. Each time Chris approached Kobus, microphone in hand, Leo pounced on one or the other of them. Eventually Kobus wrestled Leo down and, while pinning him to the ground, managed to say a few words into the microphone.

Chris started the interview by saying: 'Kobus, now this is not a domestic pet. Surely one gets injured now and again?'

As if on cue, Leo struggled free from Kobus's grip. Kobus had started replying: 'Uh, yes, Chris. One does get injured a little now and again, but ...'

Before Kobus was able to finish his sentence, Chris was flat on his back, Leo on top of him, and Kobus was rushing to rescue Chris from the lion who seemed intent on proving that he most certainly was not a domestic pet.

At least the cameraman (when he wasn't being attacked himself) got some highly interesting footage of our 'riotous pet', as Joanna called him. Leo wouldn't leave poor Wolfie alone either, and the crew were fascinated at the way the dog tolerated the lion's boisterous attentions.

Joanna asked if they might film Leo playing with our children as well. So Karin and Hettie volunteered to come outside. But Paul would not let Sandra participate. Leo was in an impossible mood, and he didn't want Sandra walking down the aisle on her wedding day covered in lion scratches.

Karin tried to play a nice, safe game with Leo, but he gave her an awfully hard time. Finally, I couldn't take it any longer. I signalled the cameraman to cut and I pounced on Leo, pulling him off Karin. I gave him a very hard smack on his bottom, commanding him to behave. But he just turned round and jumped on me, bringing me crashing to the ground. The cameraman happily swung his camera into action, so I couldn't let on how really angry I was. But I gave Leo a piece of my mind in Afrikaans...

Eventually, when Leo was exhausted or, more to the point, when we were all exhausted as well as thoroughly beaten-up, Chris managed to interview Kobus and me. By this time my hair and clothes were soaked with perspiration and I was hardly able to think coherently, let alone talk about our lion. And idiot that I am, I described him as 'a wonderfully affectionate animal'!

Surely, no one in their right mind would believe that for a moment when they saw the visuals.

The crew left at about five o'clock that afternoon, and Leo immediately turned into a good, well-behaved lion.

Paul's family, who had been watching the whole show through the windows, were rather worried by what they'd seen, and wanted to know whether Leo would not soon prove a bit of a threat to our family's safety. So we explained that Leo only became uncontrollably naughty when we had visitors, and especially if the visitors showed a particular interest in him. I believed that, in a way, Leo felt threatened by groups of total strangers, and that his outrageous behaviour was his way of telling them that he wanted to be taken seriously.

Fortunately Leo didn't seem to feel particularly threatened by Paul's family, and since they all adhered to the 'rules', he left them alone.

Late that evening, after everyone had gone to bed, I tackled my sewing again. I finished Sandra's dress some time before midnight, and mine a few hours after midnight.

When I finally went to bed, feeling utterly exhausted, I realised that the guests would start arriving in the morning, and although we had booked chalets for them in the tourist camp, they would probably want to come over to the house to say hello.

I wasn't looking forward to another day of trying to protect our visitors from Leo. Kobus would be away most of the morning, transporting the food, drinks, ice, cutlery and so on to the reception hall and getting the fires started for the barbecue. Paul would be helping him and setting up the music system in the hall. And I myself had about a million things to do before the church ceremony at five in the afternoon. So I devised a plan to immobilise Leo.

I got up at dawn that morning, went out to Leo's kitchen and removed about fifteen kilograms of buffalo meat from the freezer, adding it to the five-kilogram portion that I had removed the previous day. Leo usually got his daily meal in the evening, but I had other plans for him on this day.

So I called him and offered him the thawed portion for breakfast. Then I carried the other frozen pieces to the veranda and placed them in front of an east-facing window where the heat of the sun would soon thaw them.

At nine o'clock I called Leo for a second breakfast, offering him a chunk of meat that was almost thawed, but not quite. Leo,

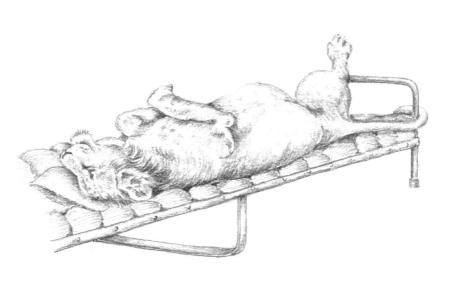

although surprised at receiving yet another unscheduled meal, didn't mind at all and happily carried the piece off in his mouth.

A while later I noticed him puzzling over the coldness of his food. He pawed it and frowned at it. Eventually he turned it over. No good. It was still cold. He tossed it in the air, and when it landed he inspected it hopefully. Still no good. It was as cold as it had been at take-off. Then he sat on it. That may seem like a brilliant move to you. But Leo often sat on things — including us — when he wasn't sure what to do next. So I believe the reason he sat on the meat was to prevent it from going away while he tried to think things through. Anyway, it helped speed up the thawing and he was soon able to enjoy his extra meal.

At ten o'clock I offered him the rest of the meat. And by eleven o'clock, when the first of our visitors arrived, his tummy was so full that it was difficult to move. So Leo flopped down next to his out-sized tummy and spent the rest of the day in a horizontal position. Naturally, our visitors were terrified of the lion and gave him a wide berth. But as soon as they realised that he was comatose, they fetched their cameras and took dozens of pictures of the serene, fat lion.

Organising a wedding is an enormous task that has a way of multiplying and breeding new, small tasks all the time. My family and I worked very hard until about an hour before the ceremony.

By the time I finally found myself sitting in the church, I was so tired that I could hardly think straight.

But as soon as the entrancing strains of Wagner's Lohengrin filled the church, and Sandra came walking in on her father's arm, a surge of exhilaration swept my fatigue into oblivion. Sandra, with her shiny red hair and radiant smile was the most beautiful bride I had ever seen. And Kobus, in a dark suit, looked so handsome that I almost cried. I hadn't seen him in a suit for ages and ages. Karin, who had never seen her father in a suit in her whole life, thought for a moment there had been some mistake. Wasn't he supposed to be in khaki uniform?

The sermon was both stirring and amusing, its theme being that faith and love inspire courage and determination. To prove his point, the minister pointed to the groom and reminded us that this young man had succeeded in winning the hand of a game ranger's daughter. 'A game ranger,' said the minister, 'who is reputed to be fiercely protective of his daughters and who also owns a lion.'

(Personally, I didn't believe it was prayers or passion that gave the young man his courage: it was his water pistol.)

When we came to the part where the rings were to be exchanged, my sister's teenage son, Kobus Frick, stepped up to the couple with his violin and played Andrew Lloyd Webber's beautiful song 'Love Changes Everything' for them. (I learned later that it was Hettie who had secretly arranged this glamorous touch.) The young virtuoso performed the melody with an exalting grace that turned it to pure magic. Paul's mother touched my hand to let me know how moved she was, and as I turned my head to smile at her, I caught a glimpse of Paul's father beside her — with a tear spilling down his cheek. (Naturally, I fell in love with him right away.)

After the ceremony, everybody got into their cars and followed us north out of Komatipoort to the reception hall in the heart of the bush.

The hall had indeed been transformed into a fairyland by Annette and her sister Lien. Blue and green tablecloths, dozens of blue and green candles, blue and green balloons, and masses of foliage and flowers everywhere. The abundance of blues and greens created a cool, forest ambience — which was just what we needed in the heat.

As soon as all the guests had been seated, Paul's oldest brother proposed a toast to the couple, and then Paul made a nice, short speech to thank and welcome everyone. A few of his bachelor friends tried to interrupt his speech with a silly song, but Paul reached for his water pistol and let them have it. I was proud of my son-in-law. He obviously knew how to deal with people as well as lions. And before anyone could interrupt him again, the speech was over.

The guests carried their drinks outside into the garden to admire the magical bushveld sunset and to enjoy the aroma of the meat roasting on the fires. A soft breeze rolled down from the Lebombo mountains and stirred the trees, bringing sweet respite from the day's heat. On the far bank of the river, a family of fat warthogs were enjoying a mud-bath, and a lone fish eagle swooped low over the bush, its call echoing through the landscape. From the wooded hills to the west of the river, the stirring cry of a jackal rose, and birds everywhere performed their end-of-day songs. The sun disappeared in a blaze of carmine and magenta behind the hills. And as dusk settled, the sweet, quavering call of a nightjar started the evening serenade.

Lowveld air is richer in oxygen than other air.

And the more oxygen humans breathe, the hungrier they get.

I don't know why.

They just do.

As soon as the meat was done, the highly oxygenated guests dashed for the serving tables and stacked their plates with heaps of home-made bread, spicy barbecued meat and salads. After second and third helpings, some were groaning with indulgence-fatigue, but they nevertheless helped themselves generously to Sandra's delicious chocolate trifle.

When everyone was full and happy, Paul and his brothers moved the tables and chairs from the hall to the patio outside. A cassette player was switched on and dance music spilled through loudspeakers into the hall.

Paul and Sandra opened the dancing with extraordinary style, gliding across the floor in perfect rhythm to the music, in perfect harmony with each other, and somehow combining grace with abandon. I was fascinated. Where did they learn to dance like that — this astonishingly handsome couple?

The rest of the young people joined in, and a striking young girl caught my eye — golden haired and ... ah! I knew that face! Hettie!

Then a gay, sunny laugh drew my attention to another incredibly lovely girl — it was Karin!

Now where, I wondered, did I get such beautiful children?

More people joined in the dancing, and the smiling faces of friends and relatives floated by — my brother, my sister, their lovely families, Paul's delightful parents, my good friend Annette, my gracious in-laws... all these charming, wonderful people, come from afar to celebrate my daughter's wedding, dancing in this forest-fairyland of music and magic.

Amazing.

How did all this happen?

A tall, handsome guy came over and asked me to dance.

'Do I know you?' I asked him.

'I hope so,' he replied. 'I'm your husband.'

'Ah, yes!' I said. 'The fierce game ranger with the lion? You are not so easy to recognise tonight, you know. The suit disguises you.'

We danced and talked and laughed, and our hearts were young and gay.

We helped ourselves to wedding cake and coffee on the patio, gazed at a million stars and enjoyed the feel of the velvet night.

Then we danced some more in celebration of all that was good: the wedding, the beautiful night, life, the universe and everything.

Moving West

During our three-year stay at Crocodile Bridge, Kobus managed to engage the co-operation of Mozambican government officials in the campaign against poachers, and by the end of 1993, the poaching problem on our eastern boundary had been dramatically reduced. So the director of Nature Conservation decided to transfer us to Pretorius Kop — a ranger's section in the southwestern region of the Park.

I wasn't sure how I felt about the transfer.

Despite all the madness of life at Crocodile Bridge, there were things that I liked about the place and that I would miss — the enchanting landscapes at the foot of the Lebombo mountains for instance, and the abundant variety of wild life in the area. And, of course, our beautiful subtropical garden.

Naturally I would not miss the hysterical telephone. Or the bats. And it occurred to me that, actually, I wouldn't altogether miss the beautiful garden too much either. There were times, especially in the rainy season, when everything grew too fast and too furiously, choking up the garden and making me claustrophobic. I like open landscapes where one can see far and wide. Our garden often got so dense and overgrown that one could see only as far as the nearest view-blocking profusion of foliage. We kept pruning and chopping things back to keep them out of our way, but the pruning only inspired more aggressive growth. It worried me sometimes that the wild tangles of vegetation appeared to be groping at me. One day the trailing stems of a delicious monster actually caught me round the throat and tried to strangle me.

The two things that I would miss most about Crocodile Bridge were, strangely enough, two people: my phantom neighbour Ilse, and my trouble-sharing friend Annette. Apparently I had become a slightly altered version of my former self who had lived so happily in isolation at Mahlangeni.

Annette and I would still be able to visit each other of course, but Pretorius Kop is almost a hundred kilometres from Lower Sabie. So we wouldn't be able to meet very often.

We moved in January 1994, about four weeks after Sandra's wedding.

All in all, saying goodbye to Crocodile Bridge wasn't too hard. There had been plenty of good times and exuberant moments but, in the greater scheme of things, my heart still belonged to Mahlangeni.

On the day that the furniture truck arrived, I again fed Leo into a horizontal state to prevent him from bothering the furniture movers.

The game guards all came over to say goodbye to Leo, and it was obvious that they would miss their feline friend. Kobus took photographs of each one of them posing with Leo, and promised to send them as soon as the film was developed.

All our children were on holiday in the Eastern Cape, so Kobus and I moved alone with Wolfie and Leo. We left in the evening to avoid encountering tourists on the road. (They wouldn't understand why we had a lion and a dog together on the back of the truck.)

It was a difficult journey. Leo insisted on travelling in regal style on the roof of the cab, his front paws dangling over the top of the windscreen and his tail hanging past the back window. There were numerous creeks along the way, and each time the road dipped down a steep bank, Leo would start sliding off the roof and across the windscreen. I would thrust my arm out through the back window, grab hold of his tail and hang on with all my weight to prevent him from falling off. When we had to drive up a bank, Leo would clutch the mounting of the roof aerial for support. We worried that the aerial would snap, so we ordered Leo to get off the roof, but he wouldn't listen.

Eventually the journey in the dark started triggering his predatory instincts. Every time we spotted eyes alongside the road, he jumped off the truck — from the roof on to the bonnet and then on to the track right in front of us — and Kobus would have to slam on the brakes to avoid colliding with him. Leo then disappeared into the darkness and we had no choice but to wait patiently for him to return from his explorations. Calling didn't help — he was in an arrogant mood. And we didn't want to risk sending Wolfie after him. Dogs are easy prey for nocturnal predators.

At the Mitomeni creek we encountered two cheetahs alongside the road, and Leo promptly jumped off the truck again. He'd never met a cheetah in person before and was eager to make their acquaintance. But the shy cats took one look at the king and fled. So Leo ran after them.

We waited... and waited... and waited...

When he finally came back about twenty minutes later, Kobus ordered him to get on the truck and to stay there, or else...

But, believe me, there is nothing much that one can do about a difficult passenger who happens to be a lion.

Pretorius Kop is about a two and a half hour drive from Crocodile Bridge, but Leo's antics kept us on the road for more than four hours, and so we arrived very late that night.

The chief game guard at Pretorius Kop, Sergeant Sambo, had been waiting for us, and as we arrived at the gate of our new home, he opened it for us, saluting smartly. We got out of the truck to shake hands with the sergeant and to thank him for waiting up for us. Leo and Wolfie jumped off the truck, but Leo took one look (or one smell) at the new house, decided it wasn't a safe place for a lion, and jumped right back on to the truck again.

Sergeant Sambo had heard about our lion, and although he kept a respectful distance, he realised right away that Leo wasn't a very brave fellow.

He informed us that the camp manager had heard that our furniture would not be arriving until the next day, so he had sent over two beds together with bedding and towels for us. We thanked the sergeant, and after Kobus had discussed arrangements with him for the following day, we bade him good night.

Clever Wolfie caught on immediately that this place was to be our new home. So he got right down to the business of marking things that needed to be marked.

But Leo remained timidly on the truck, all his earlier arrogance forgotten.

'Come on Leo,' I said to him. 'Don't be a baby. Come and explore your new home!'

He looked at me with a perplexed expression that seemed to say: 'This place smells of strange humans and dogs. I'm scared of them.'

'They've left,' I told him. 'It's only their smell that's still around. It will go away eventually.'

Leo didn't know whether to believe me or not.

'Trust me, Leo,' I said. 'It's our place now.'

He jumped off the truck and ran to Wolfie, almost colliding with him. And for the rest of the night and all the following day he would not leave Wolfie's side. He obviously trusted his friend to protect him from dangerous aliens — despite the fact that his friend weighed about a hundred kilograms less than he did.

We couldn't see much of our new garden in the dark, but it seemed huge. And there was something about the smell of the plants and the overall feeling of freshness and crispness that was nice. The altitude at Pretorius Kop is approximately 600 metres higher than Crocodile Bridge, and so the air is lighter and cooler.

We followed a paved path that wound its way amongst ferns and trees, past a fish pond, across an open lawn and up to the patio of the house. We opened the front door and walked into a very spacious room.

It turned out to be the lounge.

We discovered that every room in the house was enormous, even the kitchen and the bathrooms. But what delighted us most was the distinct absence of bats. Never again would we have to duck their idiotic crash landings.

The second best thing about the house was its huge windows that opened directly on to the outside world. We looked forward to having the daylight streaming right into the house, and to not falling over things in dark rooms any more.

Wolfie knocked at the front door. He wanted to see what the house looked like inside. So we invited him and Leo inside for a quick tour of the empty house. Wolfie gave every room a thorough sniffing-over but Leo was terrified of all the strange human smells in the house and he concentrated only on staying close to the dog.

Afterwards I fetched their sleeping mats from the truck and spread them on the front patio. Leo was so relieved at the sight and smell of his familiar mat that he immediately sat down on it to prevent it from going away. But Wolfie was in no mood for sitting around. The whole of the garden still needed to be inspected. So, off he went. Leo called Wolfie to come back, but Wolfie paid him no attention. It occurred to Leo that Wolfie would probably be a better bodyguard than his mat, so he leapt up and ran after him.

Kobus and I had the sandwiches and coffee I had packed for us, took a shower and went straight to bed. It had been a long day.

But despite my exhaustion I was unable to fall asleep. I lay watching the stars and the dark silhouettes of trees through the bedroom windows, and I wondered what the place would look like in daylight.

A barn owl called out from a tall palm tree in front of the bedroom. It was soon answered by another. I was delighted. I love the call of barn owls. They remind one of forsaken places inhabited by nothing but the wind, the moon, the stars, and barn owls.

The strains of distant frog concerts drifted through the darkness, and after a while the haunting howls of a lone hyena rose from somewhere and soared out into the night. As soon as the rising and falling echoes faded, I heard the most fascinating meowing call I'd ever heard in my life.

I woke Kobus.

'What's making that meowing call?' I asked him.

We lay quietly for a while, listening. The strange meowing call rose again, and was answered by another.

'Genet cats,' Kobus told me.

Genet cats! I was thrilled. Those dainty, shy creatures that look like a cross between a domestic cat and a mongoose — I didn't know they had such exquisite voices.

I got up and stuck my head out through the window to listen to the sweet melodies of their plaintive calls.

It was nice to be welcomed to my new home by a genet cat serenade.

At dawn the next morning I dashed outside to see if the sun was going to rise in the right place. It seemed strange not to have a river in front of the house, and for a moment I felt lost. But I remembered the route that we had travelled the previous day — first west, then north-west and then north. And some inner feeling told me that east should be behind me and somewhat to my right. So I turned, and in the dusky gloom I could make out a wide, wooded valley. And right above its horizon a splash of tangerine streaked the sky.

A wave of relief swept over me.

After three years of confusion, the sun was finally back in its proper place.

Enchanted Days

Our sunny house stands in a wooded garden of almost two acres. It doesn't have the subtropical character of the Crocodile Bridge garden — it's more spacious and open, and the vegetation doesn't look so aggressive.

The front garden faces north into a marula woodland. To the east lies a valley of silver cluster-leaf trees, and to the west is a stretch of mixed bushwillow, marula and acacia bushland. A dirt track runs alongside the southern fence of the garden, and across the track there are two houses. They belong to the two local trail rangers. Beyond these are the houses of the camp manager and other personnel.

The tourist camp is to the southwest of our house (and practically across the road), but since it's out of sight, it doesn't really feel that close. It is one of the most beautiful camps in the Park. Although it has a hundred chalets, it's a surprisingly quiet camp. It has a large tourist shop — and so I enjoy the luxury of living only a five-minute walk from a shop that sells almost everything from fresh produce to magazines, curios and books.

Even though I now have neighbours across the road, life is quieter here than it was at Crocodile Bridge. Pretorius Kop is off the beaten track. If you look at it from the air, you will see only a tiny speck of human habitation, surrounded by vast and solitary bushlands.

The Pretorius Kop section consists of five different ecozones, and so it has the largest variety of tree and plant species in the whole of the Park. One of the dominant tree species in the region is the silver cluster-leaf. It is an enchanting tree, both in the colour of its foliage and in shape. Its branches tend to grow out horizontally from the trunk and droop at the ends. The foliage, although dense along each branch, does not prevent one from seeing the lovely pattern of the branches. The long, silver-grey leaves are borne in bunches on slender twigs.

These graceful trees grow in abundance in sandy areas and on the seeplines of valleys. Their silver-grey foliage glistens like dewdrops in the early morning sun, and turns to aquamarine at dusk. In midsummer, when the trees are laden with clusters of pink fruit, the trees are no longer merely silver, but both pink and silver — like Christmas trees in a fairy-tale.

Another enchanting feature of the Pretorius Kop section is the rocky hills (or koppies) that dot the undulating landscapes. They have lovely Tsonga names: Shabeni, Manungu, Shitungwane, Matupa, Mlaleni. Our favourite outing is to climb to the top of one of these koppies and to sit there, above it all, watching the world go by.

Despite the attractiveness of the Pretorius Kop landscapes, the section is less popular with tourists than the other southern sections of the Park. The reason for this is probably the tall sour grass that covers vast parts of the area, making animal spotting difficult.

Yet the section has the biggest concentration of both rhino and kudu in the Park. It is also home to many elephant herds as well as several rare antelope species such as sable, reedbuck and Lictensteins. Giraffe are easily spotted above the tall grass, and packs of wild dogs are often seen trekking along the tourist roads. Other predators in the area are hyena, cheetah, leopard and lion.

Our garden is home to a family of barn owls as well as to many other species of birds, a community of squirrels and a variety of reptile fauna: tree agamas, chameleons, geckos and other fascinating little creatures. Regular visitors include vervet monkeys, mongooses, genets, porcupines, leguaans and tortoises. (And snakes. But I've learned to avoid and ignore them.)

Leo spent his first day at Pretorius Kop pretending to be Wolfie's shadow.

When the local game guard corps came over to meet Kobus, they found an outsize lion trying to hide behind a medium-size dog, so naturally they took him for a retarded lion.

But the only reason Leo appeared so timid that day was because he didn't yet know where the boundaries of his safety zone were.

Wolfie, of course, knew exactly where the boundaries were. So he went about marking the whole of the garden — every fence-post, outbuilding, tree and shrub. It took him the better part of the day. Leo trusted Wolfie's superior knowledge, and so he stayed close to him and paid attention.

Some time during the early afternoon, a troop of vervet monkeys scaled the southern fence of the garden, trooped across the lawn and climbed up a mango tree. When I noticed the interlopers gorging themselves on our mangoes, I walked up to the tree and warned them that if they didn't leave right away, I would call my dog. They peered down at me through the foliage and shrieked abuse at me.

'Listen,' I told them, 'I also have a lion. If you don't leave right this moment, I'll call my dog *and* my lion!'

They didn't believe a word I said and went right on cheeking me.

I turned towards the house and called Wolfie in the tone I use when I need him urgently. Wolfie and his shadow came tearing around a corner of the house. Wolfie immediately sensed the whereabouts of the intruders and launched himself at the mango tree — followed by his shadow.

For a brief moment all the monkeys were shocked speechless. Then they fell out of the tree in unison, screaming their heads off and heading for the fence at breakneck speed. Some of them were too shocked to remember where the fence was and dashed crazily all over the place. Wolfie and his shadow had a lot of fun herding the hysterical delinquents out of the garden.

By the end of the day, Leo felt confident that the whole garden — as marked by Wolfie — constituted his and his family's new safe haven. So he started relaxing more and stopped crowding the dog. Wolfie was noticeably relieved when the lion finally allowed him more breathing space.

When the game guards turned up early the next morning, they found a more arrogant lion following them through the garden towards Kobus's office. They increased their pace, glancing nervously over their shoulders. Kobus came out of the office to meet them, and when Leo spotted Kobus, he launched himself at him for a fond hug. Some of the game guards thought for a moment that Leo was attacking Kobus, and they promptly stepped forward in case he needed help.

Kobus was touched by their loyalty, but quickly explained to them that this was Leo's way of greeting him. He then gave them all a thorough lecture on how to control Leo. He warned them never to run away from Leo if he wanted to play but, instead, to stand their ground and to talk Leo out of it with an authoritative tone of voice. He also suggested that they carry a stick whenever they entered the garden. Leo had great respect for a stick — and it didn't have to be a big stick. One needed only to brandish a puny twig at him and say: 'NO, Leo!' and he would back off right away.

At the end of our first week at Pretorius Kop, all the game guards felt comfortable with Leo and knew how to control him.

We have a full-time gardener here, a man named Aaron. Leo thought he and Aaron had a lot in common since they were both interested in gardening. He enjoyed following Aaron around to see how he could help. But Aaron didn't appreciate sharing his job with a lion. So one day, when things got a bit out of hand, Aaron grabbed a wheelbarrow and charged Leo with it. Poor Leo got a dreadful shock and ran for his life.

After that he was terrified of the wheelbarrow and wouldn't go near it. And whenever Aaron caught Leo demolishing the flora, he would get the wheelbarrow and chase him with it. Leo would come running to the house, calling for help and uttering streams of complaints about the wheelbarrow. I had to explain to him that

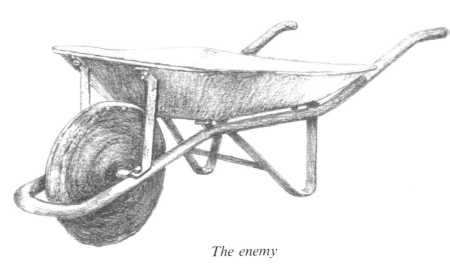

The enemy

wheelbarrows weren't normally aggressive — only when lions got destructive in the garden.

Our predecessor at Pretorius Kop had built a cement pond at the edge of the marula woodland just outside the northern fence of the garden. We keep the pond filled with water from a hosepipe. Warthog, kudu, impala, waterbuck and bushbuck often come to the pond to drink. Initially they were terrified of Leo, but as soon as they realised that he didn't realise they were edible, they lost their fear of him and paid him no further attention.

About a week after we had moved in, a troop of baboons turned up to feast on the ripe marulas in the woodland. They were busily gathering the fallen fruit under the trees when Wolfie spotted them and decided to give them a warning bark — just to let them know that he was the new boss in the area and that his job included keeping baboons out of the garden. The baboons looked up, saw the dog, and muttered to themselves: 'Goodness, what a serious-looking dog. We'd better stay out of his garden.'

Meanwhile, Leo, who had been enjoying a snooze, woke up wondering what Wolfie was barking about. He got up and went to investigate. He found the dog standing at the northern fence, keeping a watchful eye on the baboons. So he decided to go over and join him.

One of the baboons looked up again, saw something very disturbing and screamed: 'WHAZAT? A LION?'

In no time at all the whole troop had dashed up the marula trees, yelling in consternation.

Wolfie gave a few more imperative barks.

Leo only said: 'Huh?'

I was watching them from the veranda, and I decided to fetch my camera and take a few pictures of Leo and Wolfie contemplating the baboons.

All the baboons were in the marula trees now, and they were so busy screaming their heads off that they didn't even see me leaving the house and walking to the bottom of the garden. I had a zoom-lens on the camera, so I chose a spot some distance away from Leo and Wolfie in order to get a nice angle on them. I wanted to get some shots of the way their faces were reflecting their respective thoughts. Wolfie clearly took a dim view of the hysterical clowns, but Leo was having a hard time trying to puzzle out the reason for their behaviour.

After a while some of the baboons began to realise that the lion wasn't really doing anything. It just stood there, gaping at them. Maybe he didn't know how to scale the fence. The idea calmed them somewhat. So they started getting a bit braver — barking defiant battle cries while hopping up and down on the branches. A number of the larger males proceeded to display their power by breaking off small branches and hurling them to the ground.

The war-dancing and power-displaying deepened Leo's puzzlement by several degrees.

Wolfie finally decided that the sabre-rattling was just too silly for words and that he didn't need to watch it any longer, so he retired to his favourite siesta spot at the side of Kobus's office. Leo gave up trying to fathom what it was all about, and flopped down on the grass for a snooze.

The baboon concert went into diminuendo as the war-cries changed to nervous chattering. I shut my camera and decided to go back indoors. But then I looked at Leo lying stretched out on his back, and I couldn't resist the urge to go over and give him a nice hug.

I didn't stop to think of the profound shock that my actions would produce in the baboons.

The moment they became aware that I was approaching the lion, there came a murmur of panic and disbelief from the audience. What was this stupid primate doing, walking up to a lion?

Soon their screams resounded to the heavens.

I really don't know whether they were trying to warn me or whether they were reacting out of sheer dread — like an audience watching a horror movie. Whichever it was, I enjoyed myself immensely — I had never before had such an appreciative audience.

Leo was still lying stretched out on his back when I reached him, and as I sat down beside him for a hug, his huge front paws reached up and around my neck, pulling my head affectionately to his chest. The baboons got so hysterical that some of them lost their voices and could only whimper. I am sure that a number of them actually shut their eyes to avoid witnessing the sight of me being devoured by the lion.

After a while I started feeling sorry for my distressed audience, so I got to my feet to show them that I was still alive. I also waved to them.

A number of them just went right on shrieking and whimpering (I think their eyes were still closed) but others stopped their screaming, stared at me and started uttering strange sounds — which, unfortunately, I was unable to translate. But I think they were probably muttering to themselves that surely this was just a bizarre dream — it couldn't possibly happen in real life.

The two trail rangers across the road, Bryan Haveman and Bruce Leslie, soon made friends with Leo and learned how to control him, which was good because they often had to come over to Kobus's office to discuss things with him. But apart from the two trail rangers and the game guards, the rest of our neighbours chose to keep a respectful distance. They often came up to the fence, however, hoping to catch a glimpse of Leo. And Leo, who enjoyed having admirers, would amble over to the fence and graciously grant his fans the pleasure of his royal company.

We didn't want any tourists to know that we had a lion, so we asked all our neighbours not to mention it to anyone in the tourist camp. If people started flocking over to our house to meet the lion, I would be constantly having to protect visitors from Leo. Although most people are thoughtful and intelligent beings, there is always the odd one who does strange things — and who might not realise that even a tame lion can be a very dangerous animal.

And it goes without saying that, unless you are intimately acquainted with lions and know how to control them, you shouldn't try to play with them.

You might end up dead.

Hiding Leo from tourists wasn't always easy, though.

Whenever Kobus wasn't home by dusk, Leo would sit at the gate, calling for him. Although his voice wasn't capable of a full-volume roar yet, his calls could be heard over quite a distance. Fearful that tourists might get curious about the calls, I would rush outside and try to persuade Leo to do something else. Fortunately, tourists who heard Leo calling never seemed to realise exactly where the calls came from. They probably thought they were listening to a wild lion calling somewhere in the bush.

The roads in the area presented us with another problem. Whenever the family accompanied Kobus on a patrol trip, he would keep to the unmarked roads (the fire-breaks and patrol tracks) to avoid tourists. But there are a number of places where the tracks cross the tourist roads, and occasionally we would be unable to avoid encountering a tourist car. In most instances, the tourists would drive right past us before actually registering that there was a lion on the back of the truck. When they did, they would slam their brakes on and reverse at top speed, hoping to get another glimpse of us.

Occasionally people would report the unusual sighting to the tourism official on duty in the camp. And the good officer, wishing to protect us from public curiosity, would tell them that he knew nothing of such a lion and that he had no idea why it would be travelling on the back of a truck.

A baffled tourist once reported to the officer that he'd spotted a lion and a dog together on the back of a game ranger's vehicle, and he wanted to know how it could have happened. Had the lion jumped on to the truck as it passed? And, if so, why didn't it eat the dog?

The silver cluster-leaf valley to the east of our house became my favourite area for walking Leo and Wolfie. I carried a firearm on our first few walks while I studied my new surroundings. As I became more familiar with the landscape, I grew confident that I would be able to identify its non-permanent features at a distance, and so I left the firearm at home.

A patrol track leads down into the valley and up the rise, and on our second walk, I discovered that the patrol track meets a tourist road at the top of the rise. So I learned that I had to turn back just before reaching the top of the rise to avoid being seen by tourists.

But one day, just as we'd almost reached the top of the rise and were about to turn back, Leo spotted something — and off he went to investigate. He was running straight towards the tourist road. To make things worse, I could hear a car approaching. Fearful that Leo might get run over, I ran after him, calling him to come back. I estimated the road to be about another forty or fifty metres away, but I mis-estimated.

As I rushed full-speed through a thicket of silver cluster-leafs, I found myself emerging right on to the road. Leo had just crossed it, chasing after a herd of zebra. The delighted tourists slammed on their brakes to admire the lion — when stupid me came charging out of the thickets and across the road right in front of them, yelling at the lion to come back. When I realised my predicament, it was too late to do anything about it, so I just carried right on running and disappeared into the bush at the other side of the road, praying that the people would not believe what they'd seen.

Fortunately they never reported me. So I guess they probably decided it had been an illusion. Or maybe they were too shy to report that they'd spotted a lady and a fat dog chasing a lion. Who would believe them?

Despite this one embarrassing incident, our first summer at Pretorius Kop remains in my memory as a time of enchanted days. I loved my new home and its surroundings. And I guess I also realised the importance of cherishing each magic moment. My foundling prince was nearing adulthood and I would not be a lion-mother for much longer.

The Lion Man

Gareth Patterson phoned again towards the end of February, asking how long Kobus and I still wished to keep Leo. I told him that we would wish to keep him for ever, but that it was against Park policy and that we had in fact already received a formal letter from our Director of Nature Conservation, enquiring what our future plans for Leo were.

Gareth apologised for not contacting us earlier — his work in the Tuli bushlands had kept him busy. But Leo would be his first priority now, he said, and he added that he wished to meet him as soon as possible.

So we made a date for a visit.

A few days later, I drove to the Skukuza airport.

As I stood outside the terminal building, watching the two-engine turbo-prop plane come in, I wondered if I would be able to identify Gareth. I had never met him in person.

Amongst the thirty-odd passengers who disembarked, I spotted a young man whose shoulder-length blond hair resembled a lion's mane. He had the easy, graceful gait of one who spends most of his life walking. And while most of the other passengers were looking straight in front of them as they approached the terminal building, the blond-maned young man was gazing out over the surrounding bush. He was dressed in a loose T-shirt, shorts and sandals. His only luggage was a tiny battered suitcase.

I stepped forward and said: 'Gareth?'

He turned to me, smiled hesitantly and asked, 'Leo's mother?'

I nodded and smiled back at him, noting his Anglo-Saxon features and accent.

'How did you recognise me?' he asked.

'How can one *not* recognise you?' I said.

On the drive back we talked about lions, life, the good earth and everything else. By the time we arrived home we were old friends.

As we got out of the car, Wolfie came to meet us. But Leo noticed that I was not alone, so he kept his distance.

Gareth nodded a respectful greeting to Wolfie. Naturally Wolfie was impressed with this well-bred young man who had the good grace not to get familiar with him and pat him on the head.

Leo was sitting in a flowerbed at the side of the fish pond (flattening Aaron's violets), and quietly watching us.

'He's very handsome,' Gareth murmured to me.

But apart from giving Leo a brief glance-over, he avoided eye-contact and paid Leo no further attention. For a moment I wondered why. Then it dawned on me that Gareth, being a lion-person, would be wise to the fact that lions wish to be taken seriously. By ignoring Leo, Gareth was respecting Leo's right as a lion to decide the distance between himself and a stranger.

Hettie and Karin, who were both home for the weekend, made us sandwiches and tea, and we carried them outside into the garden. Leo came over and flopped down on the grass a little distance from us. Gareth still paid him no attention. Leo pretended not to pay Gareth any attention either. But I could see that he was quietly studying Gareth — and wondering about this strange human who somehow appeared so familiar.

Later, the four of us, together with Leo and Wolfie, went for a walk down into the valley.

As we walked and chatted, I noticed that Gareth habitually studied signs on the ground. When we came across fresh elephant spoor, his gaze automatically went out over the surrounding bush.

It was nice to have a visitor who reacted to the bush in the same way that we did.

When we'd walked about a kilometre or so, Leo, who was a few paces ahead of us, suddenly stopped, turned and contemplated Gareth. Gareth also stopped and looked at Leo. As Leo approached him, Gareth held out his arm to Leo. Leo inspected and sniffed the outstretched arm. Then he gave it a few friendly licks. Afterwards he briefly rubbed his body against Gareth's legs. It was a formal but warm greeting — and a demonstration of acceptance.

Kobus came home in the late afternoon, and after supper we all carried our coffee outside into the garden and spent the evening discussing future plans for Leo.

Gareth told us that his initial plan had been to propose introducing Leo into the Tuli bushlands, but he had since decided against it. Apart from the ever-increasing poaching activities in the area, farmers along the boundaries were baiting and hunting lions. So instead of the Tuli, Gareth said, he suggested the Save Valley Conservancy in south-eastern Zimbabwe.

The Save Valley — a vast private conservancy of half a million hectares — had been established by a group of landowners in the area. Their objective was to reintroduce into the area the whole spectrum of former wild animal species, including the lion.

One method of lion reintroduction used today involves the removal of wild lions from stable populations, and releasing them into unfamiliar new territory. This method creates stressful conditions for the lions.

Gareth believes (and has in fact proved) that the introduction and establishment of lions into reserves can be achieved in a different way. Hand-reared orphans and other disadvantaged lions — who have a right to the opportunity of freedom — can make the successful transition to independent, people-disfamiliarised, 'wild' lions through the processes of rehabilitation.

The Save Valley seemed an ideal area for a project such as this, and so Gareth proposed that he should talk to the landowners' committee and ask their permission to introduce a 'man-made pride' — consisting of Leo and two or three other orphaned lions

— into the conservancy. If granted permission for the project, Gareth would spend approximately two years with the lions, teaching them to hunt and to survive in the wilderness. As soon as they became self-sufficient and people-disfamiliarised, Gareth would gradually disappear from the scene. The 'man-made' pride could then constitute the core pride for future generations of lions in the conservancy.

We asked Gareth whether Leo was too old to learn to hunt. Gareth replied that he would include young lionesses in the 'man-made' pride. Lionesses are generally the better hunters, and so they would be helpful in teaching Leo to hunt.

Gareth's proposal sounded good to us. The fact that the Save Valley had no other lion populations as yet meant that Leo and his orphan pride would not have to compete with other lions for a hunting territory.

We spent the rest of the evening talking about lions, Africa's wild places, conservation and a myriad other shared interests.

It was a lovely evening. Gareth is both thoughtful and eloquent, and his company is as absorbing as a good book.

Born in England, he has lived and worked in Africa for most of his life. His lion conservation work is financed through royalties from his books and tourism-related activities at his Tuli base camp. Utterly dedicated to the conservation of wild life, all other considerations are of secondary importance to him. But his strong sense of identity and calling is underscored by good humour and humility.

Early the following morning, I found Gareth and Wolfie sharing a seat on the garden bench near the northern fence. Gareth was making notes in a book, while Wolfie just sat there, watching over his domain and keeping his new-found friend company.

I was amazed. My serious, aloof dog had actually befriended a stranger!

Leo came over and flopped down on the grass a little distance from Gareth and Wolfie. Gareth made a grunting noise that sounded exactly like a lion's greeting call. Leo lifted his head and looked Gareth straight in the eyes with an expression that seemed to say: 'Oh, you talk Lionese, do you? How nice.'

I drove Gareth back to the airport later that day. I was sorry that he couldn't stay with us longer.

He promised that he would keep in touch and let us know as soon as he had news for us from the Save Valley Conservancy.

A Memorable Autumn

Our children all came home for their autumn break and we spent our favourite season doing all the things that one should do when the bush is so bright and beautiful.

First, we all accompanied Kobus on a patrol trip along the Nwaswitshaka creek. I sat in the cab with Kobus while the rest of the family — Hettie, Paul, Sandra, Karin, Leo and Wolfie — all rode on the back of the pick-up.

It was a perfect day with soft blue skies and pastel-coloured landscapes. Even the wild animals looked soft and pastel-coloured.

The Nwaswitshaka snakes its way through woodlands, marshlands and savannahs, covering a distance of more than fifty kilometres before it reaches the Sabie river. It is essentially a seasonal creek but has many perennial pools, and so animal traffic in the area is usually heavy. On that perfect autumn day we spotted just about everything — from rare birds to black rhinos.

Actually, I'm not too crazy about spotting black rhinos. I prefer white rhinos. They're dim-witted and friendly. Black rhinos are dim-witted and aggressive.

The moment a black rhino catches sight of anything that appears alien to him, he gets hopping mad. As he hops about, you have no idea whether he is going to charge you or not. He gives no warning of his intentions. The reason for this is that the rhino himself has no idea of his intentions either, being dim-witted. The main problem with a black-rhino charge is that it's impossible to decide which way to flee. Once the rhino starts charging, he's all over the place. I think he's very myopic, so he charges blindly in every direction, relying purely on speed and agility, as well as his ability to change direction every few seconds until he has more or less covered the whole landscape and wiped out everything that needed wiping out.

The best thing to do if ever you should come across a black rhino is make sure he doesn't see you. If he does and gets mad, then press down on the accelerator and get out of the landscape. But there's no need to panic, really. You should be able to get a head start on him because he takes a while to decipher his intentions.

Fortunately the Park has only a few black rhinos. Unfortunately most of them reside in the Pretorius Kop area.

You needn't worry about white rhinos though. They're so dimwitted and friendly that you can almost pat them on the head as you drive past.

But maybe you shouldn't do that.

Because if you mistake a black rhino for a white one, you'll be in BIG trouble.

The difference between a black and a white rhino is not their colouring — they are both greyish. It's mainly their feeding habits and the shape of their mouths. The black rhino is a browser and has an elongated upper lip that overlaps the lower, giving the impression of a pout. The white rhino is a grazer and has a broad, square upper lip that gives the impression of a smile. He got his name by mistake. Originally he was called the 'wide-lipped rhino'. But people got confused and called him a 'white-lipped rhino' — and finally just a 'white rhino'. So when a second kind of rhino was discovered, it got named the 'black rhino'.

I don't know why. He's not black, just a darker shade of grey than the other one.

The black rhino is also smaller than the white one. He weighs up to 2 000 kilograms, while the white one weighs about 3 500 kilograms. But if you're not used to estimating weight at a distance, I guess this information is not very helpful to you in avoiding black rhinos.

White rhino

Black rhino

I think you should rather concentrate on the shape of the mouth. Although that may be a bit of a problem if the rhino is facing away from you. Or if it's a white rhino that's pouting instead of smiling, or a black rhino that's grimacing instead of pouting.

(A black rhino never smiles — if that's of any help to you.)

Anyway, when we spotted the black rhinos on that nice autumn day, I knew they were black rhinos because they were hopping mad. There were three of them, and after hopping about for a while they came charging at us like runaway steamrollers. About halfway towards us they got confused and lost their bearings. So they did an acrobatic about-turn and charged some distance in another direction. But a few moments later they were coming back at us again at full speed which, according to my book on large mammals, is about 45 kilometres per hour.

And Kobus had to do some clever manoeuvring with the truck to get out of their way. For a while they stupidly ran alongside us and eventually overtook us. So we slowed down. After about thirty seconds it finally dawned on them that they were charging directly away from their target instead of towards it. So they did another about-turn, and as they bore down on us, Kobus had to make another quick swerve to avoid a collision. They charged right past us and lost sight of us altogether.

I was very relieved that they didn't come back again. But the rest of my idiotic family thought it had been a lot of fun and hoped that we would encounter more black rhinos along the way.

Fortunately we didn't.

But unfortunately we had a most terrifying experience a short while later that scared not only me almost to death, but the rest of my family as well.

We were driving down the bank of a steep donga. I noticed that the track had partly caved in at the bottom of the donga, and I pointed it out to Kobus. But he told me not to worry. He knew about the washaway and he would manoeuvre the truck around it.

We were halfway down the slope when a herd of elephant appeared from nowhere at the top of the opposite bank and started crossing the track.

I didn't like that at all.

There were hundreds of them.

Or maybe fifty or so.

(Elephants tend to look more than they are.)

'Can't we turn back?' I asked Kobus.

'No,' he said. 'But don't worry. They won't bother us.'

As we reached the bed of the donga, the remaining part of the track caved in, leaving my side of the truck hanging over the edge of the washaway.

For no obvious reason, two elephant cows suddenly came tearing down the opposite bank, screaming with fury and heading straight for us.

And, for the first time in my life, I found myself in a danger situation where I had absolutely no idea what to do. And there was very little time to do it in. I had no idea what to tell my children to do either. If I told them to jump off the truck and run, the elephants might decide to go for them instead of the truck. If I told them to stay put, they'd be in danger anyway.

Kobus had grabbed his rifle, yanked his door open and jumped out of the cab (in uphill-style as the wheels on his side were suspended in the air). It was too late to load the gun and shoot, so he yelled at the elephants — in a voice so loud that the bush seemed to shudder. My eyes remained fixed on the massive faces of the two cows as they bore down on us. The expression of determination in their eyes terrified me. Masses of adrenalin surged through my system, commanding me to do SOME-THING... anything! But what?

The girls were lying flat on their stomachs in the back of the truck, their arms covering their heads. Karin was whimpering with fright — something I had never heard her do in her whole life. Sandra was trying to comfort her younger sister, murmuring: 'It's OK, Karin, it's OK.' Paul was reaching into the cab through the back window, snatching up the bullet-belt and handing it to Kobus.

All this was happening simultaneously.

My gaze was still fixed on the eyes of the two elephants, and Kobus was still yelling at them. And I remember the exact moment that I saw the expression in their eyes change from determination to hesitation — they were at that moment less than ten metres from us — about two seconds away from impact.

They came to a sudden halt. Kobus continued shouting at them at the top of his voice. After a few eternal seconds of hesitation, the cows started turning away from us and heading back up the bank. Kobus quickly checked his rifle's magazine and reached for the bullets that Paul was holding out to him. But before he even had the chance to load, the two elephants had turned around and were coming back at us with furious determination, the earth exploding underneath their smashing feet.

I could not bear to look at their faces again. And since there was nothing that I could do to protect my family or myself, I bent over, putting my head on my knees and folding my arms over my head — the posture for impact. And I was surprised and ashamed to hear myself whimpering. But even in that moment of indescribable terror, my mind was concentrating on hopeful possibilities. Kobus and I were closest to the elephants; there were only the two of them charging us — they couldn't possibly attack all of us at the same time. Perhaps they would be content to vent their fury on Kobus and me, allowing the children time to escape.

I prayed that the children would have the sense to jump off the back and run when that happened, and not be so stupid as to think they should stay and try to do anything for us. I wanted to tell them that, but there wasn't time. And even if there had been, they wouldn't have heard me — there was too much noise all around us now. About four or five seconds after I had put my head down, I realised that the moment of impact was overdue, so I looked up — straight into the eyes of two elephant faces that filled my whole field of vision. They had come to a halt, and I could see in their eyes that the crescendoing volume of Kobus's

voice was unnerving them. They backed off a little and stood contemplating us for a few moments.

And Kobus, still shouting at them, finally had the chance to load and cock his rifle. Fortunately it wasn't necessary for him to fire. The two cows turned and started heading back up the bank to rejoin the rest of the herd. There was something wrong up there — the whole herd was milling about.

But there was no time to wonder about that. Kobus was ordering us to get away from the truck and to head up the bank behind us. I was unable to get out on my side as it was hanging over the edge of the washaway. So I clambered uphill over Kobus's seat to get out. The children jumped off the back and we all started sprinting up the bank. The elephants were screaming some distance behind us, but we didn't stop to look back until we'd reached the top of the bank.

It was only then, when we'd reached the relative safety of the crest, that I thought of Wolfie and Leo for the first time.

When survival is the point at issue, the mind allows no other thoughts to distract it. Perhaps I had known subconsciously that the dog and the lion would look after themselves, and so my mind had blotted out all thoughts of them.

I saw with relief that Wolfie was with us.

But not Leo.

The idiot was on the far bank, teasing the elephant herd. No wonder they were milling about and screeching with irritation.

The children told us that Leo had jumped off the truck as soon as the two cows had come charging down the bank, but they had no idea what he did afterwards. Wolfie had apparently jumped off the truck the moment he saw Kobus getting out, and he had remained valiantly at Kobus's side throughout the whole nightmare.

We were all talking and laughing a lot now — we were, of course, adrenalin-drunk.

Actually I was the only one who was not laughing.

I was too busy sulking.

And I was preparing a speech.

My husband was in for a long lecture.

I noticed that his voice had gone quite hoarse from all the shouting. But that was not going to let him off the hook. As soon as we were alone, he would get his lecture.

Eventually the elephants moved on and our naughty lion came running back to us. He looked at us with an expression that seemed to say: 'I had such a good time. Why didn't you all come over and join in the fun?'

'You're quite mad,' I told him.

After the elephants had left, we returned to our bogged-down truck, and everyone pitched in to help lift it back on to terra firma — everyone except me.

I was working on my speech.

As soon as we were back on the road again, it was lecture time.

I started off with a reminder that I had warned about the washaway at the bottom of the donga, as well as about the elephants on the far bank — and that my warnings had gone unheeded.

After the reproachful prologue, I went on to my main theme which was about parental responsibilities. I emphasised my own personal dedication to my obligations, and I argued that, being the mother of all those children and animals in the back, I had the right to be taken seriously if I pointed out a danger situation. I added that, regrettably, men in general tended to disregard women's judgements of what constituted danger.

I concluded my argument by mentioning that it was a recognised fact that females possess a stronger instinct for survival than males. And I added that if men would trust female intuition more often, they would have a better chance of surviving longer.

I thought my main theme had sounded pretty good.

I had prepared an epilogue as well, but I decided to leave it out and to replace it with a long, cold silence.

Unfortunately we came across a gorgeous honey badger a while later. He was digging furiously for something under a tree stump, and he was so cute that I forgot my vow of silence.

I noticed, however, that my irresponsible husband had a chastened look on his face, so I decided to forgive him.

And a while later I even told him that I was grateful that he possessed such a powerful elephant-deterrent voice.

We spent the rest of our autumn vacation exploring the bushlands and climbing to the tops of all the koppies in the area. And we decided that sitting on the top of a koppie is the sort of elevating experience that changes your whole outlook on life.

The nicest thing about the koppies in this area is that they are all over the place, but far apart, so that each one of them stands in a beautiful landscape of its own and has unrestricted views in all directions.

This is how we spent our time on the top of koppies during that autumn vacation:

Kobus and the children would explore the world below with binoculars, counting up their sightings of wild animals and getting very competitive about it.

Wolfie, being his usual conscientious self, would go about his duties of patrolling the area and checking out all the signs on the ground.

But Leo and I had an entirely different agenda — one that was in a class of its own. We would sit side by side and do nothing at all with determination — nothing except dream, and watch the world go by.

One day near the end of the vacation, Kobus told us about a koppie named Matupa that he'd spotted from the air while doing an aerial census. There was something about the koppie, he told us, that fascinated him, and so he wanted to go and explore it from the ground.

Paul, Sandra and Karin were eager to go along, but Hettie had a term paper to finish, and as her classes would be starting soon, she decided to stay home and catch up on her work. I also had some work to do, so I opted to stay home with Hettie.

Kobus decided that Wolfie and Leo should stay home as well. The koppie, he explained, consisted of enormous boulders and sheer cliffs, and he didn't think that any animals other than primates would be able to climb to the top.

I warned them all to be careful, and they promised they would.

But they forgot their promise as soon as they arrived at the koppie.

Perhaps, in defence of their forgetfulness, I should mention that Matupa is a strange kind of place. It makes you forget lots of things. The moment you set eyes on it, it commands your attention and absorbs your thoughts. There's something about Matupa that doesn't quite fit in with the normal design of things in this part of the world. Perhaps Matupa was designed for some other landscape, maybe even for another planet, and got misplaced. But it's not only its design that's peculiar, it has an alien aura as well. It looks sort of wrapped-up in its own lost world.

It also looks haunted.

Legend has it that the ghost of a Watusi warrior dwells in Matupa's caves. Now what a Watusi warrior might have been doing out here in this part of Africa, I have no idea, since the Watusi people live about 3 000 kilometres to the north of Matupa on a hilly plateau in Burundi. I don't think the warrior ended up here because he got lost. Nobody can get *that* lost. He must have had some mission. Perhaps he came here in search of the misplaced koppie.

Anyway, they say that when the Watusi warrior plays his drums at night, the reverberating sounds echo upward out of the caves and roll out over the landscape. And on full-moon nights, they say, you can see the lonely warrior standing on Matupa's summit, clutching his spears and staring out over the world below.

Matupa consists of a number of GIANT round boulders stacked carelessly together, some on top of others. Whoever put them there (presumably by mistake), forgot to complete the job of building a nice koppie, thoughtlessly leaving some of the larger boulders balancing precariously on top of smaller ones. Several of the smaller boulders have already cracked under the weight, leaving all kinds of crevices and caves that will one day cause the whole structure to collapse.

Matupa has many faces. Its east side consists mostly of a bewildering array of carelessly stacked boulders. Its south-facing side has a dark and haunted look. (I can never remember exactly how it looks.) Its north face looks brighter, and is in fact quite breathtaking with its uneven high-rise wall of formidable-looking boulders. The west side consists of a sheer, unbroken vertical cliff face about sixty or seventy metres high. It's not really a cliff face though. It's the side of a single, large boulder — Matupa's main boulder. The boulder has a wide, flat summit — and it is on this summit, they say, that the ghost of the Watusi warrior appears on moonlit nights.

The reason I'm trying to describe Matupa to you, is to give you some background for the frightful encounter that awaited Kobus and the children on that autumn day when they first went to explore the strange koppie.

Their main agenda, of course, was to find a way to get to the top. So they went about searching for climbable parts of the boulders. They walked all the way round the koppie, and concluded that the only way up was from the east side. If you climbed carefully up the stacked boulders, watching your step across cracks and crevices, you could reach a ledge that slants upwards and around the northern side of Matupa until, about fifty or sixty metres above the ground, the ledge meets a wide flat surface — a sort of natural terrace that is roughly six metres wide and eight metres long. An oval-shaped rock — which is in fact a broken-off piece of the main boulder — rests on the terrace, near its eastern edge. Directly behind this rock, obscured by tangles of vegetation, is the entrance to a small cave.

Naturally Kobus and the children did not know about the cave at the time. They reached the terrace from the east side. Paul was in front, carrying the rifle. Sandra and Karin came directly behind him. Kobus was about five or six metres behind them all — he had stopped to tie a bootlace that had come undone. Paul and the girls stopped at the oval rock and decided to split up and walk around either side of it to see if there were any other ledges above or behind it that could help them get higher up the main boulder.

Sandra and Karin started moving around the west side of the oval rock, Paul started moving around its east side — and bumbled right into a lioness who was lying up in the tangled vegetation at the entrance to the cave where, of course, she was hiding her cubs.

She must have heard the party approaching, but probably decided to keep a low profile, hoping that the intruders would move on or go away without discovering her and her cubs' hiding place. But when Paul almost fell on top of her, she realised she was in trouble and decided to fight back.

With an angry roar that echoed all over Matupa she charged at Paul. He hastily backed off a few paces — which was as far as he could retreat without falling off the cliff. There was no time to cock the rifle, so Paul resorted to pointing the gun at the lioness and pretending that it was cocked. Fortunately the lioness believed him — or perhaps it was Paul's body language that saved him. (If you brandish a rifle or even just a stick at an enemy, your body language tends to say 'Hands-up!' even though your mind knows that the weapon you are brandishing is quite useless.)

Meanwhile Kobus had leapt forward, grazing his leg from knee to ankle against a sharp rock — although he didn't notice it at the time — and, reaching Paul in one second flat, he took the rifle from him and ordered him out of the way.

Just before the lioness had growled, the two girls had been studying a rock fig that clutched the boulder wall in front of them. The rock fig is a peculiar tree that grows on rocks and cliffs. The girls noticed that the uppermost branches reached all the way to the summit — about four metres above the terrace. But the boulder wall curved outwards, and the upper branches of the rock fig slanted slightly away from its convex surface so that one would have to lean over backwards if one climbed up it to the top — a rather hazardous thing to do. So the girls had concluded that it wouldn't be a good idea to try reaching the summit by climbing the rock fig.

But the shocking sound of a lion roaring directly into their ears changed their opinion in a flash. Three seconds later they were in the top branches of the rock fig and climbing on to the summit. Kobus ordered Paul to climb up after the girls.

Then Kobus talked calmly to the lioness, explaining that he and his family meant her cubs no harm. He asked her nicely to keep a respectful distance. The terrace wasn't too spacious, and there was no way down, except the way that they had come.

But the lioness refused to believe him and warned him with an earth-shaking roar that she wanted all humans out of her territory IMMEDIATELY.

Kobus tried telling her that they would all dearly love to leave, but that she was blocking the exit.

Meanwhile Paul and the girls were studying the features of the main boulder, hoping to discover some other way to get down Matupa, but they found none. The only way down was the way they had come up — past the cave entrance that the lioness was guarding.

Kobus continued to explain this to the lioness, but she was in no mood for discussions. As far as she was concerned they could find themselves another way down. She wasn't letting ANYONE near her cave-nursery. To make her point quite clear, she mock-charged Kobus. As her angry growl thundered out over the landscape, Kobus wondered what to do. Shooting the lioness was not an option. She had her cubs to think of. He glanced over his shoulder and contemplated the sheer drop behind him. No good. It was totally out of the question.

The lioness did a second mock-charge, stopping awfully close to Kobus, and he glanced over his shoulder again.

The cliff wasn't so totally out of the question after all.

In fact the drop was shrinking every second.

After the third mock-charge, Kobus saw a way to get down the cliff.

After the fourth mock-charge, the way down looked easy.

On the western side of the cliff, near its bottom, the vertical drop is broken by a ridge that slopes at a climbable angle towards the earth. A tall jackalberry tree grows high up on the ridge, and its uppermost branches reach all the way up to a tiny ledge that juts out from the cliff face — about four metres or so below the western edge of the terrace.

If they could reach that ledge, Kobus thought, they could try to get into the branches of the jackalberry tree. Reaching the ledge was the tricky part. The only way to reach it would be to jump — but if you missed it, or hit it too fast to stop, you would fall another fifty metres or so.

Kobus asked Paul if he would try to make it to the ledge — and then into the branches of the tree. If he could manage that, then Kobus wanted him to go down and find anything that could be used as a makeshift ladder and bring it back up to the ledge above the jackalberry tree. Kobus would stay with the girls to protect them from the lioness in case she decided to go up the rock fig after them.

Paul climbed down the rock fig and hurried over to the western edge of the terrace. He studied the cliff face below, spotted the ledge and lowered himself carefully in its direction. He let go and dropped to the narrow shelf below. Mercifully, his aim and judgement were good and he made a safe landing. After that he managed to reach the jackalberry tree and he climbed down to the bottom in record time.

Spurred on by the echoing growls of the lioness many metres above, where his young wife and her family were trapped, he hurriedly searched about for a makeshift ladder and soon found a climbable-looking log that was about three metres long. Somehow he managed to carry it as he climbed all the way to the top of the tree again and on to the ledge above it.

Kobus was relieved when he heard Paul calling out to them that he'd found a ladder. The lioness was at the end of her patience and was now getting really furious.

The girls hurried down the rock fig and across the terrace and, as the lioness thundered a final warning, they lowered themselves — one after the other — over the edge and on to the makeshift ladder that Paul was holding in place against the cliff face. Fortunately all went well, and after reaching the ledge they managed to get into the treetop. As soon as the girls were safely away, it was Kobus's turn. He said goodbye to the lioness, and it was obvious that she was as glad to see him go as he was to be leaving. Paul held the log steady for Kobus, and moments later they were all climbing down the tall, God-sent jackalberry tree to safety.

They spent a few minutes at the bottom of the cliff, relaxing and getting their adrenalin levels back to normal again. Karin and Sandra took quite a while to get their shakes under control. But they both agreed that their shakes were not the result of shock — lions didn't really shock them any more. Their trembling, they explained, was merely the result of adrenalin-overdrive.

(Adrenalin-overdrive, according to my daughters, happens when your instincts command you to flee but you are unable to do so because the circumstances prevent it.)

On their way back home, Kobus remembered the elephant encounter of two weeks before — and the lecture that he got from his wife afterwards. Worried that he was in for another lecture, he suggested to the children that there was no need to tell their mother the exact details of the lioness encounter.

So when my family got home and I asked how their day had been, all they said was: 'Oh, it was very nice, thank you.'

'What is the koppie like?' I asked.

'Very nice,' Sandra answered.

'Yes, very nice,' Karin agreed. 'You'll love it. You must go and see it for yourself some time.'

'But not too soon,' Sandra said hurriedly. (She was probably thinking of the lioness who would still be there for a while.)

I was about to ask why not, when I noticed the fresh scar on Kobus's leg and I exclaimed, 'Oh, look! You've hurt yourself. What happened?'

He studied his leg with a puzzled frown.

Karin said: 'A lioness growled at us. She probably gave him a fright. So he grazed his leg.'

'A lioness?' I said, surprised. 'On the koppie? She must be hiding cubs there. Did she charge you?'

'Oh, yes,' Sandra replied casually. 'It was quite exciting.'

'How nice,' I said. 'I'm sorry I missed all the fun. So, what else happened today?'

'No, nothing really,' they replied.

Kobus, who had been holding his breath throughout the conversation, couldn't believe his ears, and he wondered to what he owed his luck. Had his wife missed out on the meaning of the word 'lioness', or what?

I hadn't, of course. It was just that the semantics of the word no longer scared me. Being a lion-mother myself, I knew that lions were only dangerous if you didn't understand them.

And of course my family understood lions.

We were a lion-family.

A few months later, Kobus took me to see Matupa for the first time and he showed me the cave where the lioness had hidden her cubs. It was only then that the full dramatic nature of my family's encounter with the lioness on that autumn day struck home. And when I looked down the cliff to the tiny ledge below, and the earth another fifty-odd metres down, I almost suffered an anxiety attack.

But it was too late for a lecture then. And anyway, I couldn't help admiring my family for their ingenuity and perseverance in finding a way down rather than shooting the lioness.

On the second last day of the autumn vacation, Hettie and Leo played a game of catch. They both got carried away and played too boisterously, with the result that Hettie got injured. One of Leo's canines inadvertently cut into her left thigh, leaving a neat but very deep puncture wound.

This happened on a Saturday afternoon, and finding a doctor at that time is usually not easy in this part of the world. So I mixed one part household bleach with nine parts boiled, cooled water. I filled a sterile syringe with it and squirted the solution into the wound. We repeated the procedure every few hours. By

Sunday evening I felt confident that the wound was clean and that there were no signs of sepsis. I nevertheless urged Hettie to consult her university doctor as soon as she arrived back in Johannesburg — just to make doubly sure that the wound was clean and also to have it stitched up.

But Hettie said no: she knew the wound was clean as there was no pain. And she didn't want stitches. Band-aid would do. And anyway, she couldn't see herself explaining to a city doctor that she'd been bitten by a lion. He wouldn't understand.

On the last day of the autumn vacation we packed a picnic lunch and climbed to the top of Shitungwane — one of our favourite koppies.

We had a lovely day. And nothing dramatic happened, believe it or not.

And so I am pleased to be able to write that our autumn vacation ended on a safe note.

Bittersweet Times

Gareth came to visit again towards the end of the autumn, bringing us the news that the landowners' committee of the Save Valley had granted permission for the introduction of a 'man-made' lion pride into the conservancy. He'd also applied for an import permit for Leo from the Zimbabwe National Parks and Wild Life Department.

Gareth stayed three days, spending most of his time with Leo, getting to know him and winning his trust.

Kobus and I decided that, when the time came for Leo to go to his new home, the two of us, together with Wolfie, would accompany him and stay with him and Gareth for a few weeks to help make the transition easier.

After Gareth's second visit to us, the reality of launching Leo into his own adult world started striking home, and there were days when I could hardly bear to think about it.

I wished desperately that we could postpone the project for another year or so. But our Park Warden and his directors were getting impatient with us. We'd received a second official letter from them in April, reminding us that it was against the Park's policy to keep a lion and that they could not allow us to keep Leo any longer. If anyone got injured, they warned, the blame would be placed not only on us but on them as well.

Their fears were not unreasonable, of course.

Other hand-reared lions had been responsible for fatal accidents in the past. One of George Adamson's lions had killed his cook, and another had accidentally killed a young child while playing with it. In recent years, five cases have been recorded in South Africa of people who have been fatally injured by either hand-reared or semi-tame lions.

I wrote back to the Park Warden, explaining that we were in the process of making arrangements to take Leo to Zimbabwe and that we would be leaving no later than the beginning of June. I promised him that, until that time, I would take full responsibility for the safety of anyone who entered our premises.

Leo was a huge and powerful animal now, capable of inflicting serious injury. But he was also a gentle lion, and I did not believe that he would ever hurt anyone. Yet I could not guarantee my beliefs. And if anything happened to prove me wrong, I would not be able to live with the burden of that guilt.

Since adopting Leo I had not really been away from home. And now that he was so big, I knew that I would not be able to go away for as long as he was with us. Kobus often worked away from home for days or weeks at a stretch, and so the responsibility for our visitors' safety was mine most of the time. Even on the few occasions when I went to Nelspruit to do some urgent shopping, I would post a game guard at our gate with strict instructions not to allow anyone to enter our premises during my absence.

Even-tempered and well behaved though he was, Leo still loved to stalk and startle people. He would catch them gently, clasping them around the waist and pulling them down for a playful wrestle. But a playful wrestle with a lion could end in an accident — especially for small children or older people.

In the days and weeks following Gareth's second visit, I found myself spending most of my free time with Leo, playing with him, hugging him and talking to him, explaining to him that he was a big boy now and that it was time to think of his future. I told him that our wish for him was that he should have a very happy adulthood with a real lion family of his own.

But I wasn't being entirely honest with him, of course. What I really wanted was for him to remain with us for as long as he lived. For I believed that, with us, he would always be happy and safe.

So I would wake up at night, feeling sad and restless. Leo loved us and needed us. How could we even think of abandoning him? I paced the house, trying to think of other solutions. We could all move away to some remote wild place where no other people ever came, and live there happily ever after with our lion.

But how would we live?

We could establish Leo in some remote corner of the Kruger Park — where no one would know about him — and we would visit him as frequently as possible, often spending days camping with him in the bush.

But how would he live — unable to hunt and unable to fend for himself? Unlike the Save Valley that had as yet no lion populations, the Kruger Park has lions all over the place — wild lions who would defend their territories against interlopers like Leo.

It seemed strange to me that the lion, powerful as he is, should be the most vulnerable of hand-reared orphans when the time comes for him to be reintroduced to the wild.

During those long sleepless nights I would often think back to the day that Hettie had first gone off to university. We'd still lived at Mahlangeni then — more than 600 kilometres away from Johannesburg. We took her to the airport at Phalaborwa, and as her aeroplane started taxiing across the runway for take-off, I wanted to run after it, shouting for it to stop and bring back my child. I wanted to explain to the pilot — and everyone else — that it was all a mistake. She wasn't ready for the outside world yet. She was just a child of the wilderness, unprepared for city life . . . she would feel so bewildered, so lonely, so lost . . .

But who would listen? Who would understand?

After she'd left, I couldn't sleep or eat properly for many days.

And then, when Sandra's turn came the following year, I thought I was better prepared for it, having already gone through the whole trauma once before.

But harsh experiences don't make you stronger. They make you more vulnerable.

I decided that the only way I could prepare myself for the eventual parting with Leo was to rely on the fact that happy memories make the future bearable.

And so I set about collecting good moments with Leo to add to my memory's repertoire. And I also spent some time checking my diaries to make sure that I had recorded all the good memories of the past.

Here are a few of my favourite memories for the period March to May 1994, when Leo was between sixteen and eighteen months old.

In March Kobus went to Namibia to deliver a number of rhinos to the Waterberg National Park. He was gone for about ten days, and Leo missed him very much. He waited at the front gate every evening, calling to Kobus. On the day that Kobus finally returned, Leo pounced on him and forced him to the ground. Clutching Kobus's head between his huge front paws, he licked his face all over, almost drowning him with lion kisses.

Hettie arrived home for the autumn holidays, carrying a huge pink teddy bear. Leo took one look at the teddy bear and fell in love with it. As Hettie walked to the house, Leo ran alongside her, begging her to let him have the bear, please.

But Hettie said, 'No, Leo. I'm sorry. It was a birthday gift from a special friend.'

She carried the teddy bear into her bedroom and sat it down on her bed. Leo spent the next hour at her bedroom window, his nose pressed to the gauze-screen, staring longingly at the pink bear.

I decided to make him his own teddy bear. I searched my sewing trunk for bits of left-over fabric and stuffing until I'd collected enough to make a huge bear. Actually I didn't know how to make a bear, so I made a life-size rag doll instead. When I'd finished it, I carried it outside to show Leo.

'How do you like it?' I asked him, as I held the rag doll up for him to inspect.

His eyes said: 'I love it! I love it! I wish it was mine!'

'It's yours,' I told him. 'Come and take it!'

He looked at me with an expression of total surprise, followed by one of sheer delight. Then he pounced on the doll, clutched it to him, rolled on it, sat on it, tossed it in the air, caught it again, and ran off with it. He spent the rest of the day running all over the garden, parading his rag doll to the family, to Wolfie, to Aaron and to anyone who happened to come along. He was so proud of his doll that everyone thought he'd gone a little mad.

He even clutched the doll to him when he slept. And he spent the following few days carrying it in his jaws wherever he went.

One afternoon we went for a walk down into the valley. Leo kept tripping on the doll as he dragged it along, and eventually he found it too difficult to keep up with us. So he set the doll down and stood glaring at it. He seemed to be saying to the doll: 'Can't you walk by yourself? I'm tired of carrying you.'

'Come on, Leo!' we called to him. 'Leave your doll there. You can pick it up on the way back.'

But Leo looked at us with a pleading expression.

'OK,' Kobus sighed. 'Here, I'll carry it for you.' He walked over to Leo and picked up the doll.

And as we continued on our walk, I found it rather touching to see a fierce game ranger carrying his lion's rag doll for him.

Leo loved the rag doll to pieces, so after a few weeks it disintegrated. I considered making him a new one, but Kobus said it wouldn't look too good if Leo arrived at his new home in Zimbabwe clutching a rag doll.

One day Karin tied a three-metre-long red ribbon to a stick and invited Leo to a game of catch. Racing all over the garden she trailed the ribbon behind her while Leo gave chase, trying to catch the ribbon. But it kept slipping from his grip, so eventually he got fed-up with the game and decided to catch Karin instead. Clutching her gently around the waist, he dragged her down and sat on top of her.

Flat on her back, with Leo on top of her, Karin found she couldn't get out from under him — partly because she was laughing too much, and partly because Leo refused to move. She still had the red ribbon in her hands, so she resorted to flossing his teeth with it. Leo pulled a funny face. He wasn't too crazy about the flossing exercise, so he moved a bit, giving Karin the chance to wriggle out from underneath him.

At the age of about eighteen months, Leo had a cute-looking tuft of mane right on the top of his head. One day Karin tied a pink ribbon around the tuft of hair to make Leo look pretty, and she was so pleased with the effect that she called the whole family to come and admire Leo's new look. Poor Leo had the silliest expression on his face. He seemed to know that the pink ribbon in his hair had changed him from a noble lion into a dumb teddy bear. I took several photographs of him as a teddy bear. But I never showed him the photos. I was afraid they might give him an inferiority complex.

One day during the autumn holidays, my family and I were sitting on top of Shitungwane, watching a beautiful sunset. Wolfie was running about as usual, checking out the signs on the ground, followed closely by Leo whose only desire was to trip up the dog. Eventually Wolfie got fed-up with Leo's antics. So he spun around and issued a furious warning: 'Do that one more time, and I'll bite you!'

Leo got the message and decided to find something else to do. So he ran over to us, threw his paws around Paul's shoulders and, pressing his face to Paul's head, gave him a long and loving hug that seemed to say: 'I don't love that dog any more. I love only you.'

I hadn't brought my camera along that day, but I captured the scene in my mind: Leo hugging Paul on top of Shitungwane, surrounded by the whole family, and with the magnificent sunset over the bushlands below forming a perfect backdrop to a magic moment.

Where May a Lion Live?

Gareth phoned us from the Save Valley Conservancy in May. He'd met with the Conservator as well as with one of the landowners who had offered his section of the Conservancy for the lion rehabilitation project. All other arrangements were going well, and Lisa Hywood of Care for the Wild in Harare had offered to locate other orphan lions to make up the pride.

Kobus and I set about getting our passports in order, as well as applying for a CITES permit to transport Leo. We also applied for a visitor's permit for Wolfie from the Zimbabwe authorities.

The vet came over from Skukuza to give Leo and Wolfie the required injections together with the necessary certificates to prove that they were free of disease.

Since our CITES permit for Leo's transport stipulated that Leo would have to travel in a cage, Kobus arranged with a steel and fencing company named MEPS to build us a cage. MEPS graciously did it for us free of charge.

We needed a vehicle that could carry the cage, and so we contacted the Nissan Company in Johannesburg. They kindly offered to lend us a Nissan 4 X 4 patrol truck free of charge.

We were touched by the support and sympathy that our project received from people such as these. Without their help, the costs of transporting Leo to Zimbabwe would have put us in debt for a long time.

The steel cage arrived, and we put it on our front patio, leaving its gate open in the hope that Leo would get curious and inspect the cage, maybe even go inside it. If he could get used to the cage, then we would not need to drug him in order to get him into his cage on the day of departure. We asked Wolfie to go inside the cage — which the good dog promptly did. Then we tried to persuade Leo to follow Wolfie. But Leo refused. I tried luring him in with a nice chunk of meat, but that didn't work either. He didn't trust the cage one bit.

One day near the end of May, a phone call from Gareth turned our world upside down. The Zimbabwe Parks Department, Gareth told us, had refused an import permit for Leo. The reason they gave was that their new policy no longer allowed for hand-reared lions to be released into their parks. They believed that hand-reared lions posed a threat to field staff as well as to visitors. Gareth had faxed them a reply, explaining that part of his rehabilitation programme was to train his lions to become people-disfamiliarised. During their two-year transition period he would allow his lions no contact with humans other than himself — he would in fact teach them to flee from humans, as he had taught his lions in the Tuli to do.

The Zimbabwe Parks Department considered the issue once more, but regretted that they were unable to revise their policy.

We were devastated. What to do now? Gareth was as distressed as we were. But he promised to help find another solution.

I spent the following two weeks making telephone calls to every conservation area in South Africa, only to learn that no provincial park would take a hand-reared lion and that the Transvaal Provincial Administration had recently adopted a policy that forbade the release of hand-reared lions into private parks as well.

Gareth made about as many phone calls as I did, only to reach the same conclusion: the status of the lion in southern Africa is such that a hand-reared orphan is doomed to be homeless.

One morning at the beginning of June when I was near tears after having made about a dozen hopeless phone calls, I received a call from a lady named Rita who works for ARC (the Animal

Rehabilitation Centre) at Phalaborwa. She told me that she'd heard of a place called the Lion and Cheetah Park in the north of Zimbabwe near Harare. The owner's name, she told me, was Vivian Bristow. He kept lions, cheetahs and various other animals for tourism and filming purposes.

I recognised the name. My parents knew the Bristows. And Kobus had also met them once.

Rita told me that, although the lions in the Bristows' park were strictly speaking in captivity, they were actually as free as could be since they lived together in family groups in large camps. And she added that, according to her sources, the Bristows took good care of their animals. Most of their lion and cheetah families consisted of hand-reared orphans and their offspring. Rita also told me that obtaining a permit for Leo to go there would be no problem as the Bristows were in good standing with the Zimbabwe Parks Department. And since their animals were regarded as 'captive animals', rather than 'free animals', the Parks Department would not refuse them a permit.

After talking to Rita, I phoned my parents. My father assured me that the Bristows were animal-lovers and he believed that they would offer Leo a good home.

So I dialled the number in Zimbabwe that Rita had given me.

Vivian Bristow answered my call and said he would be delighted to have Leo. He offered to send a truck to fetch him. But I quickly explained that my family and I wished to accompany Leo to his new home and so we would prefer to bring him ourselves. Vivian graciously offered us the hospitality of his home for whatever period we might wish to stay with Leo.

He asked how much we wanted for Leo.

I was baffled. 'How much? How much of what?' I asked.

'What would you like to sell him for?' he said.

I was taken aback. We didn't own Leo, of course. He was born free. So I replied: 'He's not for sale. We only want a good home for him.'

I discussed the idea with Kobus that evening, and he thought it sounded good.

So we called the Tuli Lodge in Botswana, leaving a message for Gareth to contact us. He called us a few days later and I told him of the Bristows' park. Gareth was still sad that his plans for Leo had failed, but he reasoned that since no other option was available, the Lion and Cheetah Park seemed a good second choice.

Carol Bristow — Vivian's wife — called us two days later to inform us that an import permit had been granted for Leo and that she would fax us a copy to Skukuza.

Kobus and I spent the next few days making all the final arrangements to leave for Zimbabwe.

We were in a hurry to get away since Kobus had to be back before the end of June for urgent meetings and other appointments. Before we'd heard that the Zimbabwe Parks Department had refused a permit for Leo to go to Save Valley, our initial plan had been to leave at the beginning of June. It was now well past that date and time was running out. We wished that we could take all the children along, but they were busy with their half-year exams. Hettie had finished early — on the 11th of June — but the others would only finish in July, which was too late for Kobus.

So after some family discussions it was decided that we would leave on the 13th of June, taking Hettie with us, and return on the 27th. The other children would all be able to visit Leo at his new home at a later stage.

At least that was one good thing about Leo's new home — it would not be necessary for him to become people-disfamiliarised, and so he would always be allowed visitors.

I arranged with neighbours to give Karin a lift to her school bus on the morning of the 13th. She was still attending the Nelspruit boarding school and caught the school bus at Hazyview early on Monday mornings. I also arranged for her to stay with friends over the weekend that we would be away.

Sandra and Paul came home for the weekend before we left to say goodbye to Leo. And when Sandra hugged Leo and told him that she looked forward to seeing him again and meeting his lion-family, I realised with relief that parting with Leo would be less traumatic if we all knew that we would see him again.

Pamuzinda

In the dark, early hours of Monday morning the 13th of June, the vet from Skukuza, Dr Cobus Raath, arrived and put Leo to sleep with a ketamine injection. The steel cage was in place on the back of the truck. We had covered the floor of the cage with sand and spread the two animals' sleeping mats over the sand. It was midwinter now, and so Kobus had covered the whole cage with a tarpaulin, leaving it open only at the back.

As soon as Leo was asleep, Kobus, the vet and two game guards gently rolled him on to a canvas sheet and lifted him into the cage. Wolfie immediately jumped into the cage after Leo to keep a watchful eye on his sleeping friend.

Kobus, Hettie and I said goodbye to Karin and promised that we would phone her from Zimbabwe to let her know how things were going.

Leo was still asleep when we left.

But he woke up a few kilometres from home and was extremely upset at finding himself in a cage. So we stopped and tried to calm and comfort him. But every few kilometres or so, Leo became so agitated, that Wolfie would howl to let us know it was time we stopped the truck and talked to Leo again.

We had a long journey ahead of us — about 1 200 kilometres — and we realised that we would be on the road for ever if we were to stop every few kilometres to comfort Leo. So Kobus decided to give him a valium injection. Fortunately that settled him and he remained fairly calm and sleepy for the rest of the very long journey.

We reached the Beit Bridge border post by mid-afternoon, and after a delay of several hours at the customs office, we finally crossed the Limpopo river into Zimbabwe.

Surprisingly, there was no immediate change in the scenery, as I'd half expected there to be. Baobab trees still dominated the quiet bushveld landscapes that seemed to stretch on and on for ever.

About an hour after we'd crossed the border into Zimbabwe, the sun started setting. We stopped at the Bubye river and fed our animals the dinners that I'd packed for them: a whole, raw chicken for Leo and some dog biscuits and cooked meat for Wolfie.

We didn't stop long, as we had about another 500 kilometres ahead of us.

As soon as dusk settled, it started getting cold. And the colder it got, the more worried we became about our two animals on the back of the truck. Kobus had tied the tarpaulin over the cage in such a way that a small opening remained at the front of the cage directly opposite the back window of the cab, enabling us to peek into the cage and check on the animals when necessary. Every half hour or so, Kobus would ask me how the animals were doing, and I'd stick my torch through the back window and shine it into the cage. Kobus said that if I noticed them curling themselves up tightly against the cold, then we shouldn't continue the journey. Fortunately I never saw them doing that. They were huddled close together most of the time, but their muscles didn't appear abnormally taut.

By the time we reached the midlands, it was really cold, and Kobus stopped the truck and got out to check on the animals himself. Their noses were cold to the touch, but otherwise they seemed to be holding their own. Kobus checked the tarpaulin on all sides of the truck to make sure it was wind-proof. He discovered a spot where the edge of the canvas didn't quite meet the side of the truck, leaving a gap large enough to let a lot of cold air into the cage. So Kobus took off his lumber-jacket and, bundling it up tightly, pressed it into the gap which it filled adequately. Satisfied that the animals would be better protected now, we continued our journey.

About twenty minutes or so later, Hettie shone the torch through the back window and exclaimed that the jacket was no longer there. Kobus stopped the truck and turned it around. Thinking that the wind had probably caught the jacket and blown it away, we drove slowly back, searching for it on and alongside the road. We drove all the way back (more than 20 kilometres) to the spot where we'd first stopped to check on the animals, but found no jacket. This worried me quite a bit as it was Kobus's only jacket and I was sure that he was going to need it in the cold days ahead.

Eventually we gave up the search, but before turning back again Kobus stopped the truck and got out to check on the animals once more.

He found Leo hugging the jacket to him.

Kobus asked Leo to let him have his jacket back so that it could be used to block the gap again. But Leo said: 'Nope. It's mine now.'

We finally reached Harare at about midnight and turned west towards Norton. Twenty-four kilometres outside Harare we found the turn-off to the Lion and Cheetah Park, and a few minutes later we turned into the driveway leading to the Bristows' house.

Carol Bristow had been waiting up for us and she came out of the house to meet us. We apologised for arriving so late, but she said she knew that travelling with a lion was a difficult business and she was just so pleased that we'd arrived safely. She offered to get us something to eat and drink, but we declined. We were tired and wanted only to sleep.

I asked her if we might open the cage to let our animals out, but she said no, unfortunately not. She had no place to put them up for the night. She had her dogs in the garden and there was no telling how Leo would treat them.

I was rather disappointed as I had hoped we could unload our animals right away. They were as exhausted as we were from the long journey.

Carol explained that Leo's new home would not be at the Lion and Cheetah Park, but at their other park, Pamuzinda, about 60 kilometres further to the west. Her husband and son were waiting there for us, she said, and she would drive out to Pamuzinda with us first thing in the morning.

I had not known that. I thought we had reached our destination. Carol explained that they had decided to establish a pioneer lion pride in the Pamuzinda park. The place had no lions as yet and it seemed a good idea to start a lion family there. The pioneer pride would consist of Leo and two lionesses named Happie and Fat Cat.

Carol showed us to our rooms, and we hurried to bed to catch a few hours' sleep.

Early the next morning, Carol's cook woke us with coffee. We quickly got up and prepared for the last leg of our journey.

As soon as I was dressed, I rushed outside to the truck to see how Leo and Wolfie were.

Carol's two dogs were patrolling the truck and attempting to intimidate my animals. Wolfie paid them no attention, but Leo was threatening them through the bars of the cage, hissing and snarling at them. I had never seen Leo threaten other animals before, and was rather impressed at the awesome performance. But I also felt profoundly sorry for him that he was caged and unable to show those arrogant dogs that he was a royal prince who deserved better treatment.

Leo and Wolfie were relieved and happy to see me, but it was very obvious that they'd had enough of the cage. It broke my heart that I couldn't let them out yet. I talked comfortingly to them, promising them that they would be out of their cage in less than an hour. I brought them fresh water to drink and fed them some meat and bones that I'd saved from the previous day.

After a hurried breakfast we were on our way.

Zimbabwe is a beautiful country. We'd seen very little of it the previous day as we'd done most of our travelling through Zimbabwe at night. Now, on our way to Pamuzinda, we were able to appreciate the scenery by daylight.

But my heart was not quite in it. Half of me said 'Look at the beautiful scenery'. But the other half of me was too busy feeling apprehensive about whatever lay ahead for Leo and us.

We reached Pamuzinda's entrance gate after a forty-minute drive. A uniformed guard opened the gate, saluting smartly. We followed a dirt track that wound its way through a scenic landscape of tall grass and beautiful indigenous trees. After a few kilometres we reached the site where the new lion camp was being built.

Vivian Bristow, his son Graeme and an assistant park manager, Andy Cader, were waiting for us at the site. They had just finished building a temporary camp for Leo. It was right next to the main lion camp into which Leo would eventually go with his new lion family. At that time there were three lions in the park, but as the main camp was not yet fully completed, the lions were being kept in a temporarily fenced-in section of their new camp.

Carol parked outside Leo's camp. Someone opened the gate and we drove in and parked inside. Then we hurried to open the cage to let our tired animals out. They needed no invitation and leapt out. Leo was so happy to be out of his cage that he bounded all over the place for a while. Then he suddenly realised that the place smelled very strange, and he stopped in his tracks, looked about for Wolfie and hurried to his bodyguard.

The other three lions strolled over to the fence and contemplated Leo and Wolfie with keen curiosity.

Wolfie wisely ignored them. And for a while Leo remained quite unaware of them. But when he finally saw them, he fell down flat in the tall grass and pretended he wasn't there.

Kobus went over to him and crouched beside him, encouraging him to take an interest in the other lions. With Kobus at his side Leo felt a little braver and lifted his head to peer at them over the tall grass.

Meanwhile, the Bristows and Andy Cader were studying Leo from outside his camp, and I overheard them remarking that Leo was very handsome and incredibly big for his age. They also remarked on the fact that he appeared to be such good friends with the dog.

After a while Vivian Bristow said that he and the others would have to be on their way as they were busy with a film crew from the UK who were using some of their lions. The filming location was right there in Pamuzinda, just a few kilometres away. Vivian said we were welcome to join them if we wished. But we declined. We wanted to stay with Leo.

So they left, and we made ourselves comfortable in Leo's camp. It wasn't a very big camp — only about half an acre — but it was quite big enough for temporary occupation. It was covered with tall yellow grass and some stands of acacia trees. In one corner there was a cement pond filled with water — Leo's drinking place.

As I sat down in the grass Leo came over and sat down almost on top of me. I moved over a little and put my arm around him. He was feeling nervous and insecure.

After a while Kobus and Hettie decided to go for a walk to explore the park. I wanted to stay with Leo.

So Leo, Wolfie and I sort of huddled together in a corner of the strange camp and tried to feel at home.

At one stage one of the other lions let out an enormous roar, and we all jumped. I hugged Leo closer to me and told him that one day soon he would be able to roar just as loud.

After an hour or so, a young blonde-haired girl turned up and introduced herself as Julie Bristow, Graeme's wife. She told me that their house was less than a kilometre away, and she described how to get there. She said that we should feel free to come up to the house whenever we needed anything — the bathroom, or a cup of tea, or whatever. She added that she wanted us to come up to the house at one o'clock and have lunch with her and the rest of the Bristow clan.

I thanked her for her hospitality, and we chatted for a while. She asked a lot of questions about Leo as she studied him through the fence. She seemed a very kind and caring person, so I found myself telling her how hard it was for us to part with Leo.

It's not really my style to discuss personal worries with strangers. But the reason I was telling Julie this, was because I needed all the people of Pamuzinda to know that Leo was going to miss us, and that he would need comforting and special attention when we left.

Kobus and Hettie returned a short while after Julie had left, and Kobus decided he would go over to the film set and see what they were doing. Hettie opted to stay with me and the animals.

Leo was half asleep under the acacia tree and Hettie lay down next to him for a rest, giving me a chance to stretch my legs. I'd been sitting with Leo for a long time. As soon as I got up, Leo woke up and lifted his head to see where I was going. But Hettie stretched herself out on the grass next to him, so he relaxed again and put one front paw on her shoulder, letting it rest there.

Some time later, another young woman came over to make our acquaintance. She was Maria Cader, wife of the assistant park manager Andy Cader. She told me that their house was right next door to Graeme and Julie's, and she also offered help and hospitality.

Maria was fascinated with Leo and she asked if she could come into the camp. I was delighted that she'd asked and I rushed to open the gate for her. Leo was in a very docile mood, so I felt confident that he would not even look at Maria, let alone bother her.

Maria spent about an hour chatting with me and Hettie, and I told her — as I'd told Julie — how hard it was for us to part with Leo. She was sympathetic and assured me that her husband Andy was very fond of lions and that he would spend a lot of time with Leo as soon as his work with the film crew was over. She explained that Andy's job on the film set was to take care of the lions who were being used in the film.

I asked Maria about the three lions in the main camp. She told me that the female was Happie, one of Leo's future wives. The other two were males. One of them was very old — twenty-four years old, in fact — and his name was Trade. Old Trade had been brought over from the Lion and Cheetah Park to retire at Pamuzinda. The other, younger, male was Sam. He was a temporary visitor, an understudy for the film. As soon as filming was completed he would return to his family at the Lion and Cheetah Park.

I asked her where Leo's other future wife — Fat Cat — was. Fat Cat was at the film set. She was one of the main stars in the movie.

It had been nice talking to Maria and I was grateful that she had come to visit. She promised she would come again the following day.

At midday, Kobus and the others returned from the film set and we all went up to Julie's house for lunch. Actually, I wished that I needn't go — I just wanted to stay with Leo. But I didn't want to seem ungracious.

In the end I was glad that I'd gone. Julie's lunch was very good and I felt much better afterwards.

Leo and Wolfie had obviously been waiting anxiously for our return, and they were very relieved to see us again. Andy Cader brought over a chunk of wildebeest meat for Leo's lunch, and it pleased me that Andy came right into the camp to put the meat down for Leo. Leo ignored the meat and remained lying down, pretending that he wasn't aware of Andy either. Poor Leo. He felt so insecure.

Andy stayed and chatted to us for a while. He seemed genuinely fond of lions. He even talked to Leo. But Leo didn't understand a word. I had to explain to Andy that Leo wasn't bilingual like us. He understood only Afrikaans.

'That's no problem,' Andy reassured me. 'Leo and I will soon find a common language.' He stepped up to Leo to give him a friendly pat on the back, but Wolfie wasn't having any. He parked himself firmly between Leo and Andy, fixing Andy with a toothy glare that said: 'Don't you dare touch my lion!'

I hastily told Wolfie that it was OK, Andy was a friend. But Andy said not to worry, he would come again the following day to talk to Leo — that is, if Wolfie didn't mind.

Andy left us to go back to the filming location, and Kobus and Hettie decided to go with him for a while.

I stayed with my animals.

I picked up the chunk of meat that Andy had brought, and carried it over to Leo. But Leo only sniffed at it and wouldn't eat. Perhaps he felt too nervous to eat, or maybe it was the strange smell of the meat that put him off — he'd never had wildebeest before. Poor Leo. Everything was so strange: the language, the country, even the food.

I fetched a tin of canned dog food from the truck for Wolfie, but he wouldn't eat either. I don't think Wolfie's problem was nervousness. He simply didn't like canned food and was used to better things.

An African man turned up in the late afternoon and poured fresh water into Leo's drinking pond through the fence with a watering can.

I started to greet him in Tsonga then suddenly remembered that Zimbabweans don't speak Tsonga. Only Shona and Sindebele. Fortunately the man understood English, so we talked for a while. He told me that he'd never seen a dog in a lion's company before and he wanted to know why the lion didn't eat the dog. I explained that the dog was the lion's friend. He told me that if he was the dog, he would not trust the lion one bit. And he added that if he was me, he wouldn't trust the lion either, and he suggested that, in my own interests, I get out of the camp while I was still alive. I said that I was the lion's mother and that lions don't eat their mothers.

He shrugged and said: 'OK. You do what you want. But remember I warned you. So don't blame me if the lion eats you.'

I thanked him for his concern and promised that I would remember not to blame him if the lion ate me.

From time to time throughout the day, the lions in the other camp would stroll up to their fence and study us with curiosity. Wolfie decided it was best to ignore them altogether, but Leo remained very frightened of them and tried to hide in the tall grass whenever he saw them looking at us. I tried to show him that I wasn't scared of the lions, but he wouldn't believe me.

So I left Leo's camp and walked over to the main camp, about five or six metres away. I stood at the fence and chatted to the strange lions — just to show Leo that it was no big deal.

The lions contemplated me with mild curiosity. After a while the female, Happie, came right up to the fence and, pressing one side of her body against the wire, rubbed her head and shoulder against it, inviting me to a feline greeting. I was delighted. I stepped up to the wire and, pressing myself against it, stooped to rub shoulders with her, enjoying the moment immensely.

When Wolfie saw me rubbing shoulders with the strange lioness, he promptly gave her a warning bark from Leo's camp — just to let her know that he was watching her and that she'd better not try any tricks. The lions all made strange grumbling noises when Wolfie barked. They were obviously not used to dogs and didn't trust Wolfie at all.

I noted that all three lions looked extremely healthy and in good shape — even twenty-four-year-old Trade. It was only his shaky movements that gave away his age.

I went back to Leo and asked him if he'd noticed how friendly Happie had been. But he looked at me with a forlorn expression that seemed to say: 'Yes. But can't we all go home now?'

I put my arms around him, and there was a huge lump in my throat.

Kobus and the others came back shortly before sunset, and Graeme Bristow invited us to his house for a drink. I declined. I knew that we would soon have to leave Leo and Wolfie alone in their camp for the night, and I wanted to stay with them as long as possible. Hettie offered to stay with me, but I persuaded her to go with the others and enjoy the company.

So I sat in the tall grass between Wolfie and Leo. And together we watched the sun set. Dusk came, and we listened to the sounds of the bush. Then it got dark — pitch-black, inky dark. We huddled closer together.

Suddenly one of the lions in the main camp started roaring. I guessed it to be Sam. Then another joined in — probably old

Trade. The two of them were having a competition to see who could roar the loudest. Their thundering voices rolled over the landscape like an earthquake, silencing all other night sounds, and my two animals and I felt very vulnerable. I put my arms around them and told them not to worry — there were fences between us and the lions. What unnerved me, though, was that I could no longer see the fences. What if they had dissolved? Anything was possible on a dark moonless night in a foreign country.

In due course, Kobus and Hettie arrived in the truck to fetch me, and I asked them if we could stay with Leo and Wolfie a while longer. So Kobus and Hettie joined us in the long grass. Kobus told me that he'd met Leo's other future wife — Fat Cat — at the film set. He said she wasn't as young and attractive as Happie — in fact she was middle-aged and very fat — but she was altogether a delightful old girl, and extremely friendly and affectionate. I was very pleased to hear that. Perhaps Fat Cat would be kind to Leo — in a motherly sort of way.

Eventually Kobus said we had better get going as Carol Bristow would be expecting us for dinner.

I really hated leaving my two animals out there alone in the strange camp. I told Wolfie that we had to go up to the house for the night, but that we would return again early the next morning. And I asked him to take good care of Leo.

I fetched their sleeping mats from the truck and spread them close together in the patch of grass where we had been sitting. Leo and Wolfie seemed to understand that this meant that they were to spend the night in the camp. Even so, they walked to the gate with us and looked very forlorn when we closed the gate behind us and got into the truck without them.

My heart felt so heavy at the sight of my two animals standing at the gate, watching us drive off.

Later that evening, after dinner, Kobus mentioned to me that Vivian Bristow was concerned about my spending so much time alone with Leo in his camp.

'Why?' I asked, surprised.

'He worries about your safety,' Kobus replied.

The idea exasperated me.

We drove back to Pamuzinda very early the next morning and found Leo and Wolfie sitting close together on their sleeping mats, their ears pricked as they listened for the sound of our truck. As soon as they recognised us, they leapt up and bounded over to the gate to welcome us.

And so we spent another day in more or less the same way as the previous one. Kobus and Hettie visited the film set at intervals or went for walks in the park, and I stayed with Leo and Wolfie.

Julie and Maria came over again to see how we were getting on, and we spent some time chatting. I asked them how long the film crew would be working at Pamuzinda, and they said a few more weeks. My heart sank. I wanted the film crew to leave so that Andy could spend more time with Leo. It was important to me that Leo and Andy became good friends before we went back home. I desperately needed the reassurance that at least one person would be spending a lot of time with Leo once we'd left.

Whenever Kobus was in the camp with us, he would sit in the grass alongside the fence that faced the main camp and persuade Leo to join him. Leo would hesitantly go over to Kobus and sit down next to him. The other lions, noticing that they were being watched, strolled up to their fence and studied Kobus and Leo with curiosity.

In an attempt to bolster Leo's confidence, Kobus discussed the lions with him with a cheerful and encouraging tone of voice. Occasionally Trade or Sam, or both of them, let out a few magnificent roars, and poor Leo would crouch low in the grass beside Kobus.

Kobus would say to him: 'Come on Leo, you're a big boy too! Roar back at them — I know you can do it!'

But Leo would look at Kobus with an expression that seemed to say: 'I don't know. Those are real lions. I'm just a dog.'

We had lunch at Julie's house again, and afterwards Andy came back with us to visit Leo for a while. Wolfie didn't altogether trust Andy yet. He allowed him to talk to Leo and even to pat him on the back, but he kept a close watch on Andy, ready to set him straight if he didn't treat Leo nicely.

Andy noticed that Leo still hadn't touched his wildebeest meat, so he promised to bring Leo a chunk of fresh meat as soon as he returned from the film set in the late afternoon.

I asked Andy if it was possible that Leo could go into the main camp with Happie and Fat Cat soon — at least before we went back home. But Andy said no, that it usually took a hand-reared lion a while to realise that he was a lion. And as long as Leo didn't know he was a lion, it would be cruel to put him in the main camp with the other lions. He'd spend all his time trying to hide from them.

This was extremely upsetting news. I had hoped that we would see Leo happily established with his new family before we left.

The third day with Leo followed much the same pattern as the previous two days. Leo was still feeling nervous and he spent most of his time resting and doing little else, except snuggling up close to me or Kobus or Hettie. He would try to sit on our laps, but it was no longer possible. He was about ten times too big for that. Poor Leo. He was obviously trying to tell us that he was still just a baby and wanted to go home.

Later in the day, I went over to the main camp again, and Happie came to greet me, rubbing shoulders with me through the wire. I stuck my arm in through the fence and stroked her head. She liked that and made happy grunting noises.

On the fourth day, Hettie accompanied Carol on a shopping trip to Harare, and Kobus and I spent the day following what had become our routine: I stayed in the camp with Leo and Wolfie while Kobus divided his time between me and the animals and visits to the filming location. So the fourth day would have been very much the same as the third day, except that a terrible thing happened to me about halfway through the day.

I went over to the main camp again, and after rubbing shoulders with Happie, I stuck my arm through the fence and stroked her head. She made happy grunting noises. I turned to see if Leo was watching − I wanted him to take note that Happie was just a friendly, harmless lion like him.

And then something went very wrong. Happie's mood suddenly changed and, with an angry snarl, she grabbed my hand. I yanked it away, but my thumb caught in her jaws − gripped tightly between the upper and lower incisors. I tried not to panic and relaxed my hand, thinking that perhaps she'd let go. But I could feel her teeth going through the bone. I called to Kobus who was in Leo's camp.

'Get away from her!' he yelled and ran to the gate at the bottom of Leo's camp.

Happie was raising one paw − and I realised she was going to hook her claws into my arm.

'Get away from her!' Kobus yelled again as he raced towards me.

I yanked as hard as I could. The top half of my thumb came off at the joint as I fell over backwards. Kobus reached me and helped me to my feet.

'My thumb is off,' I told him.

I didn't want to see the wound. So I looked away as I showed Kobus my right hand.

Kobus said: 'Let's get into the truck.'

I kept my right hand covered with my left hand to make sure I wouldn't see it. In the truck I found a towel and I wrapped it around my injured hand, looking the other way as I did so.

I felt no pain. Only shock. And I believed somehow that as long as I didn't look at my thumb (or what was left of it) I would not feel any pain. It worked.

Kobus drove me to Julie's house. He asked her for disinfectant and sterile bandages. Julie immediately ran to Maria's house to fetch her. Kobus told me to sit down. I sat down at Julie's kitchen table.

Maria arrived with some first-aid stuff. Kobus filled a bowl with disinfectant and dipped my hand in it.

Julie handed me a cup of sweet tea. I said: 'No thanks.'

I was shaking uncontrollably. I wouldn't be able to hold the cup.

'You must drink it,' Maria said. 'For the shock.'

Julie helped me hold the cup and I swallowed the sweet tea.

It helped. A few minutes later I stopped shaking.

Kobus bandaged my hand and asked Maria which hospital in Harare he should take me to. Maria offered to come with us. She knew Harare well and would be able to direct us to the hospital she had in mind.

I didn't really want to go to hospital. I wanted to stay with Leo. We had only a few days left with him.

But there was the problem of sepsis, of course. I would probably lose more than just my thumb if I didn't get proper treatment.

I apologised to Julie for leaving her kitchen full of blood-soaked things. Then Kobus, Maria and I got into the truck and set out for Harare — about 90 kilometres away.

I hoped I wouldn't have to stay in hospital long.

Poor Wolfie and Leo — left all alone in their camp with no idea where we'd gone to, or why we'd departed so suddenly.

Maria suggested that we stop at the Bristows' house at the Lion and Cheetah Park and that I collect any of my stuff that I might need at the hospital.

We did this, and while I changed out of my blood-stained clothes into some clean things, Maria quickly wrote a note to Carol and Hettie, explaining where we'd gone. She gave the note to the cook, asking him to make sure that Carol and Hettie got it as soon as they returned from Harare. Maria also asked Kobus how much money we had with us. We had a few hundred Zimbabwe dollars. Maria said the hospital would require a deposit of about six thousand dollars.

We were stunned.

'Can't we send them the money as soon as we get back to South Africa?' Kobus asked.

Maria said no, they would refuse to admit me unless the deposit was paid. But she told us not to worry. She rushed off and found one of Vivian Bristow's assistants. He kept Vivian's cheque book and there were several signed cheques in it. He handed us one of the signed cheques. Maria said she would explain to Vivian about the cheque that evening, and that Kobus could arrange with Vivian to repay him at a later stage.

Maria was an angel. She thought of everything and took care of everything, allowing me to relax and think of nothing.

Once we were on the road again, she regaled us with amusing stories about life at Pamuzinda. And I laughed a lot.

But I felt so sad.

Losing my thumb wasn't so bad really.

Losing Leo was.

In a Hospital in Harare

Maria directed us to The Avenues Clinic in Harare. We learned that a deposit of 6 250 dollars was required. Maria filled out the cheque and, in her haste, made an error.

The hospital would not accept the cheque.

Maria told us not to worry. She had friends living in Harare. She asked if she could take the truck to get to their house.

Kobus offered to drive her there.

I waited for them in the hospital waiting room.

There were several other people in the room — Shona-speaking people. Their strange language made me feel ignorant and insecure. Then I overheard a mother saying something to her sick child in a language that sounded familiar. Sindebele. It sounded almost like Zulu. The mother started singing to the child. The words of the lullaby were easy to understand. The mother looked up and found me staring at her. I hadn't meant to stare. I was concentrating on the words of her song. I smiled apologetically. She smiled back at me. And life didn't seem so altogether awful any more.

Kobus and Maria soon returned, bringing with them a signed cheque from Maria's friends.

I wondered if her friends were saints or something. How could they not mind lending such a huge amount of money to total strangers — and foreigners at that?

Maria said not to worry. Her friends had obviously liked Kobus's face and decided he was trustworthy.

I was admitted to the casualty ward and handed over to Dr Gwatidzo. I worried for a moment about whether we would have a language in common, but I soon discovered that Dr Gwatidzo, as well as most of the hospital staff, spoke fluent English.

I looked the other way as the doctor removed the bandages from my hand. He asked if I wanted an injection for the pain. I said no thank you. As long as I didn't look at the wound, it didn't hurt. He asked what about my index finger.

'What about it?' I asked.

'The skin has been grazed along one side,' he said. 'Do you have any idea how that happened?'

I said no. Perhaps Happie's canines. Or the wire of the fence.

He poured the contents of a bottle of disinfectant over both my thumb and index finger. Then he bound up my hand and told someone to contact the surgeon and to book a theatre for me. Someone replied that the theatres were fully booked for the afternoon.

The doctor said: 'So book one for the evening.'

Kobus and Maria accompanied me to my room, and as soon as I was settled in, I urged them to go back to Pamuzinda. I wanted Kobus to spend what was left of the day with Leo and Wolfie.

After they'd left, I lay wondering about Happie. Why had she suddenly wanted to attack me? What did I do wrong?

I thought and thought about it. And eventually the answer came to me.

Just before I had gone over to the main camp to socialise with Happie, I had been stroking Wolfie's back. And so my hand must have smelled of Wolfie. At first Happie didn't notice the smell. I was stroking the top of her head and her neck. Then, as I turned to see if Leo was watching, my hand touched her cheek. At that moment she probably caught a whiff of the dog smell on my hand and decided I was a traitor — a dog disguised as a human.

Leo was used to Wolfie's smell, but those other lions weren't. And they obviously didn't like dogs.

I was relieved at having found the answer to Happie's sudden change of mood. I wondered, though, how I was going to convince her that I wasn't a dog. But I decided I would worry about that later.

I shared a room with three other patients. All of them white and female. English-speaking Zimbabweans. They asked what had happened to my hand. I told them a lion had bitten half my thumb off.

First they gasped with surprise. Then they laughed. Then they apologised for laughing.

It was an interesting reaction.

There was one white nurse in our ward. She had reacted in exactly the same way. (Gasp, laugh, apologise.) But all the other nurses were African women. And not one of them had laughed. Their reactions had been only of shock and sympathy.

Later, when I got home and was admitted to the Nelspruit hospital for further treatment, I encountered exactly the same responses. Every white nurse or patient who asked about my hand would gasp and then laugh at my answer. And then apologise for laughing. But the African nurses and the African patients who shared my ward were totally horrified, and would express their deepest sympathy.

Strange, this difference in sentiments.

I thought about it. And it occurred to me that the idea of a lion biting off a person's thumb is, in fact, funny. So I guess that proves that white people have a morbid sense of humour.

Later in the afternoon, a nurse brought me a form to sign: patient's permission for surgery. How would I sign it — minus a thumb and with my right hand all bandaged up? I decided my left hand would have to do the job.

I reached into my handbag for my reading glasses. They weren't there. I panicked. The nurse searched for them in my bedside cabinet. They weren't there either. So I asked the nurse to please point me to the place on the form where my signature was required. She did. And I discovered that my left hand was unconnected to my brain. It couldn't even hold a pen, let alone sign my name.

'I give up,' I told the nurse. 'This hand can't write.'

'Don't worry,' she said. 'But you must sign the form. Just make a cross.'

'Draw a cross,' I said to my left hand. It drew a shaky-looking four-legged spider.

'Not there,' the nurse said. 'Here.'

I'd missed the signature space by about half a page.

I aimed for the tiny-looking space but lost sight of it.

'Please show me again,' I asked the nurse. She did and I eventually managed to produce an insecure-looking squiggle in almost the right place.

'Good girl!' said the nurse.

I was shaken. I had become illiterate.

I spent the rest of the afternoon feeling illiterate, insecure and sad.

Mostly sad.

A nurse came to take my pulse. 'You're not smiling any more,' she said. 'What's the matter?'

She wouldn't understand about Leo. So I told her I'd lost my glasses.

'Where?' she asked, alarmed. 'When?' She grabbed a file from its holder at the foot of my bed and wrote everything down. Patient lost her glasses. Possibly in casualty ward. Approximate time: 12.15.

'Please don't worry,' she begged me. 'And please don't feel so sad. We'll find your glasses for you right away!' She rushed off.

I was startled. I certainly hadn't meant to cause an uproar over my glasses.

After that, a nurse appeared at my bedside every ten minutes or so to report that everyone in the hospital was looking for my glasses. The casualty ward had been checked, as well as the reception desk and all the lifts. But I mustn't worry, they kept assuring me. The glasses would be found.

I felt awfully guilty. And I tried to explain to every nurse who talked to me that I hadn't meant to cause them all so much trouble. But no one listened. They were convinced that my heart was breaking because I had lost my glasses.

I fixed a smile on my face.

No one was going to catch me looking sad again.

Finally the staff nurse herself appeared at my bedside and told me she had good news for me: a patient in Ward B said she had been admitted to the hospital at the same time as a patient with an injured hand.

'That would be you,' said the staff nurse, pointing at me. 'And the patient in Ward B says that before you went into casualty you handed your glasses to a lady in a green track suit.'

'Ah, yes!' I said. 'That's Maria. She and my husband brought me in.'

'Would you like us to call her on the phone for you?' the good staff nurse offered.

I said no thanks. I knew Maria would take care of my glasses and return them to me.

Everyone smiled and looked happy. I thanked the staff nurse and everyone else for their trouble, and I also asked them to thank the observant patient in Ward B for me.

After an hour or so I got tired of lying in bed with a perpetual smile on my face. So I decided to get up and take a walk.

It was then that I saw the notice attached to the rail at the foot of my bed. The lettering was large, so I was able to read it without my glasses. It read: Patient: Mrs K Kruger. Attending surgeon: Mr G A Vera.

Alarm bells rang in my head. *Mister* Vera? Why *mister* instead of doctor? Surely my condition required a doctor!

I panicked. How could a surgeon not be a doctor? Did they have a shortage of properly trained surgeons in Harare? Or what? Goodness. What would a *mister* know about stopping septi-caemia? What if he resorted to some primitive method — like amputation?

I decided the only thing to do was to make sure Mr Vera knew his job. And the only way to do that would be to refuse anaesthesia and make sure I was wide awake in theatre.

So I went off and found the ward sister. I told her that I'd forgotten to mention to her that I was allergic to general anaesthesia. She looked concerned, but came back to my room with me and recorded the information in my file.

Mr Vera turned up at 7.30 that evening and spent a while chatting to me. He seemed a pleasant person. His accent was slightly different from that of the other hospital staff. I wondered if he was originally from some other African country. Zambia perhaps. Or Kenya. I didn't ask him about his training, of course. That would have been impolite − and ungracious.

He asked me about my allergic reactions to anaesthesia and I stammered something about anaphylactic shock. I'm not sure he believed me. I sounded very unconvincing. But he told me not to worry, he would give me a few injections in my hand to induce local anaesthesia.

That was good. I could remain awake and make sure that no one chopped off the rest of my thumb.

Eventually I was wheeled down to the theatre floor. A nurse appeared and informed Mr Vera that there had not been time to clean any of the theatres, so none was available. She suggested that he use one of the pre-op waiting rooms. Mr Vera refused outright, informing the nurse that he wanted a sterile theatre and that he would wait for one even if it took all night. The nurse hastily assured him that a sterile theatre would be ready for him within two hours.

So I was wheeled back to my room again. I didn't mind. I was relieved that Mr Vera had insisted on operating in a sterile theatre.

At 9.30 that evening I was finally wheeled into a sterile theatre. Mr Vera unwrapped my bandages and anaesthetised my hand. My hand was lying on a sterile steel table next to the bed. I thoroughly avoided looking at it.

After a while I could feel my hand going to sleep. Mr Vera brought over a tray of instruments. He took a pair of scissors from it. Or maybe it was forceps. So I asked him what he was going to do with it. He explained that the tendons in my thumb had drawn back and had to be pulled back into place. I could actually feel the tendons being pulled back up. But it didn't hurt. Then he took a pair of scissors from the tray that were definitely scissors and not forceps.

'What are you going to do now?' I asked him.

He explained that, in order to inhibit sepsis he needed to cut away the severed ends of the tendons as well as other damaged tissue.

I started getting the impression that Mr Vera knew his job.

Eventually he scrubbed the wound, and then reached for a surgical needle, explaining that he would sew a skin-flap over the severed bone to keep it covered. That would also help prevent sepsis, he said.

I asked if he thought it necessary to remove some of the damaged bone as well to inhibit sepsis.

He replied that ordinarily he would prefer to do that. But the thumb is an important digit, he explained. So he would rather choose to save as much of the bone as possible. He added that hopefully antibiotic treatment would prevent sepsis. If not, he said, then further debridement would be necessary. But he believed that for the time being it was a risk worth taking.

'Will you be treating me with gram positive as well as gram negative antibiotics?' I asked.

'Yes,' he said. He looked up and added, 'You seem to know a lot about the treatment of lion bites . . .?'

'So do you,' I said. 'Where did you do your training?'

'Oxford and Edinburgh,' he replied.

'But then you're a doctor!' I exclaimed. 'A real surgeon, I mean!'

He grinned and said that yes, in fact, he was.

'So why are you called "mister" and not "doctor"?' I asked.

He explained to me that the British convention is to call a surgeon 'mister'.

'But why?' I asked.

'I suppose it's a kind of inverted snobbishness,' he replied.

'But that's silly,' I said. 'You study for many years to become a doctor. Then you study several years more and you end up as a mister again. What kind of sense does that make?'

By way of reply, he told me the following story. Back in the dark days of the Middle Ages the medical practitioners had a dim view of surgeons. The surgeons were the people who stole corpses for their research and to practise their operating skills. So they were regarded as the black sheep of the profession — the 'butchers'. And the practitioners refused to call them 'doctors'.

I liked Mr Vera.

And he certainly wasn't a butcher.

Kobus and Hettie came to visit me early the next morning, bringing me chocolates, magazines and — best of all — my reading glasses. I was so happy to see them.

Kobus told me that he'd borrowed a cheque from Vivian Bristow to repay Maria's friends. He would repay Vivian as soon as we got back to South Africa.

I was relieved to know that those trusting strangers had been repaid.

I asked how Leo and Wolfie were.

Kobus said they were fine, and he told me that Leo had had an interesting experience. Andy had brought a young lioness named Sheilah to Leo's camp to meet him. She was a few months younger than Leo and very tame. She was one of the stars being used in the film. Andy reckoned that since she was so much smaller than Leo, Leo would not be as scared of her as he was of the other lions. He took her right up to the fence of Leo's camp, and Leo was very interested in her. He studied her for a long time and eventually went closer, but hissed at her just in case she had dubious designs on him.

I was pleased to know that at least Leo had had his first close encounter with another lion. Perhaps that would help him to realise that he himself was a lion.

Kobus told me that Andy had said he would bring Sheilah over to Leo's camp every afternoon for a visit.

That was good news.

Kobus and Hettie spent about an hour with me, and then I persuaded them to go back to Leo. He needed them more than I did.

In the late afternoon, further examination and X-rays revealed that my hand was free from sepsis. So I asked Mr Vera if I could be discharged. He said he would prefer to keep me there for another day or two.

So I explained to him about Leo, and told him that I had only a few days left with him. Mr Vera understood and agreed to discharge me that evening, on condition that I contacted him the moment I suspected any indications of sepsis. He asked also that I make an appointment to see him again in three days' time, adding that I would have to consult a surgeon in my own country as soon as I got back.

I asked why. He said my thumb was in need of some cosmetic surgery. Right now it wasn't a pretty sight.

'Stop!' I said. 'Please don't tell me how it looks. It may start hurting.'

Kobus came to fetch me that evening and a nurse showed him how to clean and dress the wound.

I looked the other way. And I felt sorry for Kobus. But he said it was no problem — he didn't mind being nurse to a lion-attack victim.

It occurred to me that I'd had my turn. So now, perhaps, it was his turn. I could clean and dress the wound myself if necessary, of course, but it would be rather difficult with only one hand — and while looking the other way.

Onward, Leo

Leo was so relieved and so happy to see me the next morning that I thought my heart would break. How could I possibly leave him in only a few days' time?

I sat down in the grass with him and he kept rubbing his face against mine, uttering sorrowful groans that seemed to mean: 'Where were you yesterday and the day before? I missed you so much!'

'I missed you too,' I told him.

I put my arms around him and hugged him to me for a long time.

Maria and Julie came to ask how my hand was. And after lunch, Andy came to visit Leo again.

As we sat in the grass and chatted, Andy stroked Leo's back, and I noticed that Leo was looking a lot more relaxed with Andy.

Kobus told Andy that Leo loved riding on the back of a pick-up, and Andy promised that he would take Leo on sight-seeing drives as soon as his work with the film crew was finished.

Kobus asked Andy if we could take Leo for a drive ourselves that afternoon. And Andy said we were most welcome to do so.

So as soon as Andy left us, Kobus told Leo and Wolfie to get on to the back of the truck. Wolfie jumped up eagerly, and Leo followed, but a little hesitantly. He wasn't sure if he wanted to explore this alien land yet. He was only just starting to get used to his camp and to accept it as a safe haven. So he huddled close to

Wolfie. But after a while he started to relax and take an interest in his surroundings.

Pamuzinda is a beautiful park with both lowveld and highveld type vegetation. We came across kudu, eland, buffalo and herds of sable antelope. After a while we stopped at a creek and walked along its banks for some distance.

Leo stayed close to us, and although he remained wary, he obviously enjoyed the walk.

When we arrived back at Leo's camp, Hettie went up to Julie's house for a drink of water, and came back carrying a leg of impala — a gift to Leo from Julie. Leo was delighted with the familiar fare and got right down to devouring it. I was so pleased to see him eating well again. He'd hardly touched the wildebeest meat that had been delivered to his camp every day.

Shortly before dusk, Andy turned up with the young lioness Sheilah on the back of his truck. He drove right up to the fence and allowed Sheilah to get off into a small temporary camp that had been erected for her right next to Leo's camp. Andy wanted Sheilah to spend the night there so she and Leo could get better acquainted. She was a very pretty lioness — a few months younger than Leo and at least fifty kilograms lighter. It was obvious, though, that Sheilah was scared of Wolfie — even though Wolfie was behaving very nicely. So Andy suggested that we take Wolfie with us to Carol's house for the night.

It seemed a good idea, although I had ambivalent feelings about it. I knew Leo would feel very insecure in his camp without Wolfie. But as long as Wolfie was in the camp, Sheilah would not try to befriend Leo. And it was important, of course, that Leo started learning that he was a lion and not a dog.

So we agreed to take Wolfie back with us for the night.

I gave Leo a last hug before we left and told him that Sheilah was a very nice lioness and that I wanted him to make friends with her.

Leo looked very worried when he realised that Wolfie was leaving with us, but he kept glancing in Sheilah's direction, and I hoped that her presence would comfort him after we'd left.

I lay awake half the night, wondering what Leo was doing.

On our return the next morning we saw that the grass was flattened in a spot near the fence separating the two camps, indicating that Leo had spent the night resting fairly close to Sheilah. I wished I knew whether they had at least spoken to each other.

I asked Leo about it, but he ignored my question, pretending that Sheilah no longer existed.

Andy arrived to fetch Sheilah with the news that the film crew had decided to take the afternoon off. So he would be back in the early afternoon, he said, and he thought it would be a good time to accompany us on a drive with Leo.

I was very pleased with the idea.

Andy arrived at about two o'clock and so we spent the rest of the afternoon driving and walking with Leo.

Although Leo enjoyed the outing and appeared outwardly relaxed, I knew he was still feeling a little nervous and apprehensive. He watched us closely and stayed very close to us, almost as if he feared that he might miss some important clue if he didn't pay attention to everything we did.

Andy made efforts to befriend Leo, walking next to him and talking gently to him. Occasionally Andy would sit down and call Leo to him. Leo would turn and look to me for guidance.

'Go to Andy,' I would tell him in Afrikaans.

And Leo would understand and go to Andy, sitting down beside him. Andy would stroke his head and talk softly to him. It was obvious that Andy loved lions and that he intended to win Leo's trust and friendship. The thought gave me comfort.

Andy told us that he was very impressed with Leo. He found him remarkably well behaved and easy to control.

I told him that Leo wasn't always so docile — he could be very mischievous sometimes. But I also told Andy that Leo was extremely sensitive to a harsh tone of voice, and that he was actually a very gentle lion.

In the late afternoon we drove back to Leo's camp. And as soon as we had parked inside the camp, we noticed a change in Leo's behaviour: he seemed both relieved and happy to be back in the familiar camp, and he even got quite playful, stalking us and inviting us to play wrestling games with him.

It was good to see Leo showing some spirit again.

In the evening, Andy brought Sheilah to Leo's camp again, and so we took Wolfie with us, leaving Leo alone with Sheilah for the night.

The following day was our second last day with Leo. Kobus, Hettie and I spent the whole day with him, taking him for drives and walks, resting with him in his camp, hugging him a lot and talking to him.

Leo was starting to show more interest in his surroundings as well as in the other lions. Whenever they weren't looking his way, he studied them quietly, peering intently at them over the tall grass, nose to the wind, and a frown on his face. I wondered if it was their smell that intrigued him most. He still avoided looking at them when they roared, but he no longer tried so hard to become invisible.

On our last day I had my appointment with the surgeon. Kobus drove me to Harare while Hettie stayed with Leo.

Mr Vera was satisfied that my hand showed no signs of sepsis, and he wrote me a report to give to a surgeon in my own country.

Afterwards Kobus and I stopped at a supermarket and bought a chicken as a farewell present for Leo. We returned to Pamuzinda and spent the rest of the afternoon with Leo, staying with him until long after dark.

Then we stopped by Andy's house to tell him that we would be leaving early the next morning — as soon as we'd said goodbye to Leo. And we asked Andy if he would please, if possible, visit Leo soon after we left and stay with him a while to comfort him.

Andy promised that he would. Maria also offered to go over to Leo's camp the following morning and talk to him. She suggested to me that I leave Leo something with my smell on it — a blouse or a jacket or something. She said it would give him comfort in my absence.

I thought about Maria's suggestion that night. And I decided I would leave Leo my pillow. I had a favourite pillow that travelled with me wherever I went. It was a soft, thick, down-filled pillow, and it had belonged to me ever since I was a child. I knew Leo would love it. He loved soft things.

Early the next morning we drove back to Leo's camp for the last time.

We couldn't bring ourselves to tell Leo that we were leaving him. So we just hugged him a lot and stroked his fur.

Eventually we gave him his chicken. He was surprised and delighted at the sight of his favourite fare — but only for a moment. He knew something was wrong. He sensed our mood, and his eyes were full of questions.

'We have to go now,' Kobus said finally. He gave Leo a last firm hug, patted him on the back and then walked to the truck and got in.

Hettie hugged Leo wordlessly, spilling tears on to the top of his head. Then she too got into the truck.

I fetched my pillow from the truck and gave it to Leo. He slumped to a crouching position, clutching the pillow to his chest. And when he looked at me, there was comprehension in his eyes. He knew then that we were leaving.

It was the hardest moment of my life.

I wanted to give him a final hug, but I was afraid that he would sense my anguish. So I merely patted his head. Then I got into the truck and we drove off.

I couldn't look back.

Kobus and Hettie didn't look back either.

It was only Wolfie who looked back.

He stared at his friend until he could no longer see him.

Tears and Consolation

We didn't talk much on the long drive home.

But we tried.

We remarked on the scenery. And we stopped from time to time for tea, or to give Wolfie a drink of water. And then we commented on the scenery once more.

We arrived home in the early hours of the following morning. After a few hours' sleep, Kobus drove me to the hospital in Nelspruit. My hand was sore and slightly swollen.

The surgeon did further debridement, removing skin and other tissue, but fortunately no bone.

Two days later when I was home again, my trouble-sharing friend Annette came to visit me. It was so good to see her again.

She said she was sorry about my thumb. I told her it hardly worried me.

She said: 'OK. So talk to me about Leo. Tell me everything.'

I did. And, in a way, it helped me to get things into better perspective.

Afterwards I said: 'I miss him a lot. But I can cope with that. What I can't cope with is the idea of how much he misses us.'

'I know what you mean,' Annette said. She looked so sad.

We poured ourselves some more coffee.

After a while Annette said: 'You must try to take comfort in the fact that Leo is still young. Young people have a lot of emotional resilience, you know.'

I nodded.

'Well, I know Leo's not a person,' she added. 'He's a lion. But what's the difference? Anyway, I also believe that a happy childhood provides a good foundation for a happy adulthood.'

I thought about that. And it gave me some comfort.

Hettie went back to university. Paul and Sandra came home. Sandra shopped, cooked and cleaned the house for me. I was touched. She need not have done it. My hand wasn't sore any more. But I guess she knew it wasn't my hand that was hurting.

Friends and family called. They were sorry for me because of my thumb. This baffled me at times. What's so tragic about losing half a thumb?

After a few days I decided it was time to get on with the business of living again.

So I worked hard and talked and laughed and did all kinds of normal things.

I even managed quite well without my thumb.

Except that I dropped a lot of things.

In fact, I dropped so many plates and dishes that my kitchen cupboards began to look alarmingly empty.

But I didn't care.

It was nice to see things hit the floor and break into tiny pieces.

Insomnia was my main problem.

What kept me awake at night was the expression that had been in Leo's eyes when I had given him my pillow. He'd known then that I was saying goodbye. And he'd accepted it — quietly and stoically. No complaints. But his eyes had been so full of sorrow.

Wolfie missed his friend too. He would look at me with a big question mark in his eyes. And I would explain to him, over and over, why we had had to leave Leo in Zimbabwe. Eventually he seemed to understand that there were valid reasons, so he accepted it with a sigh that seemed to mean: 'Yes. I see. But I kind of miss the brat.'

I promised Wolfie that we would get him a new friend — a real dog, one who would look up to him and have respect for him.

I went back to hospital again for cosmetic surgery. The surgeon made slits along each side of my thumb, cutting right into the subcutaneous tissue. Then he lifted the sections of loosened skin and stretched them to cover the piece of exposed bone that was sticking out where the knuckle used to be.

When I woke up after the surgery, my thumb hurt so much that I could hardly talk. I felt rather cheated. I thought there had been an agreement between my thumb and me that it wouldn't hurt as long as I didn't look at it.

For a few days my whole hand seemed to ache. Then the pain finally went away, and I removed the bandages to look at my thumb for the first time since Happie had eaten half of it.

It was too short. And there were so many stitches sticking out in all directions that it looked like a miniature hedgehog. So I bound it up again and decided to keep it covered until the stitches came out. But when the stitches were finally out, my thumb still failed to look pretty. So I bandaged it up again.

'You can't wear bandages the rest of your life,' Kobus told me.

'I can,' I told him.

But eventually I got tired of bothering with bandages. So I threw them away and decided to ignore my thumb.

'Your thumb is not so ugly,' Kobus told me.

'It is,' I told him.

'Well, don't worry,' he said. 'I still love you.'

'You have no choice,' I reminded him. 'Your scarred leg isn't too pretty either.'

Karin said: 'Oh heavens, I have such disgusting parents — both of them chomped by lions!'

Her gay laugh always lifted my spirits. I knew she missed Leo very much too. But she kept her sorrow under cover and never allowed it to spill over into her everyday life.

Gareth phoned near the end of July to ask how Leo was doing. It was good to talk to him again. He understands all about the anguish of parting with a lion.

He was on his way to the UK for the promotion of his new book, *The Last of The Free*. I wished him luck and invited him to visit us as soon as he got back to tell us all about it.

He promised he would.

Karin taught me an alternative way of holding a pen, and so I was soon able to write again.

My main problem was typing. It took my brain a surprisingly long time to realise that it could no longer send messages to the missing half of my right thumb. 'Hit the space bar,' it would command my right thumb. And my poor half thumb would respond immediately but miss the space bar and hit the desk instead.

I decided that in future my left thumb should take over the responsibility of striking the space bar.

But it wasn't easy. In fact it was impossible. As soon as my brain sent out the message to my left thumb to hit the space bar, my right thumb would respond instead and hit the desk.

'No, not you!' I'd reprimand my right thumb. And looking hard at my left thumb I'd tell it: 'You! Hit the space bar!'

But my left thumb's response was always the same: 'Who? Me? What space bar?'

Eventually my right index finger got impatient with my left thumb for being so slow and opted to take over the job itself. The result is that my right index finger operates in constant overdrive — darting every which way to strike its own quota of keys as well as the space bar — while my idiotic left thumb just hangs there above the keyboard, doing nothing at all.

It's a pity Happie hadn't eaten my left thumb instead. It would have served it right for being so useless.

Every Sunday, week after week and month after month, I'd make a phone call to Pamuzinda. It didn't help much. Often the connection was so bad that I would have to shout down the line. Occasionally I would be able to hear a voice at the other end — Graeme's or Julie's — and it would tell me that Leo was just fine.

I wanted desperately to know more. What was he doing? How was he looking? I thought once that I heard Julie telling me that Leo had made friends with Sheilah. But I wasn't sure. The connection was so bad. On the few occasions that I got a good connection nobody was home, only the cook, and he didn't really know how Leo was.

I was seldom able to speak to Andy as he didn't have a phone in his house, and he wasn't always within calling distance of Graeme and Julie's house. But on the few occasions that I did manage to talk to him, he assured me that he and Leo were getting along well and that Leo was fine. Those few calls lifted my spirits a bit. But I wished Andy would tell me more. Perhaps there wasn't much more to tell. Or maybe Andy didn't want to tell me on the phone how much Leo still missed us.

Our telephone bills were staggering. And the frustrating nature of the calls wasn't really worth it.

Then one day at the beginning of October, something really good happened. I answered a telephone call and heard Andy's voice at the other end.

'Andy!' I called out in surprise. 'Is that really you? You sound so close!'

'That's because I am,' he replied. 'I'm at Skukuza.'

He explained that Vivian Bristow had sent him to buy elephants from the Kruger Park for Pamuzinda.

'How long will you be staying?' I asked anxiously.

'One night,' he said.

'Please, please come over and spend the night with us!' I begged him.

'That's why I'm calling,' he said. 'To ask if you can put me up.'

I was elated. 'Please hurry up and get here as soon as you can!' I told him.

I called Kobus on the VHF radio and told him that Andy was on his way to spend the night with us. Kobus answered that he'd be home within an hour or so.

Kobus and Andy arrived more or less at the same time.

'How's Leo?' were my first words to Andy. Then I realised I was being ungracious. So I hugged Andy and backtracked: 'Hi, Andy! How are you? I'm so pleased to see you. Please come right inside and tell us all about Leo.' That didn't sound too gracious either, and I felt ashamed of myself.

But Andy grinned and said, 'Leo is fine. If you wish, I'll talk non-stop about him for the rest of the evening.'

I rushed to the kitchen to get our dinner ready, and then — at last — I sat down to listen to news of my lion.

Andy told us everything, leaving nothing out.

Some parts of the story made me very sad. But I appreciated Andy's honesty.

He told us that initially Leo had missed us very much. He'd spent most of his days clutching my pillow to him and listening for the sound of our truck. For about two weeks he wouldn't eat and he lost a lot of weight. Then, gradually, he started eating again and taking an interest in his surroundings. Andy regularly took him for walks and drives all over Pamuzinda, and the two of them had become good friends. Eventually Leo also became playful again. He would steal Andy's cap and run off with it, or stalk Andy and challenge him to a wrestling game. He also made friends with one of the buffaloes who often came to graze near his camp. He would stalk it quietly, creeping right up to the fence of his camp, and then leap up and startle the buffalo. The buffalo would run off for some distance, then turn around and come charging back at full speed. Leo would flee and hide in the tall grass. Then the game would start all over again.

Eventually Leo also made friends with the young lioness Sheilah, and so Sheilah shared his camp with him for a few weeks. Unfortunately Sheilah could not stay with him indefinitely as she had to be returned to her own family at the Lion and Cheetah Park. But Leo didn't seem to miss Sheilah too much. He'd been friends with her — but in a wary sort of way. Sheilah's moods confused him. She would be affectionate and playful the one moment, and short-tempered and snappish the next. And since Leo didn't altogether trust lions yet, it unnerved him when Sheilah got quarrelsome, even though she was younger and much smaller than him.

Meanwhile, the main lion camp had been completed, and old Trade together with Happie and Fat Cat had taken up permanent residence in their new camp. Leo no longer tried to hide in the tall grass when he saw the other lions looking at him. He would merely turn his head and respectfully look the other way. But whenever they weren't looking his way, he enjoyed watching and contemplating them. It was especially old Trade who fascinated him. Trade still marked his territory every day and broadcast his dominion over it. And whenever Trade started roaring, Leo would gape in pure admiration. Leo's instincts were evidently telling him that Trade was the king — as well as his role model. Occasionally Leo would try to imitate Trade's roaring. But his voice wasn't quite up to it yet. It tended to break. And so his attempts at roaring sounded a bit like yodelling.

All in all, Andy concluded, Leo was beginning to settle down. He'd gained weight again, and he was looking well. And the fact that he idolised Trade seemed a sure indication that he was beginning to catch on to the idea that he himself was a lion.

I asked Andy if we could visit Leo in December. Andy said he didn't think we should come so soon. Leo would certainly be overjoyed to see us again, and then the inevitable parting would only be heartbreaking for all of us all over again. Lions have very long memories, Andy reminded us. Leo would never forget us. But it would be best for him, as well as for us, if we postponed our first visit to him until he was happily settled in the main camp with the other lions.

I asked Andy how long it would be before Leo would be allowed to go into the main camp.

Andy said he wasn't sure. Time would tell. As long as Leo remained scared of the other lions, it would not be safe for either him or them to share a camp. If Leo felt threatened, he might react with aggression. And then the other lions would also feel threatened and they might attack him.

'How will you know when he's ready?' I asked.

Andy smiled and said, 'Well, for one thing, when he stops hugging your pillow to him.'

'He still does that?' I asked, surprised.

'Yes,' Andy said. 'He does. It's his security blanket. It reminds him of you.'

I tried to smile, but the lump in my throat got too big. So I said: 'Let me get us some fresh coffee.' I hurried into the kitchen, closed the door behind me and wept into the dish towel.

Then I made us some good strong coffee and carried it into the lounge.

As we sat sipping our coffee, Andy told us to remember that Leo was still a young lion, just entering adulthood, with a long and happy life ahead of him. He added that Leo would always have a lion family of his own, as well as human friends. And he would always be protected, well fed and looked after. All in all, Andy assured us, Leo's life would be easier than that of a wild lion.

Dear, good Andy — he'd brought us a lot of comfort.

After Andy's visit to us I was finally able to break my insomnia.

I asked Kobus if he believed, as Andy did, that Leo's life would eventually be easier than that of a wild lion. Kobus said yes, he did. As much as he'd wished for Leo to be a free lion, he found that he could now take comfort from the knowledge that Leo would never get caught in a poacher's snare, or die from a hunter's bullet; nor would he ever go hungry, or suffer sickness or injuries — the Bristows had a vet who looked after their animals.

In the wild, Kobus told me, the average maximum age of a male lion was about twelve years.

Trade was twenty-four years old.

I like to think that old Trade's story might be an example of what Leo's life will eventually be like.

Trade was the king at the Lion and Cheetah Park for most of his life and he enjoyed the love and admiration of his wives and offspring for many years. When he eventually got too old to fulfil his role as king, Vivian Bristow moved him to Pamuzinda, together with two of his granddaughters (Happie and Fat Cat), so that he might retire there in peace.

I think it's a nice story for a lion.

And I like the idea of Leo becoming king of the Pamuzinda pride one day.

I also like the name 'Pamuzinda'. Translated from the Shona language, it means 'Meeting Place of the Royals'.

Perhaps, in the distant future, people will think the name referred to the meeting of two lion kings: Trade and Leo.

Dominated by a Genet Cat

One day in October, shortly after Andy's visit to us, a team of maintenance workers came to re-thatch the roof of Kobus's office. While removing some of the damaged straw, they discovered that a family of genets had been nesting in the thatch. The genets fled, leaving one of their kittens behind. The workers put the abandoned kitten in a box and left it inside the office, but forgot to tell me or Kobus about it.

Kobus discovered the kitten in his office early the following morning. After the thatchers had explained the story to him, Kobus came looking for me to tell me about the kitten, and to ask me what we should do about it.

The idea of being a foster mother all over again frightened me.

So I thought it over and decided that if the kitten's mother didn't come back for it, I would give it to Annette. She would make a good foster mother. And she would understand that the timing was wrong for me. I still missed Leo too much. And I also needed to be a full-time individual person for a while.

I followed Kobus outside to his office to have a look at the kitten. It was still in the box. Kobus opened the box and I peered inside. The kitten hissed at me. As I reached into the box to pick it up, it lashed out at me with sharp little claws and scratched my arm.

'Oh, you poor baby,' I said. 'You must feel so frightened.'

It fixed me with a bold gaze and tried to look fierce, but the defiant glare failed to hide the look of sheer misery on its little face.

I carried it back to the house. After filling a medicine dropper with a solution of glucose and milk, I wrapped the kitten in a warm shawl and tried to persuade it to take the milk from the dropper. Fortunately it didn't take the hungry kitten too long to get the hang of it, and soon it was gulping the milk as fast as it could. Afterwards I held it in my lap and stroked its fur for a long time, willing it to relax.

Eventually it fell asleep in my lap.

Kobus judged the kitten to be about six weeks old — old enough to realise that it had lost its real mother and to miss her very much.

Poor little thing.

And so I became a genet-mother.

That's how these things always happen to me.

I did try, however, to give the kitten back to its real parents.

I spent several nights listening to every sound in the garden, hoping that I'd hear the parents calling to their lost kitten. But no genet called. Perhaps the parents couldn't count too well and didn't realise that one of their children was missing.

One morning, a few days after we'd adopted the kitten, Wolfie knocked at the front door, asking to meet the new member of the family. So I invited him inside for a visit.

The kitten was asleep on my bed, and Wolfie approached it carefully, stuck out his nose and sniffed gently at it. The kitten woke up and promptly gave Wolfie a furious slap on the nose. Wolfie spun around and, facing me, let out a bark of surprise. The bark was not really aimed at me, of course, nor was it intended for the kitten — it was a purely involuntary bark. Wolfie is such a kind-hearted, tolerant soul. He would never dream of barking at a defenceless kitten.

When Karin arrived home on the Friday, she was delighted to find that our family had once again acquired a new member, and spent most of the weekend cuddling the kitten — spoiling him beyond redemption.

On Monday morning Karin went back to school, and I was left alone with a kitten that demanded constant cuddling. As soon as he woke up and found himself alone in a room, he would call to me with a plaintive, high-pitched voice. The soul-stirring quality of the call never failed to send me rushing to him. The kitten soon learned that the more plaintive his call sounded, the faster I would come running.

And so the kitten became my boss.

It wasn't altogether my fault. I was still feeling guilty about abandoning Leo, and the clever kitten sensed my vulnerability and took advantage of it.

After a week or so the kitten became playful, which was nice but also exhausting since he refused to play alone. I provided him with all kinds of toys to keep him occupied — a ball of string, an old rag doll, an empty tin, a rubber ball, and so on. But the kitten had better ideas. Possessed of a wild imagination, he preferred games of the make-believe kind.

One of his favourite games was to pretend that he was a man-eating tiger. He ambushed and stalked me endlessly, lying quietly in wait on the top of a bookcase or a curtain rail, a door or a cupboard until I came within pouncing distance. I acquired the habit of checking out all possible hiding places and dashing through rooms at top speed. But the tiger would launch himself at me from nowhere — often landing right on top of my head.

Another of his favourite games was to pretend that he was a mad ape. The furniture and I were all part of his jungle. So he dashed crazily all over the jungle, swinging from the curtains and leaping like lightning from bookcase to couch to table — to me. If I tried to get out of his way, he'd give chase, catch up with me and run straight up me as if I were a tree.

I was grateful that the kitten still spent a good number of hours sleeping during the day, or I might have gone crazy. Unfortunately he didn't sleep a lot at night, and he didn't want me to sleep a lot at night either. If I refused to wake up, he would lick my eyelashes or chew my hair. And if that didn't persuade me to wake up and play, he would get under the bed covers and bite my toes.

I began to count the days to the weekends when Karin would be home again to share with me the exhausting responsibility of being a genet-mother.

Not one of my previous foster children had been quite as demanding. I once raised a serval kitten, and she was the sweetest thing — so playful and affectionate — and even though she possessed some of the arrogant attitudes typical of cats, she was never as domineering as the genet kitten.

Even so, I liked the brat — especially when he curled up in my lap, licked my arms with his rough little tongue and purred with contentment.

I was surprised that he could purr. I thought that only members of the feline family purred. Genets belong to the Viverridae family. Other members of this family are the civets and mongooses. Mongooses don't purr, and I don't think civets do either.

A genet looks like a cross between a domestic cat and a mongoose. Its movements are graceful and cat-like, but it has the elongated body and shorter legs of the mongoose. It has a long tail carried straight out when on the move. The short, soft and dense coat is a light brownish-grey on the upper parts, buffy-white on the lower parts, and heavily spotted all over. Being both terrestrial and arboreal, the genet can run up a tree faster and better than most members of the cat family.

My genet kitten ran straight up bookcases and wooden doors, as well as straight up me, of course. I spent most of my days as a genet-mother covered in claw marks.

When in a calmer mood, the genet loved to ride on my shoulder. Wherever I moved inside the house, he would ride along, observing my activities. If I bent down to pick something up, he would dig his claws into my shoulder and hang on. There was no way that I could get him off my shoulder if he didn't want to get off. He especially enjoyed perching on my shoulder to watch me wash my hair. Apparently the foaming shampoo fascinated him. On a few occasions he got carried away with fascination, lost his grip and fell into the washbasin.

Although my genet kitten felt very much at home in the house, he remained frightened of the outdoors for several months. So as soon as he was old enough to start eating solids, I had to go out hunting every day to find his food for him. His favourite fare was grasshoppers, crickets, beetles and the like.

I'm not a hunter at heart. In fact, I find hunting most distressing. But that's motherhood for you.

I carried a shoe box on my hunting expeditions and put everything that I managed to catch inside. Then I brought the box back into the house, removed the lid and allowed everything to escape — giving all a fair chance. If the genet caught and ate them, then at least I didn't need to feel too directly responsible for their fate. It was also a good way of teaching him to hunt for himself.

I also knew that he would soon require larger prey such as frogs, lizards and other reptile fauna, and I had no intention of catching those for him. So when he was about three months old, I insisted that he start hunting for his own food in the garden. He still refused to leave the house in the daytime, but I eventually managed to persuade him to accompany me out of doors at night. In the beginning he was very nervous and would run straight up me at the slightest noise or movement in our surroundings. But as time went by, he became braver and learned to enjoy our nightly expeditions.

I am embarrassed to admit this, but I forgot to give the kitten a name. He didn't really need a name as I never needed to call him. He came to me at all times without being called.

The first time I realised he needed a name was during one of our nightly hunting expeditions. He got very enthusiastic about chasing a lizard or something and he disappeared into the dark. After a while I became worried about him and wanted to call him to find out where he was — I was scared that an owl might catch him. It was then that I realised that he didn't have a name. So I resorted to calling him the way one would call to an Afrikaans-speaking domestic cat: *Kietsie* (pronounced Kitsy).

Luckily the kitten responded to my tone of voice and soon came running back to me. And from that time on he was stuck with the rather silly name of 'Kietsie'.

The children came home for the Christmas holidays, and Paul and Sandra brought us a beautiful border collie pup named Jasper.

He was intended as a friend for Wolfie. Wolfie pretended that he wasn't particularly interested in the newcomer, but he didn't fool me. Often, when he didn't know I was watching through a window, I would see him playing madly with the pup, allowing it to chase him round and round a tree, or to pounce on him and bully him while he lay on his back, paws in the air, with an idiotic grin of happiness on his face.

I had never seen Wolfie behave so foolishly in his entire life, so I didn't really blame him for playing with the pup only when he thought no one was looking. In company, Wolfie was his usual composed self — he would tolerate the pup's antics, allowing it to pester him and even chew his tail, but tolerate was all he did. Playing silly games with a pup was, of course, beneath him.

In the beginning we allowed Jasper to sleep in the house. He was just a three-month-old pup, and although he enjoyed playing outside with Wolfie and the children during the day, he wanted to be near his mommy at night. And he thought I was his mommy. (All animals think I'm their mommy.)

So he slept under our bed. The genet didn't like that at all. The house belonged to him — and so did I.

At first the genet was a little scared of the dog, so it did nothing much except threaten Jasper from the safety of a bookcase or a cupboard, and then sulk the rest of the night to let me know how offended he was at having to share his domain with a dog.

Jasper got very excited the first time he saw the cat and he wanted very much to sort him out. So I had to have a serious talk to Jasper and explain to him that the house did in fact belong to the genet, and that dogs weren't allowed to bark at a genet in its own house.

Being an intelligent dog, Jasper understood and accepted the situation.

But on Jasper's fourth night with us, Kietsie decided he'd had enough, and he attacked the pup under the bed in the middle of the night. Jasper, however, wasn't having any. He barked Kietsie right out of the room and chased him all over the house.

A little while later Jasper returned, got back under the bed and flopped down to continue his peaceful dreams. But before long, the angry genet returned and attempted to rough up the dog again. So I had to get out of bed and give them both a serious lecture.

This went on for several nights until Kobus got really mad and warned me that if the nightly riots didn't stop, then either I and my brood would have to sleep outside, or he would.

So the following evening I made a bed for Jasper in the garden shed where Wolfie sleeps, explaining to him that the only reason I was changing the sleeping arrangements was because the warfare between him and the genet wasn't too good for my marriage.

The older the genet got, the more possessive he became of me, and the more jealous he was of anything that occupied my thoughts outside of himself.

From the age of four months on, his daily routine started with attacking me in my bed at the dreadful hour of about five in the morning to tell me he needed attention. I'd throw him out of the room and shut the door. But he'd scream and scratch at the door until I could sleep no longer. As soon as I was up and about, he'd either ride along on my shoulder or start playing ambush games with me — depending on the mood he was in. He possessed an amazing variety of moods: he could be riotous, bossy, arrogant, aloof, cute, frolicsome or affectionate.

At about ten in the morning, he'd eat his breakfast of minced meat mixed with egg and calcium powder. Afterwards he visited his sandbox and then went off to find himself a place to sleep — usually in a wardrobe — and I'd be very grateful to know that I would have the rest of the day free until about four in the afternoon.

As soon as he woke up he would come looking for me to tell me he was ready for fun and games again. If I was busy he would try his best to drive me crazy. The madder I got with him, the more he enjoyed the game. He'd leap on to my head, slide down my hair, disappear like lightning if I tried to smack him, and be back again in a flash for more fun.

At dinner time he enjoyed pestering the rest of the family as well — if they were home. But he was never as bold and cheeky with Kobus and Karin or any of the other children as he was with me.

After dinner it would be hunting time. Depending on how long it took us to find enough prey in the dark garden to fill his stomach, a hunting session could last from half an hour to two hours. After that, he'd be calmer and would content himself with resting in my lap while I read or listened to music.

I was pleased when, at the age of about six months, he started spending time outdoors on his own at night. I always left a window open for him on the veranda, and whenever he came in — sometimes at midnight, sometimes in the early morning hours — he'd rush straight to me and wake me up to tell me all about his nocturnal adventures.

As he got older and bolder, he started out on his nightly expeditions much earlier in the evening — and entirely on his own.

I was very proud of him.

Late one night, when Kietsie was almost nine months old, I heard distress calls in the garden. I rushed outside with my torch. Following the sound of the screaming, I aimed the beam of my torch into a wisteria tree and spotted Kietsie high up in the branches — with another genet. The strange genet fled as soon as it saw me, and so I believed that I'd saved Kietsie from a territorial fight with another male genet. I called to him to come down to me, but he gave me a disdainful look and proceeded to lick his paws in the complacent way of cats.

'OK,' I told him. 'You fight your own battles then!'

I went back to bed. But before long, I heard genet cats screaming again.

Rushing outside with my torch, I found the two of them in the top of the wisteria tree again. They didn't really seem to be fighting. My presence unnerved the other genet, and it fled once more.

'What was all that screaming about?' I asked Kietsie. He refused to answer me.

The answer came to me the next evening when the screaming started again.

A territorial fight it was not. It was a courting serenade. The other genet was a female.

When Kietsie came in at about eleven that evening, I was still reading. He jumped on to my lap, stretched himself out and started washing himself all over, purring contentedly.

'So you've found yourself a girlfriend?' I said. 'Aren't you a bit young for that?'

I had no idea at what age genets start dating. I checked my book on small mammals, but found no answer.

Anyhow, the courting continued over a period of several days, and some nights my genet didn't come in at all.

Eventually he got married and stayed out for four days. After the honeymoon he came back, bringing his wife along with him, evidently intent on persuading her to move into his house with him.

He jumped on to the sill of the open veranda window and called to her. She climbed up the wisteria tree and refused to come any closer to the house.

So Kietsie sat at the open window, calling: 'Please, please come and see my house — you'll love it! There's always extra food available — as well as free rides on shoulders!'

But his wife answered from the wisteria tree with a plaintive, wailing voice, telling him that if he didn't stop being idiotic she would file for divorce.

Kietsie tried night after night to persuade his wife to move into his house, but to no avail. Eventually it dawned on him that he would have to choose between his wife and his mother's house.

The wife won. And so he moved into her house — a comfortable den hidden amongst the large and densely packed fronds of a palm tree in the far corner of the garden. And he also started sharing her hunting territory. It comprised our whole garden as well as the gardens of the two trail rangers across the road.

Although there are times when I miss the domineering brat, I am very pleased to know that he is happily married.

And when I hear him and his wife singing to each other in our garden at night, I often think back to that first night in our new home when I'd been welcomed by a genet serenade. Those genets must have been Kietsie's parents.

Little had I known then that I would one day be obliged to raise one of their kids for them.

Something in the Air

In the same month that Kietsie got married — which was May — we heard the exciting news that Leo had also got married.

I had tried to make a phone call to Graeme and Julie's house at Pamuzinda one Sunday morning, but the lines were out of order. So I decided to call Vivian and Carol's home at the Lion and Cheetah Park. I hadn't had any news of Leo for more than a month, and I longed desperately to know how he was.

Carol Bristow answered my call, and fortunately we got a very clear line, so we didn't need to shout at each other. She informed me that Leo had been moved into the main camp in April, and that he was now living happily with the other lions. He was still a little wary of Fat Cat, but very much in love with Happie.

When I put the receiver down, it occurred to me that I was the happiest person in the whole world.

May seemed to be the month for romance, because it was also the month that Hettie got engaged.

When she phoned me one Friday morning to tell me she was bringing a friend home, I knew there was something in the air.

When the two of them arrived, their radiant faces said it all.

His name, we learned, was Kobus. Very unoriginal. But we liked the man, so we forgave him.

He is a young widower and a financial consultant for an investment firm. Gracious, wise and warm-hearted, he seemed an ideal companion for Hettie.

So when they asked our permission to get married, we gave them our blessing.

All in all, May was an exciting month, and life seemed pretty good — except that Leo was constantly on my mind and I longed desperately to see him again.

Kobus was working very hard and was seldom home. But every time I saw him, I asked him: 'When can we go and visit Leo?'

His answer was always the same: 'Soon now. As soon as I've finished this job.'

There appeared to be no end to the number of urgent jobs scheduled for him in May. And I knew that June would be even worse — he would be responsible for the annual culling programme.

Gareth also came to visit in May, and it was good to see him again. He arrived carrying his tiny battered suitcase in one hand, and — as usual — a stack of books under the other arm. Gareth possesses a very interesting variety of strange and wonderful books, and whenever he comes to visit he brings us a selection of his favourite ones to read.

As usual, we enjoyed every moment of his visit, listening to his interesting stories and attempting to answer his many questions about our views on a variety of subjects.

Being an Animal Rights person, Gareth is strongly opposed to culling, of course. So on this visit he asked us many questions about the Park's culling policy. Both Kobus and I have a lot of sympathy with the Animal Rights people, and so we wish as desperately as they do that another solution can be found to the problem of overstocked pastures.

The truth, of course, is that the earth is overstocked with humans and not with animals. We allocate our wild animals some of the tiny patches of paradise that still exist on the planet, proclaiming them conservation areas, and then we expect the animals not to multiply and outgrow their allotted space.

Even though the Kruger Park is one of the largest conservation areas in the world (it is the size of Wales), it cannot support the needs of ever-growing populations of grazers who have no natural enemies — such as the elephant. If it were possible to shift the boundaries of the Park whenever its pastures become overstocked and depleted, then culling would never be necessary.

Kobus explained the Park's culling policy to Gareth as best he could, and we talked late into the night, sharing our hopes that the future may some day bring an alternative solution.

Perhaps, one day, if sub-Saharan Africa becomes politically and economically stable, then more space and protected status might be given to our wild animals.

All through June Kobus managed culling operations and relocation programmes, taking every possible measure to minimise the trauma for the animals concerned. But the tension and the heartache of the work showed on his face all the time.

Then one day at the beginning of July, it was all over. Kobus looked at his calendar and said: 'I can take a week's leave — from the 17th of July. You can start making arrangements for us to visit Leo.'

I was so excited that I could think of nothing else in the days that followed.

Karin would be home for her winter vacation and so she would be able to accompany us. I was very pleased about that. Of all my children, she had been the closest to Leo.

I made reservations for the three of us at the Pamuzinda Safari Lodge. We didn't want to impose on the Bristows' hospitality again, and apart from that, I looked forward to spending some time alone with my family. Kobus and I had spent very little time together during the previous months, and so our visit to Leo would also be a much-needed vacation for both of us.

I wished that our other children were able to come along as well, especially Paul and Sandra who had never been to

Pamuzinda. But their classes started again on the 9th of July. We promised them, however, that we would schedule our next visit to Leo for a time that would suit them.

I had a long talk to Wolfie, explaining to him that we were going to visit Leo. I told him that I didn't think it would be wise for him to come along as Leo now had two wives — and perhaps the wives would not take kindly to a dog. I especially didn't trust Happie. I also told him that I needed someone to take care of Jasper in our absence, and I thought he was best suited for the job.

I have no doubt that Wolfie has an above-average IQ for a dog. So that day, when I explained to him about our visit to Leo, I knew that he understood at least some parts of the conversation. Afterwards he looked at me with an expression that seemed to say: 'OK, you go ahead and visit the brat. I don't think I'll come along. I have other responsibilities.'

One of Kobus's field staff, a man named Andries, gets along well with both Wolfie and Jasper. So we arranged with him to look after the dogs and to feed them in our absence.

Apart from feeling guilty about leaving my dogs at home, I looked forward to our Zimbabwe trip more than anything else in the world.

I was finally going to see my lion again.

And perhaps if I returned home with some happy memories, they would lay to rest the one incredibly sad memory that was still haunting me — the memory of that last morning with Leo when I had given him my pillow.

A Visit to the King

Dawn was just a hint of mauve in the eastern sky when we left home on the 17th of July. The sun rose over the acacia bushlands near Skukuza, revealing a bright and beautiful winter's day.

We travelled at a leisurely pace, stopping to admire animals and scenery along the way and enjoying our eight-hour journey through the Park as much as any tourist would. Or perhaps even more.

We arrived at Punda Maria — the northernmost camp in the Park — in the late afternoon, and spent the night there.

Leaving at dawn the following morning, we saw the sun rise over the Luvuvhu river, and about an hour later we left the Park through the Pafuri Gate, travelling west towards the Beit Bridge border post.

From there we tackled the 600-kilometre journey north to Harare. It was nice to be able to enjoy the vast and quiet bushland landscapes of southern Zimbabwe without feeling weighed down by the sadness that had accompanied us on our journey to and from Pamuzinda the previous year.

We reached Harare in the late afternoon and turned west towards Pamuzinda, arriving at its entrance gate shortly after dark.

The gate guard informed us that Graeme Bristow was expecting us and that we were to drive to his house before going on to the Safari Lodge.

We duly followed these instructions — and were surprised to find a whole welcoming party awaiting us. Graeme, Julie and Andy were there, as well as the senior Bristows — Vivian and Carol had driven all the way from their home at the Lion and

Cheetah Park to see us. (Only Maria was absent. She was visiting her parents in South Africa.) Another member of the welcoming party was a young girl named Fiona Nelson. Half Scottish, half English, and with a degree in Zoology, she had worked for Iain Douglas-Hamilton at Naivasha in Kenya before coming to work for the Bristows.

Although Karin, at the age of seventeen, was a number of years younger than Fiona, the two of them struck up an immediate friendship and spent the evening sharing their views on life — which, judging from their gay laughter, appeared to be of an upbeat nature.

We thoroughly enjoyed the evening and the company.

First we talked about Leo, of course. And Andy gave us the following account of Leo's introduction into the main camp.

On D-Day, Andy moved old Trade out of the main camp to Leo's former camp, and he also locked up the two lionesses in an enclosure in one corner of the main camp. Then he fetched Leo, who had been waiting on the back of his pick-up, and persuaded him to accompany him into the now lion-deserted camp. Leo bravely set foot in the alien territory, looked around for a while and, after some encouragement from Andy, started exploring the place.

Sniffing at the bushes that Trade had marked, Leo set about re-marking them in his own name. And for the better part of the day, Leo and Andy patrolled the camp while Leo checked and marked the boundaries of his new domain. In the late afternoon, when Leo was finally satisfied that the land had been adequately transferred into his own name, he sat down in a patch of tall grass not far from the lioness enclosure. And so he spent the last hours of the day contemplating his new kingdom, while stealing occasional glances at the two females behind the wire.

On the following day Andy opened the gate of the enclosure, letting Happie into the main camp with Leo. She bounded over to Leo in a playful way. Leo fell flat in the grass and tried to make himself invisible. But Happie capered right up to him and begged him with umf-umf noises to come and make her acquaintance. Leo insisted on pretending that he wasn't there, so Happie pressed her head close to his and set about sweet-talking him out of his invisible act. Eventually Leo got a bit braver and lifted his head. Happie uttered a groan of happiness and promptly rubbed heads with him. Leo had never before in his life rubbed heads with a real grown-up lioness, and for a moment it felt rather scary. But then it started to feel awfully right. So he got to his feet and they rubbed heads some more. Next they rubbed shoulders. Then heads again and, as Happie kissed him right on the cheek, it occurred to Leo that Happie was the cutest lioness this side of heaven.

Soon he was bounding after her, and the two of them started courting each other in all manner of ways.

Later, when the sun got hot, they flopped down in a shady spot under some trees, and spent the next few hours gazing fondly at each other.

Andy was pleased at the outcome of things between Leo and Happie, and so he went home.

The following morning he found them rubbing heads and grunting sweet nothings to each other.

A few days later, Andy locked Happie up in the enclosure and let Fat Cat out. Fat Cat approached Leo with an arrogant air. Andy saw trouble coming, so he hurried over to Leo's side. Leo also saw trouble coming and decided to get out of Fat Cat's way. But he wasn't quick enough. Fat Cat caught up with him and started slapping him around. Andy shouted at Fat Cat to stop, but she wouldn't. So Andy turned the volume of his voice right up and, while screaming and shouting at Fat Cat, he started whacking her with a stick until she finally stopped roughing Leo up. Andy chased her off, threatening her with murder if she didn't behave. (In case you are thinking that Andy is a really tough and macho-type person, you're wrong. He's tall and lean, gentle-mannered and soft-spoken — hardly your average lion-bashing type.)

After having chased Fat Cat a good hundred metres or so away, Andy returned to Leo and found him extremely upset and offended. So Andy sat down with Leo for a heart-to-heart talk.

Eventually Leo started feeling a bit better, and he and Andy went for a walk around the camp. Fat Cat was resting under some trees, minding her own business. Or so it seemed. As soon as Andy and Leo entered her field of vision, she let out an angry roar and went for Leo again. Leo tried to take evasive action, but Fat Cat caught up with him and, as Leo turned to beg for mercy, Fat Cat gave him another vicious slap on the nose. Without waiting for any encouragement from Andy, Leo decided he'd had enough of the fat arrogant cat, and so he slapped her right back. That seemed to put Fat Cat in her place and she immediately became more respectful.

A little while later the two lions were each resting in a shady spot, at a sensible distance from each other.

The stalemate continued for the rest of the afternoon. But by the end of the day, Andy felt that Leo would be able to hold his own against Fat Cat. So he decided to leave them to it and go home. At that stage Leo was sitting beside the fence of the enclosure, talking to Happie, no doubt telling her all about his dreadful day with Fat Cat.

On the following day Andy found Leo and Fat Cat still ignoring each other. Leo spent most of his time either patrolling his new kingdom or visiting Happie. The two of them would lie down on either side of the fence, rubbing heads through the wire, evidently discussing all kinds of things.

A few days later, when Andy felt confident that Fat Cat no longer had murder on her mind, he opened the gate of the enclosure to let Happie out. Leo and Happie were thoroughly delighted at being properly reunited again.

For another week or so, Fat Cat kept her distance. Then she started making friendly overtures to Leo, adding a good measure of female coquetry. So Leo decided to let bygones be bygones. He forgave Fat Cat and they kissed and made up.

Although Happie was evidently Leo's favourite wife, Leo was on good terms with Fat Cat now and he even appeared to have become quite fond of her.

I asked Andy if there were any signs of jealousy between the two lionesses. Andy said no, none at all. They were like sisters.

They'd more or less grown up together and they'd also raised their first litters of cubs together. So the bond between them was very strong.

Old Trade was still in good health, Andy told us. But he was very old now. In fact, at the age of twenty-five years, he was probably the oldest lion in Africa. So it had seemed a good idea to move him into his own private camp and allow him the peace and quiet that an old lion needs. He now spent most of his days eating, sleeping and enjoying regular visits from Graeme and Andy, as well as from the senior Bristows who liked to drop in for a chat with old Trade whenever they were in the area.

While we were talking about the lions, two yellowish blurs suddenly dashed through the lounge − in through one door and out the other.

'What was that?' Kobus and I exclaimed simultaneously.

The next moment they were back − another fast dash through the lounge − and we realised they were two cheetah cubs playing a game of tag. They appeared to be about six weeks old.

Meanwhile, Julie Bristow sat on the carpet in a corner of the room, surrounded by her two young children as well as three dogs and two sleepy hyena cubs.

Fascinating.

Karin couldn't keep her eyes off the hyena cubs, so Julie invited her to come over the following day to play with them.

Fiona mentioned that she was raising three orphaned cheetah cubs, and invited Karin to come over to her place the following day and meet them as well.

After a most enjoyable evening, we said our goodbyes and drove to the Pamuzinda Safari Lodge.

The agenda for the following morning was that Andy would meet us at the lodge directly after breakfast and escort us to the lion camp.

On our arrival at the lodge we were welcomed by the manager Hans Strijdom and other members of staff. They escorted us to our chalets, carrying our luggage for us and enquiring if there was anything that we needed. We were rather surprised at the royal welcome. We were also surprised by the five-star luxury of our accommodation. Both the architectural design and décor of the chalets portrayed ethnic royal culture, and the emphasis was on 'royal' comfort.

We hadn't expected such luxury and service, and it occurred to us that our visit was probably going to cost us a fortune. So we worried a little. Well, a lot actually. (Game rangers get paid mostly in sunsets.)

It was a cold night, but our chalets were nice and warm with oil heaters and there were hot water bottles in our beds.

Karin's chalet was right next to ours, and after I'd been to say good-night to her, I returned to find that Kobus was already in bed and half asleep.

'Come and get some sleep,' he murmured. 'Tomorrow is going to be a special day.'

I agreed that sleep was a good idea.

But I found that I was unable to fall asleep.

After a while I got up again, put on some warm clothes and walked out on to the wooden balcony. There were two deck chairs there so I made myself comfortable and spent the following hour or so gazing at the stars and the moon and the silhouettes of the trees that lined the banks of the Serui river below us.

When I finally became drowsy and was about to go to bed, something happened that was so unexpectedly dramatic — so overwhelming in its emotional impact — that it seemed to me the whole world would stop and take note.

A lion started roaring, his magnificent voice rolling out over the dark landscape, silencing all other night sounds.

I knew it was Leo.

I listened and listened, mesmerised by the powerful, triumphant voice that soared out into the starry night: the voice of my foundling prince — now king — proclaiming his sovereignty over that strange land.

It was a moment of magic.

He continued roaring solo for several minutes, and then another lion joined in. His voice was huskier. It was old Trade.

When the last echoes of the roaring duet finally died, I thought that sleep would probably never come to me that night.

But eventually it did, and I slept very soundly for a few hours.

At dawn someone knocked at the door, bringing us a pot of steaming, aromatic coffee, and informing us that breakfast would be served at seven.

Breakfast was an elaborate affair, served on a beautiful patio in front of the lodge and overlooking the Serui river pan. Egyptian geese called out from the banks of the river while a variety of other birds sang in the trees. A herd of graceful eland grazed on the far bank.

We met our fellow tourists at breakfast, and learned that they were from all over the world: one family was from the Netherlands, another from Australia, another from Canada and yet another from the north of Zimbabwe.

Andy arrived with Fiona while our coffee was being served, and after joining us for a quick cup of coffee, we all set out for the lion camp in a custom-built safari Land Rover.

A few minutes later we stopped at the gate of the camp. Andy opened it and we drove in.

The lions were nowhere to be seen. So we drove about the camp searching for them while Andy called out to Leo. After a while we spotted Fat Cat. She was lying in the long grass under a shady tree. As she lifted her head to peer at us over the grass, I was shocked at her size — she was enormous! Or had I simply forgotten how big lions really are?

Kobus and Andy called out to Leo again, and then suddenly Karin exclaimed: 'There he is!'

He appeared from between the trees on our right and came running towards us. My heart caught in my throat — he was so BIG, bigger even than Fat Cat, but his eyes and features were the same, and so very familiar. We all called his name, and he stopped in his tracks to stare at us, an expression of extreme puzzlement in his eyes. He recognised Andy, but he was unable to comprehend who the rest of us were.

Kobus got out of the Land Rover and walked towards Leo, softly calling his name.

Leo turned his puzzled gaze towards Kobus. And then, all of a sudden, as if struck by an immense revelation, his eyes came alive with a surge of recognition, of overwhelming surprise, and of joy. Uttering a deep, shuddering groan, Leo rushed forward, throwing himself at Kobus while at the same time turning his body sideways to lessen the force of the impact. Kobus bent forward and, with both arms, hugged Leo's enormous head to him. They rubbed cheeks, heads and shoulders — over and over — talking non-stop to each other all the time.

I was shaking like a leaf.

The moment was too big for me. The moment was probably too big for Leo as well, for he was so overcome with joy at seeing Kobus again that he didn't even see Karin and me.

So we got out of the Land Rover and walked towards him, calling his name. Leo lifted his head to look at me, and there was that same surge of recognition, of surprise and joy in his eyes all over again. As he rushed towards me, I was struck once more by his size — the top of his head would be on a level with my chin — and for a moment I feared that I would not be able to remain on my feet if he threw himself against me. So I held my hands out in front of me and said, 'No, Leo!'

He stopped close to me, looking me in the eyes, his face crumpled up with emotion, asking me for a clue as to how he should greet me. I held out my arm and he clasped it between his jaws — a gentle, loving embrace. Then I threw my arms around his neck and hugged his enormous face to mine, and we rubbed cheeks, and heads and shoulders, my tears spilling on to his fur. Then I stepped back so that he could see Karin.

She stepped forward, saying his name, and once again he uttered that deep, shuddering groan of surprise and joy. She reached out to touch him and he clasped her outstretched arm briefly between his jaws as he'd done with mine. Then Karin hugged him to her and they rubbed heads and shoulders and talked and talked.

Afterwards Leo turned around to see where Kobus was, but as he rushed towards Kobus for another greeting, something strange and frightening happened. Leo suddenly stopped in his tracks, spun around and charged at the Land Rover. Both Fiona and Andy were sitting in it. Throwing the upper part of his body into the vehicle, Leo snarled at Andy and Fiona in a threatening way. Andy was totally taken by surprise. Leo had never behaved even remotely aggressively towards him — why was he so angry with him now? Andy tried to talk to Leo about it, asking him: 'Hey Leo, what's the matter? What have I done wrong?'

Leo only got angrier and his snarls became more threatening.

Andy shouted at Leo to stop, and Kobus called loudly to Leo in order to get him away from the truck. Fortunately Leo turned and rushed back to Kobus for another fond greeting.

At that moment, Fat Cat — who was still lying in the grass under a shady tree less than ten metres from us — started calling to Leo.

It occurred to me that she might be jealous of Karin and me. Hand-reared lions, as well as lions who live in close association with people, do not always draw a clear distinction in their minds between humans and lions, and so they tend to become jealous of human members of the same sex who pay attention to their spouses.

Andy suggested that Karin and I get back into the Land Rover — just in case Fat Cat wasn't too happy with us.

Leo ignored Fat Cat's calls and continued to rub heads with Kobus, grunting and groaning with happiness.

Then, suddenly, Leo spun around and charged the Land Rover again, roaring with anger.

And at that moment I realised what the reason for his behaviour was. He wanted the Land Rover and Andy and Fiona out of his camp; he wanted to be left alone with his family from the past.

As he threw his body into the vehicle once more, snarling with fury, Andy reached for his rifle. It was a very frightening moment. Fiona clambered to the back of the Land Rover to be out of Leo's reach. Andy shouted at Leo, cocking his rifle in case he might need to fire a shot into the air. Karin and I were also in the Land Rover now, between Leo and the other two, and as Leo continued to snarl and growl at us, his jaws wide open and his face crumpled with confused emotions, I realised that not only was he commanding Andy and Fiona to leave, he was also begging Karin and me to get out of the Land Rover and stay with him and Kobus.

Poor Leo. He was so scared that Andy and the Land Rover would take us all away from him again.

Kobus finally managed to get Leo away from the Land Rover and to keep him occupied long enough for the rest of us to have a quick conference on the situation. It was obvious that, if Andy and Fiona didn't leave, Leo would continue to threaten them.

Karin suggested that she and I get out again and stay with Kobus and Leo, allowing Andy and Fiona to leave. But Andy wasn't happy with this. He was responsible for our safety and couldn't leave us in the camp without protection — there was no telling what Happie and Fat Cat might do.

It seemed that the only solution would be for all of us to leave, and then continue our visit with Leo from behind the safety of the fence. The idea broke my heart, but I didn't want things to go wrong. Leo was obviously overwhelmed and he needed to calm down a bit.

So, after Leo had charged the Land Rover a third time, it was agreed that it was time for us to leave.

Andy started the Land Rover and drove slowly towards Kobus and Leo, allowing Kobus to get on to the moving vehicle before Leo could decide to do the same. As we drove back towards the gate, Leo ran alongside us, begging us not to leave him. Kobus tried, with a reassuring tone of voice, to explain that we weren't leaving.

Meanwhile Graeme and Julie had arrived to witness our reunion with Leo, and their truck was parked at the gate. When they saw us approaching, they hurriedly opened the gate, closing it again behind us. Andy parked outside the gate. Kobus, Karin and I got out and hurried over to Leo who was standing at the fence, calling to us.

We took turns rubbing heads and shoulders with him through the wire, over and over, and we stuck our arms through the fence to touch his face and stroke his head. And all the while he uttered an endless stream of grunts and groans, as if he were trying to tell us a thousand things. Occasionally Fat Cat would call out to him. But Leo ignored her. He wanted only to be with us.

After a while we began to feel emotionally exhausted − the way one feels when joy and sorrow get all mixed up and out of control. We needed a break from it all. And so did Leo, I thought.

So we said goodbye, and Andy drove us back to the lodge.

After lunch, Kobus decided to go back to Leo. He wanted to visit him in his camp again, and Andy offered to escort him. Kobus suggested that they go in our car rather than in the open Land Rover. Perhaps Leo would object less to Andy's presence if he waited in a closed car.

I decided to stay at the lodge. I needed to be alone for a while in order to decipher my mixed-up feelings. I didn't know if I was sad or happy, or what. I needed some solitude and time to think. I don't think well in company.

Fiona invited Karin to go home with her to meet the three cheetah cubs she was raising. Karin was very excited at the prospect, and I was pleased that Fiona had asked her.

After everyone had left, I retired to the balcony of my chalet. The quiet beauty of the Serui river landscape put me in a calmer mood, and then I set about sorting out my discordant feelings.

First, I played a re-run of the morning's rendezvous in my mind and I tried to tell myself that it had been a very happy occasion.

But a huge lump settled in my throat.

Why did it make me sad that Leo had been so overwhelmed with joy at seeing us again?

Naturally I had hoped that he would be happy to see us. But the intensity of his joy had somehow caught me unprepared.

I thought about it.

And a phrase came to mind: 'Your joy is your sorrow unmasked' — the words of the Lebanese poet Kahlil Gibran.

The idea only deepened my sadness.

But then I remembered the very first expression in Leo's eyes when he'd recognised us. It had been an expression of surprise. And it occurred to me that, for Leo, the surprise factor must have been pretty overwhelming in itself. He hadn't seen us for a whole year. And he'd had no way of knowing that we were coming. We had simply appeared from nowhere — unexpected, unannounced.

So perhaps it was his surprise at seeing us again that had been so extreme, and not his joy.

I hoped that was the case.

But I wasn't sure.

Kobus returned an hour or so later and told me that the visit had gone well. At first Leo had once again overreacted at the sight of him, but after a while he had calmed down. Andy had remained inside the car, and although Leo had initially tried to chew the car up a bit, he'd finally lost interest in it and decided to sit down and enjoy Kobus's visit.

Kobus suggested that Karin and I go back to visit Leo on our own. He believed that Leo would be better able to cope with his emotions if we didn't all visit him at the same time.

So we drove to Fiona's house to fetch Karin. But there was nobody home. We drove over to Julie and Graeme's house. There was nobody there either. So Kobus and I spent a while playing with the hyena cubs. They were the cutest, craziest young animals I'd ever met.

Eventually we returned to Fiona's house and found that she and Karin had just come back from a visit to Leo. Karin explained that, after she and Fiona had bathed and fed the cheetah cubs, she had wanted to go to Leo. So they had walked to the lion camp. Fiona had waited at a distance while Karin went up to the fence and called Leo. He had come to her immediately, and the two of them spent a wonderful hour together.

Kobus and Karin drove with me to Leo's camp, and Kobus parked some distance away to allow me to visit Leo on my own. I walked up to the fence, calling his name. He didn't come. I walked some distance along the wire, but couldn't find him. He was obviously in another part of the camp. So I went back to the car and we drove halfway around the camp. I got out and walked up to the fence again. Still I saw no sign of him. So I walked along the fence for a while until I eventually spotted the three lions lying together under some shady trees. Leo lifted his head in my direction and pricked up his ears. And the next moment he was rushing towards me at top speed, answering my call with loud grunts.

As he reached the fence I pressed my head and shoulders to the wire. He put his enormous face right against mine, groaning in that deep, shuddering way of his as we rubbed heads and shoulders. Then we sat down on either side of the fence, and I stuck my arm through the wire and stroked his head and face. We talked of a thousand things, and it felt so good. Leo was in a much calmer mood now, and so was I.

While Leo and I talked, I noticed both Fat Cat and Happie watching us, and I wondered what they were thinking.

Eventually Karin and Kobus got out of the car and came over and joined me. As soon as Leo saw them approaching, he leapt up and called to them.

He greeted them joyfully, and we all sat down to a very happy family reunion.

After a while Happie got up and strolled towards us. Focusing her gaze on me, she came right up to the fence and proceeded to rub her head and shoulders seductively against the wire, inviting me to a feline greeting. I felt a little apprehensive about the invitation, but decided to humour her. She was, after all, Leo's wife. So I stood up and pressed my shoulder to the wire. But Kobus said: 'No, don't! Look at her tail!'

Her tail was straight up in the air, the tuft jerking spasmodically — signifying feline hostility and mischief. She

254

was evidently hoping to seduce me into offering her another chance to chomp me.

I was disgusted with her. I stepped back from the wire. Then I fixed her with a stern gaze and said: 'Now get this straight, Happie. I am your mother-in-law, whether you like it or not. So at least be civil to me!'

She looked at me with huge yellow eyes that seemed a little perplexed — as if she was thinking: 'Well, I didn't know you were my mother-in-law. I thought you were a dog.'

At dusk we spotted a man carrying a sack up to a far corner of the camp where the lions had their sleeping quarters. The man removed several dead chickens from the sack and deposited them in the camp. Leo and the lionesses rushed over to enjoy their supper. The man then walked over to Trade's camp, which was situated right opposite the sleeping quarters of the main camp, and dispensed more chickens.

While Leo and his wives were eating, we walked over to Trade's camp to say hello to him.

He'd been asleep at the time of the food delivery, and as we reached his camp he was just waking up and staggering to his feet. After a good stretch, he gave us a friendly but very myopic look. We moved closer so that he could see us better. He peered at Kobus and me with a look that seemed to say: 'Ah, yes. I've seen the two of you somewhere before. How are you? Now, if you'll excuse me, I'd like to have my dinner.'

Old Trade sniffed at his chickens and then sat down with a contented grunt to enjoy his meal. Most of his lower teeth were missing, so he ate slowly, but without too much difficulty.

After dinner, Trade tottered down to the bottom of his camp and stood there for a while, contemplating his surroundings. Then he drew in his breath and started roaring. His voice was husky, but still very powerful. He continued roaring for several minutes, and when he was finally satisfied that he'd done a good job of broadcasting his sovereignty to the world, he turned around to see what the other lions were doing. Fat Cat was still busy eating, but Leo and Happie were gazing at him with pure admiration. Old

Trade walked back to his lair, stretched himself out on the straw and, with a contented sigh, went back to sleep.

We said good-night to Trade, and then to Leo and the lionesses, promising Leo that we would be back in the morning. He looked sad to see us go and invited us with pleading grunts to stay the night. I told him that I didn't altogether trust his wife, Happie. Otherwise I would gladly have spent the night with him in his camp.

Andy came over to the lodge early the following morning to have breakfast with us. He was looking very pleased with himself and told us that he had just been to Leo's camp. He'd been feeling very hurt at the way Leo had treated him the previous day, so he'd decided to pay him a private visit to talk things over. As soon as he'd parked inside the camp that morning, Leo came rushing to him and gave him his usual exuberant welcome.

I was very pleased for Andy. His news proved my theory that Leo had not really been mad at him the previous day. He'd merely wanted his family from the past all to himself for a while without any interference.

We spent the rest of the week visiting Leo, relaxing at the lodge and enjoying the company of Andy and Fiona and the two younger Bristows — Graeme and Julie.

Our host and hostess at the lodge, Hans Strijdom and his wife Diana, treated us as special guests and made our visit most enjoyable.

The lodge organised sight-seeing safaris for their guests, and although we were often invited to join them, we declined. We wanted to spend as much time as possible with Leo.

Initially Hans, his wife and the two safari guides were the only people at the lodge who knew the real reason for our visit to Pamuzinda. We decided to keep it that way and not to mention anything to the tourists. We didn't want to be the centre of conversation at every mealtime.

But Hans had two little dogs (half Maltese and half something else) who changed all this for us.

They never barked at any of the other guests — only at us. Every time we arrived back at the lodge after a visit to Leo, the two little brats would bark their heads off.

The reason, of course, was that we smelled of lion.

To make matters worse, they followed us to the dinner table and spent the entire mealtime sniffing our legs under the table, and making growling noises.

One of the guests eventually remarked that the dogs appeared to have some special interest in South Africans, and so Hans came out with the truth and explained the real reason for the dogs' behaviour.

After that, of course, there was no getting away from it: we became the centre of attention and every mealtime was dominated by questions about Leo.

We found, however, that all the guests were moved by Leo's story. And although they had all been to the lion camp at some stage or other during a sight-seeing safari, every one of them expressed the wish to see the lions again. So the safari guides promised to take them on another visit to the lion camp.

One of the guides later told us that Leo was fast becoming the most photographed lion in Africa.

One day, while we were having tea on the patio with some of the other guests, Karin decided that she wanted to explore the scenery on the other side of the river pan. Unaware that guests were not supposed to leave the area around the lodge unescorted, she set off and walked down the river bank. Although there was some water in the pan, it was the dry season and the river itself was low.

All conversation on the patio suddenly ceased as the guests turned their heads to watch Karin walking off into the dangerous wilderness. Some of them voiced their concern, but Kobus reassured them, explaining that, having grown up in the wilds, Karin was more than capable of looking after herself.

There was a sign nailed to a tree on the river bank bearing the legend: 'Danger: Do not go beyond this point.'

Karin reached the tree and stopped to read the sign. Having done so, she promptly ignored it and disappeared over the far bank of the river. She knew that, apart from crocodiles, no other man-eating carnivores roamed Pamuzinda. Leo and his family were the only big cats on the estate, and they, of course, lived in their own camp.

While Karin was gone, four young elephants turned up to drink at the pan. And as we sat watching them from the terrace, the guests got even more agitated. What if the elephants were still there when Karin returned? How would she get safely past them?

The elephants did in fact stay on, spending most of the afternoon grazing on the river bank. But I wasn't worried about Karin. She would see the elephants, of course, and find another route back to the lodge.

Having done just that, Karin returned an hour or so later and reported that she'd spotted a lovely variety of animals on her walk.

On the evening of our last day at Pamuzinda, Kobus and I went to Hans's office to settle our account. We were pleasantly surprised to learn that Carol and Vivian Bristow had arranged with Hans to charge us only half the normal price. And even the normal price was not as high as we'd expected it to be. We were even more surprised — and touched — when Hans informed us that he'd decided not to charge us anything for our last day at Pamuzinda.

'But why?' we asked.

'Because you're Leo's parents,' he replied.

We appreciated the kind gesture immensely.

Early the following morning Andy arrived to escort Kobus to the lion camp for a final 'inside-the-camp' visit to Leo. The plan was that we would all visit Leo again after breakfast to say our goodbyes through the fence. But Karin suddenly wanted desperately to go along with Andy and Kobus and visit Leo inside his camp. So I gave my permission, if rather reluctantly, making her promise that she would' stay close to the car and watch out for the lionesses at all times.

I longed to go with them as well, but my problem was adrenalin. Every time Happie fixed me with her mischievous gaze, I'd become jittery. And I didn't want to smell of adrenalin while inside the camp with the lionesses — things might go wrong. To an animal, fear and aggression have the same smell: that of adrenalin. So it's not wise to smell of adrenalin in a wild animal's company — your fear might be mistaken for aggression.

I stayed at the lodge and finished our packing.

When Kobus and Karin returned from their visit, I noticed that Karin was looking rather sad. So I asked Kobus about it. He said that Leo had been in a boisterous mood. As soon as Karin got out of the car, Leo was all over her, begging her to play with him. Karin was quite willing to play, but Kobus and Andy agreed that a wrestling game with Leo was no longer safe for Karin. Leo weighed more than 200 kilograms now. Moreover, the lionesses had sensed Leo's boisterous mood, and they'd appeared a bit restless. So Karin had been ordered back into the car.

I felt so sorry for her. I could well imagine how much she longed to play with Leo again. I had that same longing.

After a quick breakfast, we said goodbye to everyone at the lodge and packed up to leave.

Andy came to the car to see us off.

As Karin opened the back door to get into the car, I was surprised to see a gaping hole in the seat's upholstery.

Kobus explained that Leo had done it. That's how boisterous his mood had been that morning.

I wondered if our insurance people would believe the story.

We said goodbye to Andy, and thanked him for everything he'd done for Leo and for us. He promised to keep in touch with us and to let us know as soon as there was any indication that Leo was to become a father.

Kobus, Karin and I arrived at Leo's camp for our final visit.

We found the three lions enjoying the early morning sun in a grassy patch near the south fence of the camp. Leo leapt up and came running to us. After the usual happy greetings, we all sat down and talked.

We talked of many things — Wolfie, Hettie, Sandra and Paul who had all sent him their love, and all the good times of the past. Leo gave us his full attention, his gaze focused on us with warmth and affection.

It was altogether a very lovely visit.

Eventually Fat Cat called to Leo. He answered her with a grunt. Then he looked at us with an expression that seemed to say: 'Excuse me, I have to go now. The wife is calling.' He got up and walked back to the lionesses, flopping down in the grass next to them, but keeping his gaze focused fondly on us.

I wanted some photographs of Leo and the lionesses, but they were too far from the fence for nice close-ups. So Kobus offered to go into the camp and take the photos for me.

As Kobus walked up to them, I watched the lionesses closely, but they seemed unperturbed by his presence.

While Kobus was taking the pictures, I thought of the photos we had taken of Leo at Pamuzinda the previous year: there had been a lot of tension in his eyes and in the lines on his face then, and for many months afterwards I had been unable to look at those photographs without feeling incredibly sad.

Now, as he posed for photographs with his wives, he looked regal and handsome, and the expression on his face was of contentment and well-being.

I looked forward to having my new photos of Leo, and to placing them in my photo album right next to the sad ones of the previous year. They would provide my photo album as well as my memory album of Leo with a happy ending.

Eventually we called Leo back to us to say our goodbyes.

We all rubbed heads with him through the wire, and when my turn came, I sat down and talked to him for a while, explaining to him that we had to go home now, but that we would be back to visit him again as soon as we were able. I told him how good it had been to see him again, and how much the memories of our visit would mean to me.

All through my speech he paid attention to the tone of my voice, and when I had finished he tilted his head to one side — in the same way that a human does when smiling at a loved one — and his rust-coloured eyes grew warm with love and trust.

I knew then that Leo was happy: happy to be a lion, and to be amongst lions, and happy that we had visited him and shown him that we had not forgotten him.

Fat Cat called to him again. She was evidently getting to be a rather possessive wife. Leo got up and walked back to his wives.

As we drove off, we leaned out through the windows, waving and calling goodbye to Leo and his family.

And so I buried my heart at Pamuzinda.

All Things Wild and Wonderful

Shortly after our return from Zimbabwe, a rogue elephant bull got into the habit of vandalising our neighbours' gardens at night. I knew that our garden would soon get its turn, but I hoped it wouldn't happen before Kobus got home. (He was attending a meeting somewhere in the north of the Park.)

Naturally, my luck didn't hold.

I was woken one night by the resounding clanging of a steel fence in trouble. So I got out of bed and rushed outside, calling to the dogs to come and help me.

They obligingly barked at the elephant as loudly as they could, while I shouted at him at the top of my voice. After a while he finally got the message and turned away from the fence. By that time he'd already broken a fence-post, pulled part of the wire down, and demolished half a tree.

He came back again the following night, bringing a friend with him. Fortunately Kobus had returned home, so I woke him up.

'You have a better elephant-deterrent voice than I have,' I told him. 'Please go and talk to the elephants.'

Kobus jumped out of bed, pulled on a pair of shorts and rushed outside, calling to me to bring him an egg.

'An egg?' I thought. 'Now what does the man want with an egg?'

But I didn't argue: I took him the egg.

He threw it at one of the elephants, hitting it square on the shoulder. The elephant lifted its trunk and pressed it to its shoulder, sniffing at the spot where the egg had splattered.

'AARGH!' he screamed, and fled into the night, followed closely by his friend.

They never returned.

I liked what I'd learned.

Next time, instead of yelling my lungs out, I would simply hurl a couple of eggs at the intruders.

A few nights later we were woken by lions roaring so close to us that the whole house trembled. Kobus leapt out of bed like a bolt of lightning.

'Where are you going?' I asked in alarm.

'I forgot to close the gate,' he replied.

I thought of our dogs and our horses, and I jumped up and ran after him.

Kobus was in such a hurry to get outside to close the gate that he didn't waste time putting on a pair of shorts first. (He doesn't own pyjamas. Excuse me for mentioning this, but it's relevant to the story.)

'Shall I bring some eggs?' I called after him.

But he didn't hear me. He was already outside and heading towards the gate at top speed.

It occurred to me that a naked human might look very edible to a hungry lion, so I tried to find my pistol, but it was locked in the gunsafe. Time was running out. I grabbed my torch instead and ran after Kobus, wondering if I would be able to stun a lion by hitting it on the head with a torch. The roaring started up again, and I felt as if I were running straight towards an earthquake.

As soon as I rounded the bend at the fish pond, I saw two enormous lions standing right at the open gate.

I lost my nerve.

Stopping dead in my tracks, I started screaming at Kobus to come back.

But I needn't have bothered. The lions took one look at Kobus and fled. And they didn't utter another sound all night. Apparently they'd never seen a naked human before, and they were shocked speechless.

I suppose there is something to learn from this episode as well, but I think I'd rather stick to the egg trick.

It was late winter now, and the grass cover in the veld was getting sparse. A herd of impala and a few bushbuck took to grazing in our garden. Naturally we were delighted to have them. They eventually got so tame that one could actually walk right up to them and have a chat. Our dogs have been trained not to harass antelope, and they left them in peace.

Actually we didn't need to train Jasper. Wolfie trained him.

Being a border collie, Jasper is, of course, also a herding dog. And his herding instincts are so strong that he even gets into our fish pond to herd the fish.

At first he tried to herd everything that moved. But Wolfie soon set him straight and taught him the rules:

- Antelope may not be disturbed.

- Leguaans, tortoises and other reptiles may be studied from a respectful distance, but are not to be herded.

- Guinea fowl, mongooses and squirrels may be herded for fun — but within limits.

- Baboons and monkeys are to be kept out of the garden at all times with an authoritative tone of barking. If found in the garden, they are to be herded out at top speed.

One afternoon in late winter, Karin took the dogs for a walk down into the valley. A herd of impala suddenly came fleeing out of the bush, crossing the track right in front of her. Karin and the two dogs stopped, waiting to see what the impala were fleeing from. A pack of wild dogs came charging out of the bush, also crossing the track right in front of them, but they slammed on their brakes to stop and stare curiously at Karin and her two companions.

Karin commanded Wolfie and Jasper to stay with her and be quiet — which the good dogs promptly did. Wolfie stood

protectively between Karin and the wild dogs, keeping a very watchful eye on them. Jasper, who had never met wild dogs before, tried to look invisible behind Karin's legs.

The wild dogs studied Karin and her companions for a while, and eventually the leader of the pack started edging towards them, curiosity written all over his face. Wolfie wasn't too happy about this. So he took a few steps forward, his hair bristling and his upper lip lifted in a warning gesture that said: 'Don't you dare come any closer to Karin.'

Karin wasn't scared of the wild dogs. She knew that they were only curious and that they intended her no harm. She was, in fact, delighted to make their acquaintance.

Unfortunately, as soon as Wolfie started moving towards the leader, the whole pack suddenly became restless which, in turn, made Jasper even more nervous.

As Karin sensed the change in the pack's mood, she realised that the situation might get out of control. And there was no way that she would be able to protect her two dogs if the pack came for them. So she flung her arms into the air and shouted at the wild dogs to go away. They turned and fled.

Karin was disappointed that the meeting had to end this way, but she'd nevertheless enjoyed the unique encounter, and she hoped that she would someday get another opportunity to talk to wild dogs and to make their acquaintance in a more peaceful way.

The spring rains came early, and a funny thing happened right after the first rains. In the evening, as I was feeding the fish, a little terrapin climbed out of the fish pond and studied my foot.

Not believing what I was seeing, I bent down to have a closer look at him. He lifted his funny little face and looked me right in the eyes.

Perhaps I was being over-fanciful, but I could have sworn that the expression on his face said: 'Are you my mommy?'

'No,' I told him hastily. 'I'm not. I'm a primate, see? A mammal. We're not even distantly related.'

He looked down at my foot again, and took an experimental taste of my toe.

'Oh, you're hungry?' I said. 'OK, I'll get you something to eat. But that still doesn't make me your mommy!'

I fetched him a few slivers of chicken from the fridge. To my surprise, he ate it right out of my hand.

And ever since then, every evening when I feed the fish, he gets out of the pond and demands that I feed him as well. I keep telling him that I'm not his mommy — just the lady from the Welfare Society. But the silly little creature appears to have bonded with me. Whenever I try to introduce him to Kobus or the children, he gets shy and ducks into the water, and then I have to feed him under water.

Now what is it that makes this crazy terrapin think it's my duty to feed him?

It's not that I mind. The trouble is, though, that a terrapin has a lifespan of a few hundred years. Which means that it probably has a very long childhood. About fifty years or so. I don't want to be a terrapin-mother for the rest of my life.

Annette says my problem is that I have this aura about me that transmits a message to all strays and orphans that I'm their mother.

It's worrying.

How can a person get rid of such an aura?

The other day while I was gardening, a young leguaan crossed the lawn behind me.

Karin said: 'Quick, mom! Don't let him see you. Get into the house!'

'Why?' I asked, startled.

'He might think you're his mother,' she said.

I've been thinking about this aura. I don't think such a thing really exists. I think animals are just extraordinarily good at spotting idiot humans like me who are programmed to believe that their sole reason for being is to care for hapless creatures.

Believe me, animals are far cleverer than we think they are. They sense things that we don't even know about.

Which reminds me of something that happened back in 1994.

A few weeks after we'd returned from our first visit to Zimbabwe (the one when we'd taken Leo to Pamuzinda), I drove to Hazyview one day to buy some groceries and I forgot to stop at a fourway intersection. Unfortunately, at that very moment, another motorist also forgot to stop at the intersection. And so we collided right in the middle of the crossing. Fortunately no one was injured, but both our cars were badly smashed up and had to be towed away.

I felt just awful. I'd never before been involved in a car accident. And I knew that the only reason I'd had the accident was because I'd been thinking of Leo instead of paying attention to my driving.

I spent the rest of the day feeling incredibly sorry for myself. When I got home, I paced the garden — up and down, up and down — wondering why life was treating me so badly.

Eventually, when I got tired of pacing, I sat down on the grass and stared into the marula woodland. And there stood a waterbuck bull, contemplating me with an expression that seemed to say: 'Lady, what IS the matter?'

So I told him what the matter was, explaining how I'd lost my lion as well as my thumb and my car.

He just went right on staring at me with wise soulful eyes. After a while I asked him, 'Well, aren't you going to say anything?'

He walked off into the bush.

But it didn't matter.

A therapist would have looked at his watch and told me my time was up. And he would have sent me a bill. And he wouldn't have listened to my story with such soulful eyes.

And, anyway, I was feeling much better.

We have a beach cottage in the Eastern Cape, and shortly after our return from our second trip to Pamuzinda it occurred to

Kobus and me that we hadn't been to our beach cottage for almost four years. I guess we'd been too busy raising orphans and getting chewed by lions. We decided to plan a family holiday at our beach cottage for the coming summer.

So, as soon as all the children had finished their exams, and Hettie and her Kobus had got married, we packed two cars full of people and dogs and set out for Paradise Beach. (I considered taking the terrapin along as well, but Kobus vetoed the idea. So I arranged for a neighbour to put out food for the terrapin in my absence.)

Paradise Beach is a lovely, quiet place. It has no tourist facilities, only a few privately owned beach houses. Several species of small mammal — bushbuck, genets, monkeys and mongooses — share the place with us, while seagulls and dolphins and many other sea creatures abound in the area.

We had a truly splendid vacation.

Clever Wolfie, who always knows what life is all about, spent most of his days sitting on the beach — on a beach towel under a beach umbrella, contemplating the sea. (All he needed was a pair of sunglasses to complete the picture.) Jasper had a great time chasing waves and herding seagulls. The children swam and surfed, and they went fishing and snorkelling and supplied us with all kinds of delicious seafood.

One day, while Kobus and I were walking along the beach, we spotted a school of dolphins swimming round and round in a wide circle just beyond the breakers. We went through the surf and swam out towards them. They allowed us to come very close and circled us for a long time.

It was magic.

We could hear the mothers calling to their young, and at times they were so close that we could have reached out and touched them. But we didn't — in case they didn't want us to. They were taking such care not to touch or bump into us, so they probably expected the same courtesy of us.

Looking back now, I realise that without the dolphins and the seagulls and all the other animals, including our two dogs, the holiday would not have been nearly so wonderful.

We all need animals.

Just think how lonely the world would be without them — as Chief Seathl wrote in his letter to the United States President in 1855: 'If all the beasts were gone from the earth, man would die from great loneliness of spirit.'

One of the first things we did when we got back to the Park was to go for a drive and check whether the animals in the area still looked well and happy.

We were pleased to find that they did.

So afterwards we climbed to the top of Shabeni to watch the sun set. A troop of baboons sat on a cliff-top nearby, discussing us and other things amongst themselves.

The sun set lazily, hovering above the horizon in a blaze of pink and magenta.

I looked out over the quiet bushland landscape, and its beauty touched my soul. The last rays of sunlight played on stands of silver cluster-leaf trees, turning them into wispy clouds of aquamarine. I listened to the gentle rhythm of the wind and to the bird calls rising from the vast silence of the bush. And the words from a poem by Joseph von Eichendorff came to mind: *O wie mich das freut, ... Die prächtige Einsamkeit* (Oh the joy that I find, ... in such exquisite solitude).

My thoughts wandered to Mahlangeni and lingered there a while. I realised that part of me still belonged to that wild and lonely Eden.

But I no longer regretted having moved away. The years after had brought us to other Edens, and had filled my heart with new and precious memories.

A booming bark interrupted my reverie. It came from one of the baboons on the nearby cliff-top, presumably the leader, who wished to remind us who was boss in the area.

Kobus answered him with a friendly salute.

At the foot of the koppie, a handsome giraffe couple emerged from the thickets and started sampling the greenery along the southern slope of Shabeni. Soon they were munching their way up to the trees higher up the koppie.

We sat so quietly that they didn't notice us until they were within thirty metres of us. Stopping mid-munch, with leaves dangling from their mouths, they fixed us with puzzled gazes.

Shortly afterwards, a magnificent martial eagle landed on a rocky ledge near us. It folded its wings and, turning its head towards us, fixed us with an imperial stare.

The baboons, of course, were also still studying us.

'We are being watched,' I murmured to Kobus.

'Always,' he said. 'The bush is full of eyes.'

It occurred to me that we'd had this conversation before – in fact on many occasions.

Years ago, when we still lived at Mahlangeni, someone once asked me if the idea of being totally alone in the wilderness never worried me. I replied that it was more often the idea of *not* being alone that worried me. Time and again, when I would think that I was alone, I would hear a strange noise or sense a movement, and discover that I was being watched.

But one gets used to the idea of being watched. And in time the idea grows on one until it acquires a very comforting dimension: 'I am not alone. I am known. I am part of nature.'

Most people who live in the cities have probably lost this primeval feeling – this awareness of the company of animals and plants. And so they must often feel abandoned and alone – even among crowds of other people.

The sun disappeared over the distant hills, leaving splashes of crimson and carmine in the western sky. As we sat waiting for the smoky blue hour of dusk, I wondered about city people, about their stressful lives and their loneliness.

I wondered if they still recognised within themselves the longing for wilderness and solitude; if they still remembered the soothing harmonies of nature, the repetitive refrains of the seasons and sunsets, the exhilaration of each new dawn, the sweet delight of making the acquaintance of a wild creature.

If they have forgotten this, then they might think of conservation merely as a necessary exercise to preserve the planet's finite resources and to prevent our eventual extinction. And the whole effort would seem such a joyless one.

But if they remember, then they will know that conservation is also about preserving the magic that nourishes our souls; a cause, therefore, that also holds a promise of joy.

In the fading light of dusk the landscape below us became hazy and ethereal, like a view of a fantasy world. The stirring cry of a jackal rose from somewhere between us and the night — reminding us that the darkness belongs to predators. So we said goodbye to the baboons, to the giraffe couple and to the eagle, and started climbing back to earth.

But just before we did, I stood for a moment to absorb the full enchantment of everything around us.

And a phrase came to mind.

Ici reste mon coeur.